SEVEN SECRETS OF SUCCESSFUL WOMEN

DONNA L. BROOKS

LYNN M. BROOKS

MJF BOOKS

NEW YORK

Published by MJF Books
Fine Communications
322 Eighth Avenue
New York, NY 10001

Seven Secrets of Successful Women
LC Control Number 2001-130247
ISBN-13: 1-978-465-6
ISBN-10: 1-56731-465-1

The sponsoring editor for this book was Susan Barry and the editing supervisor was Caroline R. Levine. It was set in Fairfield by Victoria Khavkina of McGraw-Hill's Professional Book Group composition unit.

Manufactured in the United States of America.

MJF Books and the MJF colophon are trademarks of Fine Creative Media, Inc.

QM   10 9 8 7 6 5 4 3

To Frank, for his unwavering belief, support, and motivation.

CONTENTS

PREFACE

Lynn, my co-author, and I are really excited about this book. A lot of our friends and colleagues have shared work-related stories through the years, many of them ending in riotous laughter with the inevitable "can you believe this one?" We've all had the "horror stories" about crazy bosses, dealing with difficult colleagues, having incredible deadlines, and too much to do with too little time. Probably most of you have shared similar experiences with your friends and family, maybe at dinner, at family gatherings, or over margaritas and nachos after work! The scenarios may be different, but the story is often the same.

In our work environments, many of us probably consider ourselves "average" or even "well above average," but many of us can't really identify with the really successful superwomen we read about. We may wonder how they manage to do all the wonderful things that they do. Well, they're probably doing many of the same things that we all do, just on a different scale. It's all relative! But what are *they* doing that *we're not* doing? How have they become so successful?

When you think about what you actually do in your life, you may begin to see things differently! Many women who consider themselves average are actually doing incredible things. They work, take care of family, volunteer, go to school, and take care of things on the home front. They drive their kids to sports events, work in the PTA, make Halloween costumes, prepare meals for the family, make dazzling presentations to their clients, prepare budgets, write reports, run departments, manage staffs. What we really need to do is to just learn a few tricks of the trade from those who are very successful and then follow their lead. *These strategies really do work!*

Lynn and I started talking about this book quite awhile ago, when I was starting to do research for my doctoral dissertation. I was always very interested in what made some people, especially women, really successful. What made them different from the rest of us? Lynn and I looked at the project from different perspectives. She has been in corporate America for about 12 years, while I have spent most of my career in education, both secondary and higher ed. I often tend to see the lofty, theoretical side of issues, and Lynn has provided a more down-to-earth counterview. As a result, when I start looking at success at the highest level, that anyone can become a CEO of a major corporation if they want to, Lynn will often bring in a more realistic approach, specifically that most people probably don't really want to be a CEO. They want to enjoy their work, be successful on several levels, have balance in their lives and, in some cases, simply learn how to hold on to their jobs in times of downsizing. This combination of perspectives has proved to be an effective mix of enthusiasm and the belief that anyone can do anything, and the realistic tasks of building the foundation to reach your goal. So interestingly enough, despite being identical twins, even Lynn and I have very different views of what success really means.

We have had different roles in the project. Lynn has done a good deal of the background research, has done a number of the interviews—especially in the international arena (her specialty)—and has contributed to much of the discussion which generated various directions in the work. I have done much of the actual writing and many of the interviews, and will serve as the narrator in the book. (We thought that it would be too confusing to always be saying "we, us", etc.) Frequently when I say "I" in the book, it really means "we."

As you read this book, we hope that you can see yourself in many of the same situations that we and many of our friends and colleagues have experienced. You will also most likely identify with some of the experiences of the successful women and men we interviewed. Their experiences and insight will undoubtedly help you focus in your own career path. In addition, we hope that you will find the strategies helpful in your work life, and maybe even in your personal life. We really believe in these strategies. They've worked for us and for many of our colleagues as we move ahead in our careers. So, here's to success!

Donna Brooks
Lynn Brooks

ACKNOWLEDGMENTS

We would especially like to recognize all the participants in the research, both those who were named and those who chose to remain anonymous. In addition, we would like to thank our many friends and colleagues, who have always encouraged us and given us great ideas and advice. Thank you, Frank, for always providing encouragement—it couldn't have happened without you. Thanks so much to Carol Stuckley, who has not only been an incredible role model, but who never fails to make time for friends in her whirlwind schedule! And to Mary Ruff, Clairemarie Caffrey, and Becky Boyd, who have shared so much with us all these years. To Dr. Elsie Chu, our cousin and first role model, who was able to teach us all about success and fulfillment, despite incredible adversity. Thanks also to Dorothea Palsho, as well as fellow EWMD board members, who have become such great friends and advocates. Our thanks to Susan Barry and Carol Levine at McGraw-Hill who have been so wonderful to work with during our first literary experience. And special thanks to our family—Mom, Dad, Bud, Craig, Suzanne, Matthew, Gregory, Stephen, and Peter.

INTRODUCTION

One of the main reasons for writing this book is an absolute commitment to the concept of success. Most of the books about success recount stories of exceptional people who have achieved exceptional things. If you read the biographies of many famous and successful people—men and women—you will frequently encounter the same themes: drive, ambition, overcoming adversity, and unfailing commitment to achievement. While it is easy to admire these successful people and applaud their accomplishments, we may sometimes have a difficult time identifying with them—they seem to have more substance than the rest of us.

But this book is different. It's for "average" people who can achieve success on many different levels. Exactly what is success? I frequently ask this question in my classes and seminars. Think about what it means to you. Some people say that success is being happy and balanced in their lives. Others say success is money. Still others say it's achievement and recognition in the job, or raising children well, or personal and professional accomplishments. Well, it can surely be all those things. But what is success to you? For me, success means being able to do things that I wouldn't have believed possible at one time in my life. It means challenging myself, achieving professional and personal accomplishments, and gaining the feeling that I can do things that I wouldn't have thought possible 5 or 10 years ago.

The meaning of success is highly unique to each individual. We all have different needs, different aspirations, different talents. One very important fact to keep in mind, however,

is that not everyone aspires to become a CEO or college president or corporate superstar, or highly visible politician. There
are choices and consequences for every decision we make. For
many people, success at work may also mean holding on to a
job in a time of downsizing, or getting a new job from an interview, or simply getting recognition for a job well done. These
are big successes, too!

When I used to read about successful women, I sometimes
thought about the differences between them and me. I was
average and they were extraordinary. They were accomplished
and I wasn't. I was reading about them, but I couldn't have
included myself in their category. They did all the right
things—they were usually first-born, competitive, focused, and
had parents or role models who encouraged and challenged
them. Sometimes I felt that it was too late for me—I didn't
have those things growing up. We tend to think that other people always have it together; they know what they're doing, they
have a career path, they're on track.

Think of how many of us were raised. If you don't fit the
traditional leadership model, you'll identify here immediately!
Your mother may not have worked. She was a great homemak-
er, took care of the family, scoffed at other women who
brought "store-bought" cookies or cakes to luncheons or teas
with friends, and made sure that her house was clean as the
ones in commercials. Sound familiar? If you're a baby boomer,
you grew up with Barbie and Ken, vacuous sit-coms on TV
(*Bewitched, I Dream of Jeannie,* and *The Brady Bunch*), and
the idea that you went to college to find a husband, without a
clear career path in mind. OK, there are exceptions, but
they're most likely the women in the traditional leadership
profile—the ones not reading this book!

If you went to college, you probably didn't have too clear of
a career path upon graduation. (All right, confess. How many
psychology/sociology/English/foreign language majors are
reading this book right now? I was a French-Italian major in
college!) We were probably doomed from the start! All of a
sudden, we were thrown into the cold reality at graduation
from high school or college—we didn't really know how to do
anything!

I came across an interesting comment when I was reading the classic book *Games Mother Never Taught You,* by Betty Harragan. Written in 1977 (the year we graduated from college and exactly 20 years ago), the book reassured me that some things are still true no matter how many changes have taken place. Harragan wrote:

> It will take at least twenty years before significant numbers of women begin to reach the higher echelons of business, but they will come from today's expeditionary forces of working women. It is important that volunteers in this force don't get deflected, distracted or discouraged simply because they don't know the ground rules of what is essentially a boys' game—playing corporate politics.[1]

Most women didn't know the rules 20 years ago and many still don't know them today! And Harragan was right—it has taken 20 years for women to really start making changes in organizations.

But what I have found most often is that most women flounder around for years trying to figure out what they need to do to get ahead. I'm not saying that doing so is always *all* bad. Reflecting back over the last 10 years, I have seen changes that I couldn't have believed possible. A lot of my female friends and colleagues were feeling the same way. But as we talked, I realized that most of us were making blind decisions. We stumbled into jobs, didn't plan career moves, didn't have anyone guiding us or mentoring us. There were some good decisions and some bad decisions. Were there things that we would change? Sure! But I realize that even with this uncertain and rocky background, it's definitely not too late for any of us to learn *now* what we need to do. Learn and practice. . . .

A DIFFERENT WORLD

When I talk to many talented, ambitious women over the age of 28 or 29, there seems to be a surprisingly common thread. I think that we're trying to undo years of socialization which taught us to be like our mothers as we were growing up. But that world no longer exists for most of us. Our mothers may not have worked. Today, dual wage earners or single-parent breadwinners are the norm, not the exception. Our mothers probably didn't have to be risk takers, worrying about balancing home and work, understanding the politics of the organization, or finding a mentor. So they didn't—and indeed couldn't—prepare us for the workplace and life that was facing us.

It's no wonder that many of us are extremely uncomfortable in a competitive environment—even healthy competition (it wasn't ladylike!). We don't feel comfortable letting others know about our talents and accomplishments (people don't like braggarts or stuck-up snobs!). We feel stressed trying to balance everything and be superwomen. Most of us didn't have mentors. What were they? Who cared? We didn't even know the questions to ask, let alone what the answers were. So many of us drifted around trying to figure out where we belonged. We were no longer in our mother's world, but we hadn't evolved enough to enter "a man's world."

Where does that leave us today? Many of us lament that we didn't have much guidance as we navigated our careers. But we can and should learn from women who have made it. Who are they? What are their secrets? What can we learn? These women can be from myriad backgrounds—corporate America, politics, higher education. I decided to find out by doing some research.

THE ORIGINAL STUDY

Several years ago, I conducted research for my doctoral dissertation using senior-level women in female-friendly organizations to determine if they had reached senior positions as a result of their own characteristics and political savvy or a result of organizational support—or both. In my original research I concluded that it was a combination of individual and organizational efforts that allowed these women to advance.

These women displayed a surprising consensus as to what

helped them become successful, a consensus reflecting my specific plan to address individual and organizational differences. I established diversity of industry (banking, airlines, pharmaceuticals, publishing, and insurance, just to name a few), geographical location, age, race, and department within the organization as factors. I conducted intensive personal interviews, administered quantitative instruments, and gathered personal and organizational data on dozens of very senior women managers. Seven major areas seemed to keep coming up as a result of the interviews. These themes are the success strategies that form the basis of this handbook.

One very important issue that must be addressed while discussing success strategies for women is that women are not all alike. If you look around, you will see a wide diversity of age, background, race, culture, social and economic status, education, and so forth. Women cannot—and indeed should not—be categorized into a generalized group, for several reasons. So consider the widely individual approaches and situations as you read on. We have all heard the generalizations: Women are more emotional than men, they aren't tough enough, they can't make decisions, they don't like conflict. The list goes on and on. Does that mean that *all* women fit that description? Or does that mean that *all* men are tough, unemotional, conflict-seeking decision makers? Of course not. For some women it is true. *Some* women don't like conflict, *some* women are not decision makers. But many women don't mind conflict; in fact, they may enjoy challenging encounters. Many women are excellent decision makers, tough enough, and so forth. The main idea here is that *sex role* rather than *gender* is a greater determinant of the type of approach a person will use. What is the difference?

Sex role is the amalgam of characteristics of an individual, either a man or a woman. Some women show tendencies toward more masculine characteristics of being more analytical, tougher, and more competitive than other women. The converse can be true of some men. I gave the participants in my original study an inventory that indicated sex-role identity as masculine, feminine, or androgynous. About one-third of these successful women showed male tendencies toward management skills and other broad traits which had generally indicated effective leadership behavior in past studies. However, two-thirds of the women were identified by more feminine characteristics or an effective combination of masculine and feminine in their skills and traits.

Even in this group of very senior corporate managers, there was a tremendous diversity in outlook, style, and leadership approach. It is, therefore, most important to understand yourself well and to get a sense of what your strengths are and realize what your weaknesses are—and work on them. That's a major aspect of your learning. You can ask others you trust to help you evaluate yourself, you can make a list yourself, or you can take a test such as the Myers-Briggs inventory to isolate individual traits and tendencies. You may also wish to attend workshops and engage in similar kinds of activities. Such programs are frequently available at colleges, professional associations, and conferences, or even on tape. If you can truly evaluate yourself, you will be on the first step toward your evolution to success. I began to realize that many women have to take control of their own career success. But the most important step is step 1—you just need to get started!

The strategies identified in this book seemed to work well for the women I interviewed, although many of them very well may have become successful despite their apparent opportunities in female-friendly organizations. They possessed the necessary confidence, political savvy, and drive for success. Many of them were probably born with these characteristics—or developed them at a very young age. But not *all* of them! Some of the women identified particular individuals or situations that pointed them on to the road to success. They learned what they needed to know for success.

So I started to think about what "average" women could do if (1) they didn't have a personal background that was congruent with what many top women experienced, or (2) they didn't work for an organization committed to their success. I began to realize that many women have to take control of their own career success. In numerous articles, books, and media information on leadership and success profiles, successful individuals have frequently stated that if people work really hard, they will be noticed and get ahead. However, I think that there is more to success than this. Of course, it is always assumed that we need to work hard—many women say that they work far harder than men! They may also have a high energy level and a certain amount of luck, but we already knew that! Still, a number of other factors were probably involved in their success, factors that they may have taken for granted without even considering them as components of success. But these may be the most essential keys to success! The women may have been naturally competitive and driven, effective networkers, and good communicators with strong mentors. So for everyone who doesn't have someone as a guide to the right path, here's the first step!

WHAT ARE THE SEVEN SECRETS FOR SUCCESS?

Most people are very interested in finding out the secrets of success. Research makes it fairly easy to identify the major skills and strategies for success. The hard part is to integrate them into our own personal situations! As with most things, it just takes determination and hard work.

So what exactly are these seven secrets? Most of the women I interviewed agreed that it is essential to have characteristics such as high energy, tenacity, a certain amount of toughness, a sense of humor, and flexibility. These are all really important traits; however, they are often innate characteristics rather than strategies that can be learned. The seven primary strategies in this book are secrets that *can* be learned. See how you measure up in these areas.

Secret 1: Successful people realize the importance of a mentor or an advocate.

Secret 2: Successful people know how to increase their visibility.

Secret 3: Successful people know how to develop an effective network.

Secret 4: Successful people have learned to communicate effectively.

Secret 5: Successful people can balance home and work.

Secret 6: Successful people know when to take smart risks.

Secret 7: Successful people understand the politics of the organization.

Do you have these skills? If not, you can learn them! We will examine the importance of each of these areas and how you can develop and practice them in your own career and life.

HOW MUCH WILL I NEED TO CHANGE?

Now, some of you may feel that you need to change your personality or behavior to try to act like a man or to make yourself fit in. Well, yes and no. This book is about personal challenges, discovery, and self-examination, among other things. It may indeed necessitate changing or at least modifying your behavior and personality. But remember that everyone is an individual. What works for some people doesn't work for others. Some women can be very successful displaying more masculine characteristics. There are others who would find it so out of character that the attempt would backfire. Individual organizations, as well, may dictate your behavior. If the organizational culture espouses risk taking, values differences, and tends to be more gender-blind, you will probably feel more comfortable with a more feminine style. If it's a male-dominated industry or organization which fosters a tough, no-nonsense environment, you may need to make a choice: Do you try to fit into the existing culture, do you try to change it by yourself, or do you leave for a more promising environment? It's an individual decision.

I recently read a book about gender differences in organizations that looked at various forms of exclusion based on sexism: the organizational activities, how decisions are made, meeting formats, business trips, sales incentives, and the like.

It examined how women are ignored, and how so many women grumble about the terrible atmosphere that is frequently found in such organizations. While I will emphasize that in many cases this is absolutely true, when I read the book, I spontaneously wrote in the margin, "Do something about it!" It is true that many organizations still do not foster a positive environment for women. It is true that there is discrimination and bias in many organizations. But that doesn't mean you are forever condemned to endure this kind of environment. It can mean starting to look at strategies to change the environment, discovering how to work within the environment to create change, finding advocates at the top who can help create change, learning what you may need to do to move ahead or adapt, or finding out what you need to move on. But we can't just complain about it. It's far too stressful, frustrating, and unproductive.

Learning these secrets can help you identify what you want or need to work on individually so that you may be able to apply it organizationally. So it's also an opportunity to see what works and what doesn't, what kinds of changes or compromises you're willing to make and what is nonnegotiable. Maybe you don't want to dramatically change your behavior. Maybe you do. Maybe you don't yet know enough about what you need to do to actually formulate a plan. This is a path of discovery, an ongoing process, not a one-shot "how to" book. Different people will view this book and use it in different ways. When women ask if they have to change their values and act like men to get ahead, the answer is absolutely not! A very large number of the women I interviewed noted specifically that they are still very much themselves. They have just learned to adapt more easily to various situations and environments. Women need to learn what aspects of both masculine and feminine behavior will be the right combination both for them as individuals and for their organizations.

Flexibility is critical to our learning. Diane, a senior executive at Gannett, Inc., the publishing giant, said that women have to learn how to change gears, to be able to adapt to a variety of settings.

This advice is very important. In some situations, it can be a true asset to have more "feminine" traits of communication, nurturing, and teamwork. But when you need to be tough—in negotiations, for example—you may have to shift gears and draw on more "masculine" characteristics of tough, direct, unemotional behavior. (Again, even here it depends on the *type* of negotiation. There may be various scenarios.) So let's learn which skills we can capitalize on and which ones we need to hone to develop a package that can work most effectively for us! Keep in mind that for each of the seven success strategies, there is a common thread necessary to succeed. Let's start the ball rolling and talk about it!

USING THE FOUR P'S IN YOUR SUCCESS STRATEGY

Every success strategy has four essential components. I call these the "four P's." Really using the four P's can help you achieve success in each one of your seven strategies. You will probably reflect on the four P's very often as you develop your success strategy—I know I do! In order to make these strategies work, you need to have *performance, perseverance, practice,* and *patience.* If you apply these four P's to each one of the success strategies, you will definitely see the results! Think about many of the situations that you have found yourself in during your life. What has either been challenging or frustrating and what has led to your success? The first thing is that you probably have had to work very hard to prove yourself: *performance.*

Think about when you get a new job or a promotion. In your job, you probably know all your coworkers and they know you. You probably have a reputation of being a hard worker. You are known and respected for your performance. This is an assumption for successful individuals. The majority of the individuals I interviewed underscored the need to work hard and do their jobs well. However, women may have to work harder than men just to be perceived as equals. Performance must be flawless and topnotch. Remember that many women, especially those at the top, need to set the standard and create a positive environment for the women following them.

Many of the women interviewed said that they concentrate on doing really outstanding work. They don't want to leave any room for doubt that they were well selected for their position and that they are doing a great job. Many of these women stated that they are very aware of setting the standard for women following them. Many are in highly visible positions requiring risky or controversial decisions to be made. It's sometimes easy for critics to find fault if women aren't doing a first-rate job. You have heard the line from these critics if one questionable or controversial decision is made: "See, we put a woman in the position and look what happened. She blew it! I told you that women aren't tough enough to make these kinds of decisions!" Although there are inevitably times when even the most prepared person can be questioned about his or her decision, you can't make allowances for poor preparation or incomplete work. It's got to be right!

> *Lynne Abraham, the district attorney of Philadelphia, said that when she was a trial lawyer, she really knew each case and really knew the law. She was always extremely well prepared. She humorously added that she was so well prepared for each case that she knew more about the crime than the criminal!*

Perseverance, as stated in the dictionary, indicates a commitment to a goal following a particular course of action, frequently withstanding some difficulty or resistance. Sound familiar? How many times have people told us, either overtly or covertly, that we shouldn't or couldn't do something—that we weren't experienced enough or tough enough, didn't have the right background, needed more education, had kids, needed better connections? The list goes on. Most people have probably had these things said to them. But what makes successful people different from less successful people is the perseverance not to lose sight of their ultimate goal and to look at these potential setbacks as challenges rather than barriers. Think about it. Have you been dissuaded from accomplishing a goal by the comments or actions of others? I know that I have! But you can learn from past experiences and become more persevering—you have to or you will never to be able to face adversity and continue on. Look at people you admire and see how they have overcome adversity and met challenges.

> *Most of us remember speed skater Dan Janssen's experience in the Olympics several years ago as he fell in key races—losing all chance for his dream of a gold medal—just after the tragic death of his beloved sister, Jane, from leukemia. The whole country shared his grief and incredible disappointment. But who can forget the ultimate triumph and joy in the 1994 Olympics when, after years of disappointment, Janssen won the gold medal and skated around the rink with his baby daughter, Jane? That's perseverance!*

A major aspect of perseverance is setting a goal to strive for. Many women don't set goals. But this is absolutely critical for success! How can we benchmark and assess the progress we're making to achieve our goals if we haven't set any? I probably set my first real goal in my early thirties, so it's never too late to start! It's amazing. When you set a goal and chart your progress, you actually have a chance of meeting it. What a concept!

> *A friend of mine keeps his list of goals in his pocket every day. He says that he periodically pulls it out, reads it, and sometimes revises it, depending on new challenges or having met certain other goals. He always knows it's right there in his pocket, just as a reminder!*

One of the P's that some people overlook is the importance of practice. When they say that "practice makes perfect," they're not kidding! Think about outstanding athletes. When we watch the tennis championships at Wimbledon, Olympic ice-skating finals, or downhill skiing events, we see the culmination of years of practice. We don't usually see the hundreds of times athletes have lost, fallen, gotten frustrated or angry, or wanted to quit. So don't forget that most practice involves a few steps forward and a couple of steps back. It's not necessarily going to be a direct upward path!

So what do we need to practice in order to become more successful? Well, of course, among other things, we need to practice the seven strategies for success! Specifically, we need to practice taking some risks; we have to practice not giving up when we meet challenges. We can practice saying no more often to find balance in our lives and practice *not* saying "I'm sorry" so often! We can practice trying to increase our visibility and developing effective relationships with influential people. We can practice having a sense of humor more often and not taking ourselves so seriously at times. And that's just the beginning. As you continue to read, remember that you do indeed need to constantly practice to achieve your goals!

Patience is for me, and probably for most other people, the most difficult of the four P's. Once I get an idea in my head, I want it to happen immediately. I always think that if I work really hard, I can determine my own destiny. But the problem is that we frequently must depend on outside factors to facilitate our efforts. How many times have we all been ready to start a project, a job, or other task and been held up by others (for whatever reason)? It's very frustrating! But it's also a fact of life, so patience really is a virtue. There are times when you are rewarded for patience and other times when you lose if you're too patient. I don't have the answers, but I think that we need to be *more* patient when we are at the mercy of others and *less* patient when we depend on ourselves to accomplish our goal.

So think about these 4 P's as you begin your journey toward success. Be sure to apply them to your success efforts.

- *Performance* must be flawless and top-notch.
- *Perseverance* means continuing to try, despite setbacks and disappointments.
- *Practice, practice,* and *more practice* does make perfect—or at least a lot better!
- *Patience* is a virtue when you can't control an outcome, but whenever possible you need to set the pace!

PART ONE

THE SEVEN
SECRETS

SUCCESSFUL PEOPLE REALIZE THE IMPORTANCE OF A MENTOR/ADVOCATE/ CHEERLEADER/COACH

Research shows that mentors can play a crucial role in career development. My research suggests that mentoring is one of the most important factors—if not *the* most important factor—in success. Without someone helping you along the way, either through direct influence or through advice and guidance, your chances of success may be quite slim. Mentors or advocates frequently facilitate a process of developing future leaders, as opposed to managers. They aid in the socialization of the protégé (i.e., learning the politics) and increase the protégé's visibility. Having an effective mentor may be even more important for women than for men, since many men on the "fast track" have received informal coaching for much of their lives, whereas many women may not experience the same advantages until they enter the workplace. Having a mentor will help the protégé learn the dos and don'ts of the organization. Those who don't have a mentor may be left on their own to figure it out for themselves. (Don't most of us have experience with just guessing what we should and shouldn't do to get ahead?) Although we can navigate our own career journey, it surely is much easier with a guide.

Recently, 461 female executives and 325 CEOs (all male) responded to a Catalyst survey, which included information on mentoring.[2] Some 44 percent of the men thought that formal mentoring programs were an effective strategy for advancing women, while only 2 percent of the women agreed. However, 37 percent of the women thought that *informal* mentors were essential to success. Many women preferred male managers as mentors to female managers.

> One survey respondent stated, "It's still a man's world . . . . It's very helpful to get a perspective from a man." Judith Rodin, president of the University of Pennsylvania, agrees that mentors are crucial to success. Mentors give advice, identify roadblocks and barriers, serve as sounding boards, and help you think for yourself. However, she adds that the gender is not important.

Most successful women state that they have had mentoring relationships. However, the concept seems to have gained acceptance only recently, in the last generation or so. I read an interesting definition of a mentor while I was doing my research. It stated:

> The mentor relationship is one of the most developmentally important experiences a man can have in early adulthood. The mentor is usually several years older, [with] greater experience and seniority in the world the young man is entering. Other terms have included counselor, guru, teacher, adviser, and sponsor.[3]

Interestingly, even in this definition, it is evident that most mentor-protégé relationships have traditionally been among men ("one of the most developmentally important experiences a *man* can have"). So we need to take it from the experts—successful women in the know—that mentors can really make the difference in career strategy!

THE IMPORTANCE OF A MENTOR/ADVOCATE/ CHEERLEADER/COACH

A 1984 longitudinal study of AT&T female managers found that women who had mentors advanced more rapidly in the organization than those who did not have mentors. Further, women who were initially evaluated as not having advancement potential, but who had mentors, advanced as far as or farther than those who were identified as having potential, but who did not have mentors.[4]

The mentors in the AT&T study assisted the women with promotions, encouraged them to continue their education, and provided them with advice. They also facilitated their protégés' advancement, not only by adding a certain credibility and "legitimacy" to them, but also by helping change the way in which their protégés were perceived by coworkers. You can just hear it: A respected senior manager saying publicly, "Wow, that Jane sure is a go-getter! Do you know that she's even heading up a big conference for her professional association in addition to her job here? She's definitely going places!" Of course, as you will see as you read on, *you* could even arrange for an advocate or mentor to say that kind of thing as your "publicity agent." No one will know that it's not just an off-hand comment! This is the type of thing that your advocate or mentor can do to increase your visibility and high-level image.

Women at any level below the upper executive echelons may at times be mistaken for lower-level employees. A mentor can provide "reflected power," indicating to the organization that the woman has powerful allies and resources. When a senior executive mentors a female protégé, he or she makes a public commitment to that individual which encourages the organization to further accept women as bona fide members of the power structure in the organization. It becomes a signal to other managers, as well as to lower-level staff, to take this person seriously.[5]

The participants in my study agreed that one of the key

factors in their success was mentoring. In fact, several senior women interviewed at AT&T discussed what they learned from their mentors, and especially what they have done as mentors themselves.

> *Gail McGovern of AT&T has mentored a lot of people in her career—five to six at a time. She has promoted a lot of women and is very sympathetic to child-care issues for women and men, especially since she has her own young son.*

> *Another senior executive at AT&T feels that women can help promote other women. She gave a colleague a list of 20 qualified women for a VP position when he couldn't think of a woman to recommend for an interview. She considers herself an advocate and raises awareness for women. She feels that she is a role model for men as much as for women and tries to be balanced, make choices, and live by them. She doesn't say "I should have."*

> *Another manager had a discussion with her boss about her being "too soft." She learned a lot about her leadership style, which is collaborative—she did what she felt she needed to do. She feels that some of the early women in leadership positions were not role models, since they had to take on male characteristics, but that things are changing now. The organization encourages more balance, family, community, and so on. A new role model is emerging for both men and women.*

Women in other organizations have had similar experiences.

> *Jane, a senior executive at a major utilities company, said that the president originally didn't want to promote her because she was a woman. He was hesitant to give her the position. However, her boss (a man) said that he would change the president's mind—"just give me a little time." Six months later Jane got the job. The boss helped her "fix" the situation by intervening and promoting her visibility. The president just had to get used to the idea of a woman in the position.*

> *Diane, an executive at a major newspaper, said that her mentor told her to relax a little in her management style: "You're doing OK." She is tough as a manager, but is now more willing to let her feminine side show. She has not been on specific committees for the advancement of women, but has been integral in the growth of many of her lower-level employees. Diane has guided street-tough employees, encouraged education, and made a*

*"celebration" of an employee just having received her GED. She
adds that mentors are good for women, not only nurturing
mentors, but also kick-in-the-butt types!*

*Edwina Woodbury, the chief financial officer at Avon, said that
her mentor is the company chairman. He handles crises that come
up, then moves from priority to priority quickly. He has taught her
how to manage her time and prioritize. He doesn't work late and
has few meetings. She has one role model for managing time,
another for managing people.*

If I were to choose the most critical success secret, I would
have to say that having an effective mentor or advocate is it!
When I teach management classes and discuss the changing
roles of employees in organizations, I frequently underscore the
importance of the mentoring relationship. At the end of the
class, as the students are about to leave, I always ask them, "So
what's the one thing that I want you to remember, if you remember nothing else from this meeting?" They all chime in, "Get a
mentor!" and then laugh, because I've told them many times
during the class that I want them to remember that advice.

What exactly is a mentor? Definitions include a wide array
of terms: counselor, coach, adviser, and advocate, among
many others. In essence, a mentor is often a more senior individual, frequently within the organization, although not necessarily, who shows a newcomer or protégé the ropes. Mentors
assist the junior manager in knowing the proper protocol, who
the key players are, who makes the decisions, and whom the
protégé will need to meet and impress. Mentors give the protégé an opportunity to become more visible by letting decision
makers see her work and potential. They give the protégé the
opportunity to stretch herself. They advise the junior manager
on how to handle specific situations or make career decisions.

Mentoring opportunities available to women have not kept
pace with the number of women who need or want these mentoring relationships. So what do we do? Well, one solution
may be to redefine who a mentor is and what a mentor actually can do. Does a mentor really have to be an older, more
experienced person who has seen and done it all? Or can a
mentor be an advocate who simply knows a lot from experience and who is able and willing to help us in our careers?

We would prefer to be a bit less structured in our definition of what women need in a mentor or advocate. So many of us are getting hung up on the definition of what a mentor is that we don't think about how a mentor or an advocate can help us. We may need different people to help us with different situations. We may need someone on the inside track at work to help us with general information in order to make more intelligent decisions. We may need these or other people to put in a good word for us so that we'll be recognized for a promotion or plum assignment. Sometimes we just need someone to ask advice of, or to blow off steam with, or to be supportive. That someone may be a single individual or different people: Does it really matter if it's an "official mentor"? You may look at these people as your support network, as cheerleaders or coaches. Whatever you call them, they're just people who care about you and what you do, and ideally they're well connected and respected!

THE ROLE OF THE MENTOR

What do mentors actually do? People who are advancing in organizations have various skills that they should learn. Mentors can assist them in their learning. In addition to offering insights into company politics, mentors can help their protégés learn the values, history, norms, and standards of the organization—the organizational culture.

> Lynn learned "values" from colleagues at Rosenbluth International. She discovered that humor was a very important element of the culture, as was a certain degree of informality (certainly in dress and communication) and flexibility. She didn't realize that the people on the inside track were privy to this information and capitalized on it. Although she knew that it was a fairly relaxed working environment, she didn't know that you needed to really participate actively in situations in which your humor and flexible style would be visible to senior management. It's the kind of thing that you think you know, but you may not focus on until someone points out just how important it is to know the values and norms of the organization.

Mentors can also tell you what skills and education you may need in order to advance. In other words, what do you need to do to be able to reach the next level in your career? Women often have difficulty in formulating this kind of career strategy. We don't set goals as frequently as men do. But if we don't set goals, how can we possibly achieve our expectations? An advocate can help.

Michelle, a lawyer and senior executive, said that one of her mentors asked her, "What exactly are you going to be doing in 5 years?" She described him as a kick-in-the-butt kind of mentor, which all of us need sometimes. Other advocates may provide a more nurturing direction.

Mentors and advocates help us identify the path to advancement, as well as the blind alleys. They can give us advice on which positions to take and which ones to avoid. They can also help us identify the possible barriers to our advancement. Advocates can help increase our visibility within the organization. They can let more senior people see how great we are and make sure that we are on important committees, teams, and projects.

Gena, a senior manager at Merck, gives credit to her boss and mentor for getting her involved in highly visible teams. Her boss is an advocate of diversity and he saw her potential. He values the need to represent a variety of perspectives in decisions, which reflect not only Merck's employee makeup, but its customers as well. Gena admits that she not only gained terrific experience and increased visibility within the organization, but also acquired a greater sense of self-confidence from the exposure.

Mentors can facilitate your acceptance into the inner circle of the organization. They can make sure that, as an "insider," you meet all the right people and are exposed to the right environment. They see to it that you are considered for the right assignments and promote visibility for your performance.

As we will see in Part Two, many women have difficulty giving and receiving feedback, especially negative feedback. This may be an area in which an advocate can provide much-needed advice in an environment of trust. Sometimes we may be doing something wrong at work, but no one tells us about it until it's too late! (Keep in mind that those who are envious or competing with us for recognition may even be making a conscious or unconscious attempt at sabotage.) By then, we have already done possible damage to our career. Wouldn't you rather have someone you trust and admire be the one telling you what you need to do along the way? I would! Not only can you maintain your feeling of well-being; you may very well salvage your career in the process! Sometimes a mentor or advocate will be frank enough to tell you if you're doing a good job—or not such a good job. In the case of the latter, the mentor may make suggestions to get you back on track and make progress. Remember, it's an ongoing process.

THE STAGES OF A MENTORING PROCESS

What does a mentoring process look like? While it is unique to each person or set of circumstances, some predictability can be expected. A mentoring relationship usually begins with the realization that there is a commonality between the two parties. They get along; they have a fair number of things in common, possibly similar personalities, and ideally similar values. (I'll talk a little bit more later about the benefits of choosing an advocate or a mentor, rather than being assigned someone in a random way.) The mentor often takes on the role of coach and begins to provide information, challenges, and visibility to the protégé, presumably a younger, less experienced individual.

For several years, both people will probably benefit from the relationship, becoming better friends or confidantes. However, in the event of a transfer, promotion, or similar separation, the relationship may change for both. The protégé may have new-found feelings of independence and success, while the mentor may experience feelings, even deep-down, of a possible threat or change in the dynamics of the relationship. He or she may no longer be the only expert. There may be a temporary period of discomfort, but after that the relationship will probably be redefined in a more collegial, peer-like friendship. The protégé may then need a new mentor or advocate to reflect the change in her new situation.

As with any other developing relationship, it is important to realize that emotions certainly are involved, and a feeling of trust and sharing should be developed. Don't forget that, in this type of relationship, you'll probably be telling your mentor or advocate things that you may not tell other people. Also remember that the relationship is a two-way street. You will want to give as well as take. Remember, as situations change, the relationship may change with new and different needs of those involved, especially the protégé. This is a major reason that it is especially important to have advocates or mentors whom you can really trust and feel comfortable with.

CHANGING WORKPLACE, CHANGING EMPLOYEES

Another key point is seen in the dramatic change in organizations. It used to be that hierarchies were the accepted path for success. You started out as a junior manager, and as your older, more experienced mentor showed you the ropes, you proceeded to move up in this traditional environment. You may have continued on as an assistant vice president or director, then finally made it to vice president after a certain number of years. In a traditional bureaucracy, that's just the way it was. However, the world of work is changing so dramatically today that this path may no longer exist. Instead, you have temporary workers, employees who stay with a company for a few years and then leave, either voluntarily or involuntarily. There are younger employees managing older employees, women managing men. The new work environment is becoming so totally different that the traditional process may no longer apply.

Look at technology companies, for example. Most of these companies are scarcely 20 years old, and they are usually owned and run by young, energetic, frequently unconventional people who barely know what a bureaucracy is! These organizations are more open, flexible, dynamic, and forward-thinking than many older organizations. Can you imagine expecting the same kind of mentoring situation at Netscape or Yahoo as at General Motors, for example? (Yahoo, the Internet search engine, was founded by two young graduate students in California a few years ago, just to find an efficient means of accessing the Internet for their friends and fellow students. They wore shorts and T-shirts—and still do—as they worked in their cluttered offices. But business took off so fast that these computer geniuses had to hire an experienced president to run the operations side of the company. The president is a more mature, conservative, middle-aged type. Interesting, isn't it? Who's the expert or mentor in this situation? It depends on whether you're talking about the computer side or the operations side. See how it will be more interesting from a mentoring perspective in the future?)

From a general perspective, can you imagine a 25-year-old director of marketing in one of these young, high-tech organizations depending on a traditionally minded 50-year-old vice president who doesn't know much about computers for information on developing a career? It wouldn't happen. Who's going to be the expert? These organizations rely far more on team approaches and less on hierarchical environments. It's much more of a peer support system and process. So don't we really need to assess what's going on at work and design a new mentoring strategy for the changing workplace? Things are changing very rapidly at work. We'd better start to make changes in our own minds—and organizations!

In addition, women may find that learning only from those who are at a higher level in a hierarchical structure may not entirely suit their learning style. When you think about a formal mentoring program, it seems more like a proliferation of the traditional patriarchal situation—like "dad" telling you what to do without much interaction, and the assumption that you don't really know a lot. It's a power struggle. I don't know about you, but this approach still makes me cringe!

While it has traditionally been true in organizations that younger employees have learned from older employees, then copied their behavior in order to be recognized and promoted, it is definitely not necessarily true any longer. Further, women frequently just prefer nonhierarchical relationships, such as teams or other, more equal environments. So keep your eyes open for a mentor or advocate who suits your lifestyle!

FINDING A MENTOR

One question that some of you may ask is "How do I go about finding a mentor?" If you are in an organization that fosters this type of relationship, the answer may be relatively easy. You may be assigned a mentor, take advantage of a mentoring program in place, or be able to network with people who are willing to work with you. But for many of us, especially if we are either unaccustomed to seeking out such a person or hesitant to go looking for one, the experience can be daunting. Sometimes it is a result of luck, sometimes of planning. Some of the people we may relate to most effectively are simply good friends and family. For general professional advice and support, I often seek out colleagues, such as members of the European Women's Management Development Network, an international management development association of which I am a U.S. board member. Professional associations can be an excellent resource for obtaining information, establishing effective contacts, engaging in research, and conducting a job search. These resources can be an excellent means of finding information or gaining support outside your organization, for the most part.

Inside the organization, the people whose advice I seek do not necessarily have my promotion or recognition as their number-one priority. But I do feel very comfortable with the relationships I have tried to develop with certain of my peers so that I can ask the more organizationally focused questions. Is this the ideal scenario? Maybe not, since it does not really constitute having a mentor, but then I still get the support, visibility, advice, and guidance that I need. And isn't that what a mentor does? Some people may argue—and they may very well be right—that this type of peer advocacy cannot be nearly as effective as a true mentor. But what if there is no one at your organization who is willing to be a mentor in the more comprehensive way? What if you don't feel comfortable asking someone to make the time and emotional commitment to you? It's still better than not having guidance, visibility, and support at all!

When I think of what having a true mentor would have done for me, I am certain that it would have put me on the right track a little faster. I have learned many things by trial and error—as have most of my friends and colleagues. But I try to be extremely generous with my time and advice—whatever help they may be to others—to many people who ask. I have developed more of a "mentoring" relationship with some people, but I feel good about the fact that I have at least helped other people by pointing them in the right direction and taking the first step.

> One of the most influential people in getting me started on the right track was a woman I met only twice. I haven't seen her in years and I'm not even sure that she would remember me. When I first started taking my doctoral courses, I had met a very impressive consultant to my college. She already had her PhD and I just called her to ask what she would recommend that I take as additional electives. She suggested taking as many business courses as I could—something I had never really thought about before. I thanked her and did as she recommended. I discovered that I really enjoyed the courses and had a natural affinity to management. I didn't speak to the woman after that, but she really made my career direction take a dramatic turn for the better.

So you never know where you'll get the best advice! Take advantage of any situation in which people are willing to help you—and don't neglect to pass along what you have learned to others. Remember, this is a relationship-building network!

Interestingly enough, I am beginning to find that not only younger women but also younger men are starting to seek out the advice of more senior women. The younger men probably feel quite comfortable with the professional relationship between men and women to begin with, and may also be very interested in gaining a diverse perspective. I have had several younger men ask my general advice and my opinions on organizational issues. Conversely, I have felt very comfortable asking their opinions or advice on various matters. It's very refreshing to see that the next generation of men seems to have largely lost their predecessors' attitudes about women in the workplace. The younger men are so used to having women in their classes and on their teams that, for the most part, they are much more at ease with the role of working women in general. This kind of relationship can be very helpful for all parties concerned.

Still, to gain the benefits of a traditional mentoring relationship, a formal mentor is required. Finding one can be difficult. To the frustration of many women, some mentors, generally men, have traditionally chosen a protégé according to such criteria as having the right style, playing the approved sport, belonging to the right clubs, or attending the right schools. Rosabeth Moss Kanter has called some mentoring relationships "managerial cloning."[6] Most senior men know a great deal about how younger men can become successful—they've done it themselves. But they know very little about the everyday dilemmas of professional women: the balancing act between home and work, between being tough enough but not too tough, between not being too feminine but maintaining your sense of self. Most senior men have never had to face these situations.

There may be potential barriers for women who want to develop mentoring relationships. One may be a lack of access to information networks. Women often have limited contact with potential mentors. A possible reason is that some women may have limited knowledge of how to develop informal networks (see Success Secret Four). Women may also tend to interact more frequently with others of similar status, rather than higher-level people. In some situations, certain women may even be excluded from potential networking groups which form the source of mentors. Stereotypes and biases may still exist within an "old-boys' network" that precludes women from being recognized for their talents and being asked to become protégés. The last barrier may just be the discomfort some men feel in mentoring women. You know how it is: Men usually feel more comfortable around other men for the camaraderie, the sense of bonding. Some men may just not see the possibility of women fitting the same mold, or they truly just don't want women in their group. They may not say it, but some men do think it. It often takes a long time and a lot of energy to change attitudes among such people.

Have you ever had a mentor? I have never had one—nor have most of my friends. Does that mean, however, that I haven't had people help me, listen to me, or support me? Definitely not. Many of us have had family, friends, colleagues, and acquaintances who have helped in various ways. We probably wouldn't have accomplished as much on our own. However, I will confess, it would have been easier if I had been able to identify someone to fulfill all these roles. On the other hand, what happens if our mentor leaves or in some way we must disassociate ourselves from that person? It's probably better to have a number of advocates or mentors.

DEVELOPING MENTORING RELATIONSHIPS

Research has shown that many women do not have the opportunity to work with a mentor—for a variety of reasons which will be discussed in greater detail later in the chapter. One recurring reason is that, because of people's natural inclination to seek out others like themselves, a mentor-protégé relationship may develop as the result of two people discovering similar backgrounds, interests, and goals—either coincidentally or by design. It has traditionally been accepted that young men on the fast track, for example, may be identified by a senior manager and invited to an impromptu lunch, golf outing, ball game, or similar informal gathering—a situation that may develop into a type of male bonding. Conversely, an ambitious young male manager may realize that moving ahead on the fast track is enhanced by the choice of a well-connected senior executive and subsequently may begin to develop a rapport with such a manager. Many younger men just assume that this opportunity is available to anyone.

A while back, a newspaper reporter interviewed me for a story about my research. During the interview, we started talking about some of my findings. I explained that women frequently don't know the necessary strategies for success, such as the importance of a mentor. The reporter was surprised at this statement. I asked him if he had a mentor. He said, "Yes—as a matter of fact, it was one of my professors at school." I asked him what this professor did for him. He said that he encouraged him to write for the college newspaper, made sure he received invitations to events when prestigious authors were in town, and helped him get his first job out of school. I said that most women don't have mentors to help them out in those ways. He said, "Really? I just assumed that everyone had people like that to help out."

The son of a colleague, Eric, had a similar experience. When Eric began his real estate career after finishing graduate school at NYU, his new boss put him on the right track. He taught him how to deal with clients, got him into private clubs, recommended the right racquet/health club to join (male bonding), and taught him the clothes to wear and the other necessary points of doing business. What a great asset!

However, many women have not had the opportunity to experience the informal association and rapport of senior managers, who are primarily men, without the baggage of office gossip or underlying rumors. In addition, many senior managers may not identify young women as candidates for the fast track—probably not as a malicious intention, but as an oversight. As noted earlier, people tend to gravitate toward people most like themselves—it's just human nature.

The reporter I just mentioned asked why women don't seek out mentors themselves. Good question. He was right. Most women do not seek out mentors, possibly because they don't realize the importance of a mentor to their career, or possibly because they just don't know anyone senior enough to serve as a mentor. Another reason is the possible discomfort of seeking out a relationship—albeit as a mentor—with a more senior (probably older) man and risking the rumors that may ensue. This may not be an unlikely scenario, since the majority of senior-level managers are still men. In addition, there are probably just not enough senior women to serve as mentors if a female protégé feels more comfortable seeking a woman's advice. For many women, this remains a frustrating situation.

> A senior executive of Bell Atlantic was told by her former (male) boss, a good friend, "You know, I could never go out to lunch or dinner with you—just you—in the same way I can with another male executive." He was right. People would probably have jumped to conclusions.

It is also an interesting question of whether it is more beneficial to be assigned a mentor or to let a mentoring relationship develop on its own. For some people, an assigned relationship works out wonderfully, but for others it can be a source of anxiety.

> In one major accounting firm, a young man just beginning his career was very pleased with his assigned mentor. They worked together well and had a lot in common. However, I asked him if his female colleagues felt the same way. He said, "You know, now that you mention it, some of the young women were not looking forward to their first official meeting with their mentor." He said that the women clearly felt some discomfort at having been randomly assigned to a mentor.

In my graduate classes, I often ask students if they would rather be assigned to a mentor or choose one. These classes are generally quite well mixed in terms of gender and race. Many of the students feel that they would rather choose a mentor, although their reasons often differ. For example, a female student said that she would feel more comfortable with someone like herself. On the other hand, a male student stated that he would like to be in a mentoring relationship with at least one woman so that he could learn a different perspective from her and continue to effectively understand the differences—and similarities—between men and women. Another male student said that he would rather choose a mentor (or several mentors), because he wouldn't want to get a "loser" for an advocate. When I asked him what he meant, he said that he would consider someone a "loser" who wasn't as smart or motivated as he would like. He added that he wanted a mentor who was into technology and computers, since he would like to learn more about them. There should clearly be a comfort level between mentor and protégé, and this "fit" may differ depending upon the people involved. Therefore, it may be preferable for an organization to allow for a choice of mentors, whenever possible.

The selection process may illustrate one of the difficulties in establishing an effective mentoring program in organizations at this point in time. Unfortunately, many of the decision makers, including those involved in determining the structure of mentoring programs in organizations, may continue to feel that the way mentors and protégés are chosen is highly effective for all participants. However, with the increasing diversity within the workforce, the mentor-protégé selection process may become outdated. As a result, it may be effective for an organization to establish database pools of potential mentors and protégés among its employees. Employees wishing to participate as either mentors or protégés could give pertinent information, even anonymously at first if they wished, such as interests, age, department, and goals, and then check the database for a match of their choice. In this way, participants could develop a better professional rapport with those with whom they would have the most in common or from whom they could learn the most.

Don't forget, a mentoring relationship is a two-way street. In addition to the information that the mentor may impart to the protégé, the protégé is likely to provide insight and understanding to the more seasoned manager on his or her frame of reference. It can become more of a symbiotic relationship. Whatever their position in the organization, employees may wish to suggest this approach to their human resources department to help alleviate the current discomfort of being assigned a mentor who has different interests and background from the protégé.

BARRIERS TO MENTORING RELATIONSHIPS

Barriers to mentoring relationships for women can be both internal and external. Women may not choose to seek out mentors, or mentors may not seek them out. Why don't women seek out mentors? The most likely answer is that women fail to recognize the importance of a mentor. They may think that if you work hard enough and are smart enough, you'll get ahead. And even if women do recognize the importance of obtaining a mentor, they may not feel comfortable or experienced enough to assume an assertive role in initiating a mentoring relationship. In a 1983 study of almost 400 women, 61 percent said that they "fell into" a mentoring relationship, 20 percent were selected by mentors, but only 19 percent sought out mentors.[7] Why this reluctance to seek out a mentor?

First, a woman may feel uncomfortable starting a mentoring relationship with a male manager for fear of having it misconstrued—either by the mentor himself or by the organization—as a sexual approach. The male mentor, as well, may feel more comfortable with another man initiating the mentoring relationship, since he's "one of the guys." A man can casually invite another to have lunch, to play tennis or golf, or to go to sporting events. But if a woman does the same thing, does it become a date in the man's eyes? It may be that the very strategies used by men to develop mentoring relationships may not work for women or, worse, may even work against women.

External factors working against women include the fact that female managers generally have fewer formal and informal opportunities to develop mentoring relationships than do their male counterparts. Since many women occupy lower-level positions, even in management, it is likely that these women will not be as visible as their male counterparts. They frequently do not have access to potential "bonding" opportunities, such as on golf courses, over lunch, or even in the restroom.

> *Mary, a talented and experienced editor, recounts that after a morning strategy meeting, her male boss and male colleague headed into the men's room, talking and laughing—you know, the male-bonding thing. She went back to her office to get some work done over lunch. A couple of hours later, the two men come rolling in from an obviously pleasant lunch, at which they probably continued the strategies from the morning meeting. Mary felt clearly left out of the process. Whenever they had decided to get together for lunch, she wasn't told about it and was*

not invited along. It was obviously an impromptu decision, made in the men's room. How do you compete with that?

In addition, women cannot always develop friendships and socialize with their mentors in the same way as their male counterparts do. When women do not have access to more senior managers who may serve as effective mentors, they may utilize peer relationships for social support, fulfilling the need for relationship rather than direction and guidance. But there are just some times when you really need to have a senior manager for guidance and advice, not just someone to listen patiently to your situation.

Another barrier to women in management is that male mentors, because of their own perception of societal bias, may view a female protégé more as a wife or daughter than as a professional colleague. When a mentoring situation appears more "safely" as a father-daughter relationship rather than a potentially romantic encounter, it may still be counterproductive, since it takes on a paternalistic-dependent cast that may keep women from developing and moving on to more effective mentoring relationships.

What about women serving as mentors to other women? Although things are gradually beginning to change, there are still not all that many women in senior enough positions to mentor women who are moving up in organizations. My research has shown that the senior women who are really terrific—talented, approachable, well connected—are usually overwhelmed by requests for mentoring. While many aspiring female managers may feel that they lack support from the senior women in their organization, the truth may be that there just aren't that many mentors to go around! The reasons for not taking on a protégé include lack of time, nonsupportive environments, too much dependency on the part of the protégé, and the risk of choosing the wrong protégé. However, a number of senior women underscore their commitment to developing younger women and men.

The former president of Bryn Mawr College cites a commitment to support people once you've taken a chance on them—and to provide feedback. There is a critical obligation to the next generation to provide information and guidance. From her own experience, she thinks about how someone else would do a task she is faced with. She has often figured out who was doing things well and mirrored them.

Gail Blanke, a senior vice president at Avon, considers herself a team player, not territorial. She likes people, likes to motivate people, likes to get her team promoted and recognized, and likes them to have more money. She considers herself very nurturing and believes in informal mentoring groups. She would like to see more reaching out and feels that positive reinforcement is a critical piece.

But, as I mentioned, there is a possible risk on the part of any mentor, male or female, in choosing a female protégé. Since greater emphasis and visibility are placed on the success of a woman, a mentor could be taking on a greater risk to ensure her success—even if the protégé turns out not to have what it takes. Keep in mind that even if a woman has as much going for her as a man, many people may still harbor the expectation that a man will be more successful. So if a woman succeeds, it probably won't be as recognized as success for the mentor or for the protégé. But if a woman fails, for whatever reason, the visibility could be far greater for both parties. The failure may be perceived even more keenly if both parties are female. Since female executives may be in more precarious positions than their male counterparts as it is, it's possible that there will be a greater risk to take on a female protégé, who may conceivably be seen as a "liability." In addition, some organizations may perceive the partnering of a female mentor and female protégé as a "female coalition," a situation that may be viewed as a negative in the organization. (Uh-oh, they're ganging up on us! They're probably going to start that "feminist stuff"!)

Are there advantages and disadvantages to male or female mentors? Women wishing to move ahead in organizations may view some female mentors as warmer, more empathetic, and better role models than men. In addition, the likelihood of encountering sexual issues is greatly reduced. On the other hand, male mentors have been traditionally viewed as more powerful and better connected than women in organizations, whether or not it is actually true. Men may also be able to give their protégé a certain credibility or legitimacy as a result of their real or perceived position.

Unfortunately, as it stands now in many organizations, female protégés may have difficulty in being selected by either male or female mentors for several of the aforementioned reasons. Therefore, it is very important for women to understand how to develop effective networks that can translate into future mentoring opportunities, rather than relying on traditional mentor development. Although things are changing, female mentors may serve as effective role models and coaches to women in the earlier stages of their careers, whereas male mentors may be more effective in later career stages, when women need more emphasis on developing organizational influence.

THE QUEEN BEE SYNDROME

Do women make poor mentors? My personal experience says no. Almost all the women I interviewed make it very clear that they consider it a priority to help women—and men—following them in the organization. But other women tell a different story. The Queen Bee syndrome has been widely studied—the idea that once women have moved ahead in the organization, they pull the ladder up behind them. This is still a hotly contested issue. In some organizations, especially bureaucratic ones with a traditional leadership pattern (i.e., based on a male military or sports model), it may have been necessary for women to conform to the accepted leadership style in order to get ahead. It is important to note here that masculine-feminine sex-role identity may be a better indicator of leadership style than a person's actual gender. With this thought in mind, it makes sense that women or men who succeed in a particular organization are most likely quite similar in their leadership approach. Thus, the question of women or men as inherently effective or ineffective mentors is probably more an issue of what their sex-role identity is. (Sex-role identity indicates certain traits, characteristics, or tendencies that are characteristic of masculine behavior, feminine behavior, or a combination of the two—for example, athletic, competitive, compassionate, nurturing.)

Maybe I'm lucky, but I have had a couple of really terrific female bosses. They have encouraged me in challenging and stretching myself, offered advice, and made an effort to develop my strengths and skills. However, I know that other women tell horror stories about working for women. I think that, in all honesty, there are both good and bad male managers and good and bad female managers. This could be where luck comes in: Sometimes you get a great boss and sometimes you just don't!

But, as I mentioned, the majority of women involved in the study specifically noted that they were extremely interested in developing the skills of all their employees, both women and men. Some were especially pleased when their encouragement, advice, or recommendations gave other women the opportunity to advance. However, it was clear that an essential aspect of their management style was to develop their staff.

In the old days (and still occasionally today), some women felt that if they had to tough it out and fight their way to the top, well so did everyone else who followed them. In a recent article in *Fortune* magazine, seven extremely successful and well-known women were interviewed about their success. Only one of the seven indicated that she specifically identified talented women to develop. The others felt that they should be gender-blind and that if you worked hard and made a name for yourself you would succeed.[8] I personally disagree. We have seen time and time again women who are working just as hard as their male counterparts—or even harder—and getting nowhere.

Although employment ideally should be gender-blind, there may be a number of skills or characteristics that otherwise very talented women are lacking or that are underdeveloped. If fully developed, these skills can make women extremely competitive in a gender-blind environment. Some women, on the same track and with the same qualifications as their male counterparts, may just need a little extra direction or advice. The very competitive women in the article probably learned other extremely valuable skills that they do not necessarily take into account when looking at their success, and they may feel that it's up to other women to make it on their own. Perhaps they were lucky and had very supportive parents or other mentors and advocates in their careers that other women have not had. Maybe they had a less traditionally feminine socialization. Maybe they were just tougher. Maybe they were greater risk takers. There are so many variables that it is unfair to assume that if these women could make it, others should be able to make it as well. It doesn't mean that only those women whose fathers and mothers taught them to be tough, competitive, athletic, or effective risk takers deserve to be successful. We can't change our early socialization—we have very little control over what our upbringing is like. However, we can certainly change our present.

Among the women I interviewed, the feeling of exclusion is not the prevailing thought. Most of them try to identify high-potential female subordinates as well as equally promising male subordinates who have skills that may need to be developed. It is a scenario of inclusion, not survival of the fittest. However, that survival-of-the-fittest mentality may be simply more indicative of the more competitive, military- or sports-based structure of many organizations. If women seeking top positions years ago didn't play by those rules, they didn't get ahead. It may be true that some organizations are still like that and compliance to such a structure is still essential to get ahead. However, most management gurus now espouse the team-based environment thriving on communication and trust as the most effective organizational structure. In such an environment, women and men can more easily afford to exhibit a more nurturing, open, and supportive management style.

Part of the possible misconception may come from personal management style and individual socialization. If you go back to the differences between how men and women are socialized (e.g., participative team sports versus nurturing games), it may be that many women are not used to the typical confrontational encounters in a business environment and therefore are not entirely comfortable with certain interpersonal interactions. For example, many men are quite comfortable with shouting at one another (either figuratively or quite literally) one minute and hanging out as friends the next minute. That's just the way men are socialized and it's no big deal. However, women may become confused or hurt by such an encounter and may not bounce back in the same way. As girls, they may not have experienced an environment which facilitated this type of encounter (by participating on a sports team, for example). Consequently, these women can't always just brush it off and forget about it. It's bad enough when such an encounter occurs and the boss is a man. But take it a step further to a female boss who happens to share the same masculine characteristics and management style. Some successful women who have been socialized in a similar fashion to men, through sports teams or leadership positions, may have learned to participate easily in this type of "masculine" management style. Their behavior could create conflict or even resentment among other women—they see the same physical gender, but not the behavior typically associated with that gender.

Successful women who have been socialized in the same manner as successful men are often called "no nonsense" or "tough as nails" types, yet men exhibiting such characteristics are not given the same labels. The female subordinates of these women may not feel entirely comfortable with this gender disparity, since in truth it is still not common for women to be in power positions as frequently as men. The more junior women may not be used to women who are so different from them in their management style.

> Diane, a director, talked about what she saw as the importance of women being able to work easily with men by developing an understanding of the differences between the genders—and also an understanding of women who possess masculine sex-role characteristics (i.e., leadership style). One of the roles of a mentor, for example, may be to facilitate the understanding of differences in management styles and appropriate reaction and interaction.

However, it is also important to understand that women who have been socialized in a more competitive, "masculine" environment are not necessarily less willing to facilitate the advancement of other women—or men, for that matter. Their willingness may just be less outwardly apparent as a result of their overall characteristics or personality, which may be less "warm and fuzzy" than that of other managers, women or men. (Again, let's not make gender generalities.)

It was very disappointing to read a recent article about a female executive from a financial services firm who refused to promote the visibility of her top performer to the chairman of the company because the top performer was a woman. Likewise, she would not serve as her mentor, which effectively cut the younger woman off from the fast track of the organization. The female executive said that she would consider it a mistake for a woman executive to choose only to develop other women. However, that did not seem to be the issue. She should have been developing men as well. I had to question both the motives and the possible sense of insecurity of the executive. Was she so insecure in her position that she felt it would derail her career if she pointed out that her top performer was a woman? It's one thing to exclude a person—either a man or a woman—out of ignorance, but quite a different story to systematically shut out a fast-track employee because she is of the same gender. If I were the executive's subordinate, I think that I would be looking to move! Fortunately, this type of narrow-mindedness was rare among the women I interviewed, most of whom were in exactly a position to promote the visibility of both their talented male and female employees. They really worked to promote their employees' advancement as a critical part of their leadership role. I see this as the more realistic perspective of effective leaders.

Instead of stereotyping some successful female managers as Queen Bees, it may be enormously effective to ascertain the characteristics of these women that were beneficial to learn and that may help you in your own career. Although you may feel that you don't want to emulate certain characteristics typical of many men, you don't have to adopt any or all of the elements of their management style. But certainly an understanding of how some managers manage successfully can serve only to improve communication and overall organizational effectiveness.

KEY FACTS OF MENTORING

As Lynn, my co-author, was learning about the whole concept of mentoring—the hard way, of course—she realized a couple of key facts. When she had moved into a new company, she decided to really look at what it takes to be more successful. We talked about a strategy and did some reading and discussing with other people to find out what to do to facilitate her success. Among other things, Lynn determined that she would get to know the senior people right from the beginning. She did. She met most of the key decision makers and spoke to them on a regular basis. She considered herself at an advantage to have her office on the executive level, which put her into the same physical space to interact more effectively. However, although she had a good relationship with many of the top executives, the situation didn't seem to be as beneficial as she thought it would. She wasn't always in the information loop for key decisions or updates, and she felt that something was missing. She was right. But what was it?

A male colleague who was in the "inner circle" made a recommendation about 6 months later. He suggested that, although Lynn knew the key people, they really didn't know *her*. She didn't "hang out" with them—have lunch, play golf, and so on. He said that she had a good reputation for being a hard worker and smart, but they didn't see her personal side—her good sense of humor and the ability to adapt to any situation. (People who really know Lynn often see a very different side of her than those who do not.) Coincidentally, in this organization, a major success factor was sense of humor and ability to be one of the guys! So Lynn decided to ask her colleague to include her in the key players' plans to get together socially or for lunch. For example, if they were going to get together, he could put in a good word or invite her along. In this way, senior management would be able to get to know Lynn in a different light. Her colleague was becoming her unofficial advocate. He could help her become more visible and better known, which in an organization such as Lynn's was essential for advancement. This was very valuable inside information.

So it is essential to go beyond simply knowing more senior members of the organization. Not only do we have to make the effort to go out of our way to meet the key people (which can be intimidating in itself in some organizations!); we also have to use this segue to get to know people well enough to be "one of the guys." (Now, of course, I mean this figuratively, not literally.)

It can really help to find others, preferably more senior members of the organization, who will help you first identify what is important in the organizational culture. What is it in your organization that gets people noticed? Is it hard work (i.e., whoever arrives the earliest and stays the latest wins)? Is it teamwork and a collegial environment? Is it a sense of humor and the ability to laugh at yourself occasionally? Once you have determined what qualities are most valued at the organization, you can continue by identifying those who can help you practice these skills, become more visible, and invite you to participate in, at least to some extent, the higher levels of the organization. You generally need to be "invited." Most people cannot just admit themselves into the "club." And that is one of the major roles of your advocate or mentor.

Although it may be difficult or even painful, it is helpful to ask those in a more senior position (whom you trust) for constructive criticism. They will frequently be able to see the big picture and how you fit into it. As them directly: "Am I doing the right things to get noticed? What experience do I lack? Do I have the right education? What might I be doing wrong? Do I need to change any behaviors?" (This will be a big one for many of us!) No one likes to be criticized, but if done constructively, criticism may be the most effective way to identify and correct potential problems. Look at it this way. If certain issues seriously need to be addressed, other people are going to see them, even if you don't! So wouldn't you like to have someone, whom you trust, work with you in a supportive environment to help facilitate your professional growth rather than be coldly and brutally told about your faults without a means to constructively work on your development?

It is especially salient to note here that many women have difficulty separating business from personal feelings. Many of us feel that if people are our friends or acquaintances at the office, they have the same commitment to us as our personal friends. They frequently don't! That's why when we are criticized, fired, laid off, demoted, transferred, or reprimanded by those we like—and who supposedly like us—it almost seems like a betrayal. "I thought that she liked me. How could she eliminate my position?" With that in mind, it may be devastating to have the cold, hard, critical truth thrown at us by someone we like. We can possibly prevent the situation by preparing ourselves before a potential crisis arises. An effective mentor or advocate can help us out.

A lot of what I've been talking about concerns a very nurturing kind of mentoring. But several participants in the research mentioned the need for a "kick in the pants" type of mentor—someone who really gets us fired up and thinking about what we're doing or what we need to do.

> *Several of the women in the study said that they had had mentors who bluntly told them, "Look, what are you going to be doing in 5 years? You better start thinking about that now!"*

It may not be the easiest way to receive helpful advice, but there may be situations in which we really need someone to "jump-start" us. Otherwise, we may risk being lulled into a false sense of security.

This may be especially true in an organization experiencing downsizing, for example. People know it's going to happen— they may even know it's going to happen to them. But frequently they don't do anything about it! You may need someone to say, "You're going to lose your job. Who's going to pay your mortgage? What are you doing to get a new job? Let's go, get moving!" Again, business is business; don't take things personally. However, many women probably do take this kind of approach personally, and they must learn the hard way to overcome their sensitivity. We frequently don't have sports or military experiences that prepare us for this type of approach, so we just have to practice understanding it by thinking about the rationale behind it. Some people are just not "touchy-feely" kinds of people. They don't treat *anyone* with kid gloves. If you understand their way, you will tend to be less offended or hurt and put off when they treat you coolly. Ask yourself: "Are they treating anyone else any differently?" We really need to get tougher and thicker-skinned in the workplace. Remember, we're constantly dealing with people with many different types of personalities. We cannot take it personally and wear our hearts on our sleeves. In a perfect world everyone would be fair, considerate of feelings and a great communicator. But so far that does not exist. So this may be yet another reason to have several mentors or advocates. Some will be nurturing and others the kick-in-the-pants types. One kind can appeal to our more sensitive side and the other will help us develop our thicker skin!

MENTORS AS CHANGE AGENTS

Women in the workplace may express less confidence, have lower career and pay expectations, and take fewer risks than their male counterparts. There are times when we all feel that if people tell us often enough that we can't do something, we begin to believe it. We begin to question our skills, our talents, our abilities. However, the converse is also true. If someone is constantly reassuring us that we can do something, we start to really believe it. We may need to counteract any self-esteem issues, and a mentor can certainly help point us in the right direction.

As I mentioned earlier, one of the roles of the mentor is to help us understand what really goes on within the organization. Women frequently have less experience in organizational politics than men and may also have fewer female role models, so that they may be at a decided disadvantage in developing strategies and going for powerful positions. How are we supposed to know whom to talk to, which jobs to go for, what kinds of experience to get, what educational background is appropriate, and how best to get the job if we don't know who the key players are? Why do men often get the plum jobs that we never even hear about until newly filled positions are announced? Their mentors are helping them out. Well, my motto is "When in Rome, ..." Learn what you need to start getting noticed, and I bet much of that will be facilitated by a mentor.

> *Former Congresswoman Marjorie Margolies Mezvinsky agrees that you can't do it without mentors. Politicians don't generally have role models. She recommends that you find yourself about eight people you respect and admire. You can't be successful if you don't let yourself be mentored.*

> *A friend of mine at Merck agrees that attitudes have really started to change in the last 5 years or so. Her boss, an Asian male, was one of the first managers to address the diversity issue head on. He has been a tremendous guide and inspiration for her. He is smart, talented, hard-working, and well connected, with a great insight for future trends. White male managers would ask, "Why are we doing this diversity thing?" He would "shut them down with extraordinary grace." A program was set into place to select high-potential employees for mentoring and career development. My friend believes that if all employees are developed equally, the cream will rise to the top.*

CROSS-GENDER MENTORING

Although cross-gender mentoring may certainly happen with an older female mentor and a male protégé, especially in many of the newer or high-tech organizations, the traditional scenario has been an older male mentor and a younger female protégé. Many, if not most, of the women I initially interviewed cited male mentors as a critical advantage in their advancement in organizations.

> *Diane at Gannett talked about a male colleague, a former military officer, as someone who was instrumental in helping her career—and still does today. Carol at Pfizer says that a number of*

her male bosses and colleagues accepted her and encouraged her throughout her advancement at the company.

It is not grounded in research, but my general feeling is that women who are senior enough to be considered mentors by younger men are probably much more experienced and aware of the issues that their young male protégés experience than are senior men who attempt to empathize with their female protégés. Senior women have had to adapt far more to the male model than senior men have had to adapt to a "female" model of sharing, communicating, and nurturing.

Even with all these positive benefits, if mentors are approached properly and with the right attitude, the situation can be really tricky. There is no room to approach it naively. You really want to be prepared if you wish to seek out an effective mentor across genders. If you aren't prepared, you run the risk of derailing your career. I don't want to persuade you not to seek out a mentor, especially a male mentor. Far from it! However, it is enormously important to understand the best ways to approach this tremendously beneficial relationship.

First, it is critical to have a fair understanding of socialization and the dynamics between men and women. If you're a woman, don't go any further in seeking a male mentor before you really understand this issue. I'm not a sociologist or a counselor, but this is really important stuff! For a socialization overview in this book, refer to Part Two. Deborah Tannen[9] does a terrific job of describing the differences between men and women in her books, as does Carol Gilligan.[10] I really thought I understood a lot of the differences between men and women until I read some of these works. They opened my eyes!

Some of the successful women I spoke to thought that I shouldn't underscore the differences between women and men in my book. They felt that doing so would exacerbate the gap between genders. On the other hand, some women felt that the book should celebrate the differences between women and men, without making too big a deal about it. They felt that it was wrong to ignore the positive diversity in attitudes and the way people look at things. Both opinions have merit. (But it is interesting to see yet again that gender does not always dictate attitudes. Not *all* women feel the same way. Not *all* men feel the same way.) However, despite the surface attitudes that men and women reflect, at a deeper level we may find that men really do think differently from some women, and I underscore the word *some*. Men are often socialized in a different way. They may play by different rules than women do. The goal may be to talk to a lot of your male friends or colleagues, people you can trust and confide in, and find out what they really think. With my very close male friends, I can hear their politically correct approach. They may certainly appreciate male-female differences—they are very accepting of women and very supportive—but sometimes I still catch the deep-seated way that they really feel, even if only occasionally. There may be a very traditional attitude, feeling, or thought lurking deep inside that occasionally comes out. It's like going back to their instincts, or something! So you may just want to be aware that this could affect a mentoring situation in the future.

From what I can see, having a mentor is one of the most critical aspects of becoming successful. However, it is important to realize the implications of such a relationship as well. Of course, depending upon the people and the situation, there may be certain risks in a mentoring relationship.

As I mentioned, the risks may be especially salient for women who have male mentors. Of course, there may be talk within the organization of a sexual, rather than professional relationship. In addition, the mentor, especially if assigned through a formal mentoring program, may not have the talent to perform in that capacity. The mentor and protégé may have personalities or goals that are too dissimilar, or too much alike, so that conflict may arise in the relationship or even competition for the same positions. Then too, if you have a mentor or advocate who is really terrific but tough, you'll have to be ready for greater workloads, responsibility, and scrutiny. But many successful women have underscored the importance of having a mentor and they have established positive, professional relationships, so most likely the negative situations are far outweighed by the enormously positive ones.

Another fact that must be mentioned is the physical and emotional side of cross-gender mentoring. It would be irresponsible of me not to bring this issue up. Remember, this is the development of a relationship. You and your mentor will probably spend a lot of time together. Ideally you will grow, share, communicate, have disagreements, and enjoy successes. There is always the possibility of a romantic or sexual side to the relationship, despite your original expectations.

Potential problems could include sexual attraction, marital disruption, and damaging gossip. It may be a difficult balance, because on the one hand you have the desire to develop effective professional relationships; on the other hand, you may feel the need to keep your distance in order to avoid complications or gossip. It may not be an easy decision. You may feel a great deal of anxiety as well, so you may need to examine your own expectations. Many women will agree that it is probably not a good idea to get romantically involved with anyone at work, especially your boss or mentor. Emotions aside, it could be a serious impediment to your advancement. What happens if the relationship goes wrong? Will it become uncomfortable? Will you be able to work productively and separate your professional and personal feelings? Will your professional relationship or your reputation be damaged by gossip? Perhaps your concerns about developing a romantic attachment may lead to avoiding a mentor who could actually help you or lead to decreased effectiveness in your work. Both the internal aspects of the mentoring relationship (your emotions) and the external aspects (what others may think and your reputation) need to be addressed. These are all questions which may arise in any work setting, and the issues probably won't be exacerbated by developing a mentoring relationship with the opposite sex. But, again, you really need to know all the aspects of such a situation so that you don't enter the mentoring relationship naively.

It may be difficult to develop an appropriate level of intimacy in a professional mentoring relationship. The parties may have different expectations of how close they should become. It is absolutely critical to define the boundaries of the relationship. If a romantic attachment seems possible, the two parties must agree on the necessary strategies to maintain a professional relationship. But many, many men and women have very successfully maintained a purely professional relationship, attitude, and demeanor. This can be successfully achieved with careful examination of your views, attitudes, and expectations, as well as those of your mentor.

Your organization can help you through its human resources department. The organization can establish effective programs through which mentors and protégés can choose a suitable match on the basis of similar interests, goals, and expectations. This approach should certainly be more effective than an arbitrary match such as exists in many current mentoring programs. Keep in mind, as well, that many older male mentors can gain valuable insight from female protégés with regard to women's leadership styles, preferences, and professional and personal needs (the need for flexibility and child care, for example). In fact, this may be an excellent opportunity for women to begin or continue to effectively change the organizational culture by contributing their perspectives to more senior executives who are, of course, more instrumental in providing direction and commitment!

Mentoring may prove to be a critical issue if women in organizations want to make some serious changes. Many women may truly question whether they can make it in their organizations. Some women leave because they become frustrated at the lack of understanding and sensitivity to what they're going through as women. There is the frequent bias, even covert bias, against women in some organizations, the lack of flexibility, and the lack of commitment on the part of senior management to family and personal issues. Some women may say that it's not worth trying to change management, because nothing ever changes anyway. Well, this may be an opportunity to try. By working with an influential mentor, a female protégé may not only influence the senior executive, frequently a man, but subsequently begin to change senior management's perspective on what women experience. Executives may take this new perspective back to the boardroom or major committee and begin to change the organizational policies pertaining to these issues.

Another potential outcome is that, with the help of influential mentors, women may gain the credibility, exposure, visibility, and position to initiate some of these same changes in attitudes and policy within the organization. Such changes have already begun to occur in numerous organizations. It can certainly be extremely rewarding and exciting when you start to change the values and attitudes of your organization!

ORGANIZATIONAL ROLES IN MENTORING

In addition to what we as individuals can do to develop effective mentoring situations, we may want to look at what our organizations can do to facilitate the situation. It may be extremely helpful for women if the organization can provide opportunities for them to interact with potential mentors in formal and informal settings. Such opportunities can increase women's access to more senior executives who may serve as potential mentors. At Rosenbluth International's annual company picnic, the senior executives don aprons and become the barbequers and waiters and waitresses. It is an excellent opportunity for the employees to interact positively with the senior staff and develop a potential rapport.

Many organizations have ongoing job shadowing, and training can be provided to allow women to see opportunities in mentoring relationships as well as ideal scenarios and time lines for a mentoring process. Many women may not realize the importance of using mentoring as a serial process, with different people assisting as the women move to increasingly responsible positions. The benefits of mentoring can also be highlighted. Succession planning, or who will be prepared for which positions, can start earlier in women's careers. How can we plan for our future role if we have no idea of what that role may be? By knowing our role, we can identify people earlier who may be able to assist us in our advancement.

Madelyn Jennings and Terri Sullivan have greatly influenced their organization, Gannett/USA Today, through their innovative initiatives in the human resources department. Terri was instrumental in establishing an inclusive mission statement of USA Today. Many of the programs are exciting, forward-looking opportunities. Terri always had the opportunity to use USA Today as a ground-breaking laboratory. The publisher of USA Today, Tom Curley, very much agrees with Terri's agenda. They are breaking a lot of barriers to women's advancement. Madelyn, whom Terri recognizes as one of the driving forces at Gannett, created most of the human resources programs at the company.

Gail Blanke, at Avon, was instrumental in developing LifeDesigns, an opportunity for women to learn about themselves and how to have an impact on their future lives. These kinds of programs can really make a difference for a woman.

ADVOCATES: KEEPING YOUR SUCCESS MOTIVATION ALIVE

Have you ever gone to a motivational seminar or workshop or heard a speaker talk about all the things you can do to become more successful? If it's a good speaker and program, you get excited, psyched up, full of energy, and ready to embark on your mission of success. But then, after a day or so, you're back at home or at your job and realize that nothing is really different. The same rules still apply, and you quickly lose your motivation to do things differently. It's really disappointing and frustrating. It's like going on a diet. The first couple of days of healthy eating are fine, but then you pass a McDonald's and the lure of a cheeseburger and fries is too great. So you go back to your former bad habits. It almost reinforces your feeling that you can't change, which makes you feel even worse.

A fad diet is not a quick fix—what you really need to do is change your lifestyle. In the same way, you need to realize that changing the behaviors and attitudes that have taken 5, 10, 20, or 30 years to develop cannot be accomplished overnight. Remember this is a process, not a program. A class or seminar is not going to do anything without constant support and reinforcement. So here is where the importance of a mentor, advocate, cheerleader, or support group really comes into play. Everyone has down days—everyone! At times we all feel unsuccessful, overwhelmed, uninspiring, fat, ugly, boring, stupid, old—you name it, we feel it! Only a very special few people have the ability to always psyche themselves up without outside assistance. So be sure always to have people who can listen to you, advise you, and put you back on track. Sometimes, it may just mean someone helping you through the tough times.

During the last couple of months of finishing my doctoral dissertation, I was working full time, dealing with stressful family issues as well as all the normal things that had to get done in my life, then getting home in the evening and writing at the computer until 3 or 4 o'clock in the morning. (So what else is new? Sounds like a pretty typical situation for most women I know, just with slightly different variables!) I had no life and was really burned out. Very late one night, as I worked on my dissertation, I began talking to a friend on the phone and I broke down in tears, saying that I didn't think I could continue at this pace any longer. He reassured me that I could finish my degree, and after I hung up, a fax started to come through on my fax machine. He sent me a computer clip art picture of a cat hanging on to a branch with one paw, under which he had written "Hang in there, Donna, you're almost done!" Years later I still have that fax and it reminds me of how much one little thing helped me. It really got me through.

What most of us are trying to do isn't easy. If it were, we would have done it long ago! We're changing basic assumptions, behaviors, and values in our lives. We're trying to do a balancing act. We all need people in our lives to help us accomplish this task, both at work and at home. In all honesty, without mentors, advocates, supportive people, and cheerleaders, we probably could not succeed in making the significant changes in ourselves.

Most of the advice that I received from research participants regarding the importance of mentors applies to all of us. Almost all the participants did have a mentor or several mentors, so what can we learn from them? First, it helps to find someone who will become a true "buddy." This means someone to chat with, hang out with, go to lunch or play golf with, and so forth. If it turns out to be a fairly senior member of the organization, so much the better! A well-positioned mentor or advocate can be a true political ally. Mentors know who the decision makers are; they can increase our visibility and help us understand how the organization works. But if we can also have people who believe in us and support us, we can really make it.

SUMMARY

- Mentors have been described as influential senior members of the organization with experience and knowledge which can be of assistance to younger protégés. They provide training, information, political savvy, support, and direction to the protégé. They help create visibility and credibility for the protégé. They provide effective feedback in an environment of trust and open communication. They are often seen as essential for the advancement of women.

- Be sure to ask advice of a number of people, even if you have an official mentor. You may gain insight and advice from diverse sources.

- Don't forget to help others along the way with your advice and time. You may be the person who gets someone started or excited about a new direction.

- Establish a network of people who can help you and whom you can help. These people can be from work, from professional organizations, or from friends or family.

- If your organization does not have an official mentoring program, ask your human resources department to consider putting together a mentor-protégé pool—a database of those willing to help upcoming employees and those interested in learning. It can even be an informal process of interested participants.

- Women may need to be aware of barriers to developing mentoring opportunities, such as the lack of access to information networks and senior-level people. In addition, the old-boys' network may still apply.

- A mentoring process goes through changes as the needs of the protégé and mentor change: as both parties develop, get promoted, and gain experience and confidence.

- Changing organizations and changing employees are creating new dynamics for mentoring. The mentor may not necessarily be the older, more experienced manager, but the younger technology expert, for example.

- You may find coaching or advice from unlikely sources. Use your network to gain insight and information on mentoring opportunities.

ACTION PLAN

Describe what you would look for in a mentor or an advocate (personality type, gender, age, race, interests, position, department in the company, and so on).

How do you plan to identify this person?

Is she or he in your company, a personal friend, an acquaintance?

How will you approach this person as a potential advocate or mentor?

Will you just seek out one person, or will you identify several people who can help you with different aspects of your career?

What will your expectation be of this relationship? What do you expect to gain? To give?

What kind of information can you provide that may assist your mentor or advocate? (Think about different perspectives on specific issues, points of view, information about your possible areas of expertise and skills.)

Are there possible negative impacts regarding your choice of a mentor?

How much time and energy are you and your mentor willing or able to commit?

Can your organization help you with this choice? How? If your organization doesn't have a mentoring opportunity, how will you encourage it to start?

What barriers may you encounter? Can your mentor or advocate help you?

SUCCESSFUL PEOPLE KNOW HOW TO INCREASE THEIR VISIBILITY

Visibility may be almost inextricably connected to networking and vice versa. A number of the research participants identified many situations in which they gained greater visibility as a result of their formal or informal networks. They were able to develop more effective networks because people knew who they were—they were visible. There are many situations in which people can gain greater visibility and recognition if they just take the chance to stand out.

> *The former president of Bryn Mawr College advises taking an interest in wider business areas that will carry you into situations with more senior people. She recommends taking advantage of teams and committees, volunteering, and engaging with people socially. She sees the need to develop partnerships.*

> *Congresswoman Eleanor Holmes Norton agrees. She says that it can be difficult for a woman to speak up in a room—especially in a political environment. It takes some gumption to jump in. But women are bringing in a certain culture, how they behave.*

Think about it. When you're on a team project or presentation and someone has to make a report, do you volunteer? Who is noticed among the team members when the report is given to senior management? The team leader or presenter is the one who is most visible in the group and who will tacitly or outwardly receive the credit for a good job. Of course, there is always a risk that senior management won't like what your team is reporting, so be sure that you're as prepared as possible to make a positive impression. But that's part of risk and reward—and this may be a good time to practice the skill of risk taking! (See Success Secret Seven.)

Another way to become more visible is to request that you be part of a highly visible team, preferably one endorsed and initiated by senior management. This is a good way to interact with senior-level decision makers, learn some of their skills, be able to see the bigger picture in the organization, and also give more senior managers a chance to see your talent.

> *One of the research participants recounted a story of a young woman who gave a team presentation at which, unknown to her, the president of the company was present. He was so impressed with her poise and delivery, that he specifically requested that she be put on the "fast track" via a highly visible position and increased responsibilities. Another participant in the research attended an industry social event and began chatting with the CEO of a major corporation. Six months later, when a highly visible position became available in the CEO's company, he specifically requested that the woman be put on the interview list. She got the job!*

I've asked to be included on several teams, which really helped me develop a deeper understanding of how the organization runs, as well as get to know people whom I would not ordinarily have had the opportunity to meet. I have also tried to keep abreast of new areas and opportunities for getting involved on a good committee or team. You may want to contact the person in charge of the project and announce that you're interested.

You may think "Right, at my organization I'm never going to be asked to be included in higher-level meetings!" Well, this may be an especially good opportunity for you to practice your networking and develop your skills in a mentor-protégé environment. You may want to identify advocates, or at least more approachable senior managers, and tell them that you're interested in learning more about the organization from a different or higher-level perspective and that you're willing to work very hard on the project. If you have a mentor or an advocate, you may want to find out which are the best teams, which ones will help you the most, and how your mentor can help you get on the appropriate team. On your part, this requires the commitment to preparation and hard work, and the willingness to take some risks.

> Barbara, a senior vice president, says that early in her career she was an airline reservation agent. She worked for 3 or 4 years in this capacity, traveling and seeing the world. She worked for very helpful people and was given the opportunity to succeed, achieving visibility. Each success gave her more opportunity and more visibility. At her airline there are opportunities to take on positions as team leaders. These are perfect opportunities to be viewed by senior managers, peers, and subordinates in a leadership role. Barbara recommends that, whenever possible, you choose to work with talented people and that you make your own opportunities and create visibility for yourself.

> Washington lawyer Pauline Schneider was asked to be on the White House staff at someone's suggestion, thanks to Pauline's visibility and effective networking. But her natural instinct is not to talk about herself too much; she still feels uncomfortable with that.

When I've asked to be included in key meetings or on committees, the response is usually surprise that I would actually want to go to more meetings. (Most people are trying to get out of so many!) I've also asked to be included in meetings as a job-shadowing opportunity, which many companies either endorse or even promote. Many managers are pleased when someone wants to go the extra mile to learn more about the company. Provided that the meeting doesn't include confidential or sensitive material, people may feel very comfortable having an extra attendee. Committees, in fact, are frequently very happy to engage a volunteer, rather than coercing someone.

You can also make an opportunity to ask for more responsibility. It may help at first to discuss your longer-term plans with a more senior advocate or mentor. There may be a fine line between asking for more responsibility and just getting more work. How many times have you (or people you know) been told that you will be assigned more responsibility—which will determine a raise, title change, or promotion after a specified time—only to be put off and told that it's not going to happen on schedule? Meanwhile, you have the responsibility of a higher-level position with its accompanying workload, but nothing to show for it. It is important to clarify your goals and expectations when asking for a more responsible assignment. Input from a senior decision maker and mutually agreed-upon goals and expectations may help define the expected outcome. If you have someone at a higher level pulling for you, the chances of your raise, title change, or promotion may actually materialize!

> *Karen, now president of a large publishing company, wanted to be recognized earlier in her career. However, she realized that there were many ingrained ideas within organizations. Men talk to men more often. Men's names are mentioned in decisions more often. They're just more visible. Women are not often as deft at self-promotion.*

You may want to analyze the areas in your department or organization that may require your expertise and make a proposal on how you can fulfill that need in order to gain visibility. Some people have been very successful at writing their own job descriptions. This is especially true when doing so can reduce costs or improve productivity.

> *One director successfully wrote a new position for herself when she analyzed ways in which her division could save $250,000. An expert in computer systems, she happened to be discussing various issues with her boss and started to work on a process that would improve the company's bottom line, which she could manage. She successfully made a proposal for a position in which she would effectively utilize her talents at a higher level and salary.*

> *Another director at a publishing company parlayed her bilingual capabilities, strong South American contacts, and strategic geographical location into an interesting position that suited her needs. Living in Miami, she was not thrilled about commuting to the northern New Jersey headquarters when she started as the company's South American sales and marketing director. So she analyzed the benefits of maintaining an off-site location (in Miami) by underscoring the reduced cost, along with time saved, of her flying directly from Miami to South American cities versus similar trips from New York. She showed that she*

could make much better use of her time and the company's budget by setting up a regional office in Miami.

Companies are always interested in plans that can improve productivity and the bottom line. This can be done either through more effective use of existing resources or through cost reduction.

A young colleague of mine, Faith Hamilton, recently started a job at a large university, where she felt she would have the opportunity to advance more quickly than at a smaller institution. During her application process for that position, she and I frequently brainstormed and devised strategies on how she could secure the job offer. I recommended doing an informational fact sheet about herself, in addition to her résumé, which highlighted various accomplishments, committees, projects, and programs she had conducted. She loved the idea—and got the job!

Remember, you often only have a very brief time to get yourself noticed via a résumé, so a fact sheet is an effective addition, which interviewers may like. I recently served on four search committees within a month, with about 500 résumés to read, so believe me, I can appreciate how much information you need to digest in a very short period of time! With this same resource, Faith was able both to provide concise information to the search committee and to reduce her interview anxiety by not worrying that she had forgotten to mention significant information during the interview. (Many other colleagues have used the fact sheet suggestion—they really love the concept!) You may have interviews within your organization, as well as outside the company when you're seeking a new position, so it may be wise to update your information sheet periodically and let various decision makers in your organization be aware of your skills and talents for their succession-planning needs.

A few weeks after she got the job, Faith called me on a Friday afternoon, all excited. After our conversation about ways to increase her visibility at the new university, she had tried out some of our strategies. She heard about a new committee on which only two representatives from the university would sit. The committee would be very visible and have representation from highly respected members of Ivy League universities. Faith contacted the vice

president in charge of the committee, presented her résumé,
personal information sheet, and professional portfolio, and reviewed
why she felt that she would be an excellent addition to this visible
committee. Several days later, she received word that she had indeed
been appointed to the committee. Keep in mind, she had been there
for less than 3 weeks! At first Faith thought that she might be
perceived as too pushy, but I reminded her that people in very senior
positions don't get there by being anonymous. The committee was
probably very impressed by her assertive behavior and top-notch
credentials. We agreed that our strategy really worked!

THE PROFESSIONAL PORTFOLIO

One very effective way to increase your visibility and let others
know what you're doing is to develop a professional portfolio.
As we just discussed in Faith's situation, this is a wonderful
tool which is relatively easy to develop, but is frequently not
utilized. Most people have résumés which highlight their
accomplishments on the job or in professional organizations.
But it is a limited documentation of them as people. An interviewer once asked me, referring to my résumé, what it was
about myself that I especially liked or was proud of. When I
told her, she pointed out that it was nowhere on my résumé.
She was absolutely right. Realizing that interviewers for jobs,
either internal or external, truly do take only 20 or 30 seconds
to scan a résumé, you need to make sure that your résumé
effectively demonstrates your abilities and experience. You can
certainly take advantage of books, workshops, and so forth to
develop an effective résumé. But an outline of your accomplishments accompanied by a professional portfolio is an outstanding addition to your résumé when you have reached a
possible second stage—the interview.

As anyone who has ever conducted interviews will tell you,
candidates start to look alike after a while. What can you do to
make yourself stand out? What skills can you demonstrate to
the decision maker in a department that you aspire to? What
will excite the interviewer about your accomplishments? What
can you add to the team or committee? First, you can put

together a brief outline of your accomplishments—outstanding sales targets you have met or exceeded, special projects you have completed, seminars you have conducted, programs you have designed, courses you have taught, training programs you have completed, special skills you possess which do not appear on a résumé. In this way, potential employers or bosses can get a sense of what you can bring to the team or organization in a very brief period of time. Professionals can include many things in a folder or notebook which identify their accomplishments: special articles, press releases, or letters of commendation for projects. Have you worked effectively on a successful political campaign or chaired a volunteer committee for a school, church, or synagogue event? Have you run a United Way drive at work or coordinated other volunteer activities? Are you active in your local PTA or professional or civic association? Have you been involved in running conferences or hosting foreign students in an exchange program? These also constitute a large part of your experience and who you are as a person. Such information increases visibility in an organization, yet many people neglect to include it. A young colleague of mine, Steve Stefanovich, mentions on his résumé that he has completed the U.S. Marine Corps marathon. That's the kind of really interesting information decision makers pick up on!

TOOTING YOUR OWN HORN—SUBTLY!

A friend was "assigned" to practice visibility skills as a test case. It's always a real learning experience to practice "tooting one's own horn" without seeming too contrived or pushy. This is where your support system can be especially helpful to encourage you. My friend has always been hard-working and smart, but like many of us she didn't know how to play the political game really well early in her career. In sales and marketing, she was responsible for bringing in multi-million-dollar clients, generally attained as a result of having built professional relationships with her customers over the years. She left one job after a number of years, during which time she was well paid and very well liked by her peers and bosses; but she had not been on the fast track, since she was not at the company headquarters. I didn't know if this was the key variable or if she needed to address other areas as well. So we talked about the ways to change in her new position and discussed her new strategy.

After my friend had been at her new company for about 2 months, I happened to be in her office for a visit when a fax came in informing her that she had just closed a sale for $1.5 million after 2 weeks of work. Not bad! Only 5 minutes earlier, the senior vice president had been in her office chatting with her. The client's name came up in the casual conversation as a potential sale. When the information arrived in the fax minutes later, I suggested that she go to the VP's office and casually mention what a coincidence it was: "I just got this sale after we were talking about it!" Her initial reaction was to say no and simply send a memo about it. I suggested that she strike while the iron was hot and give herself the credit—in a very subtle and casual way. She agreed and stopped by the VP's office. He was very pleased and suggested that she tell corporate communications so that the sale could be mentioned in the company update. (He knew how to make his department visible in a positive way!) The strategy worked. Even if the VP hadn't been there, she could have sent a memo: "Just thought that you'd be interested in this update. . . ."

It may also be very helpful to analyze the desired behavior—see not only how your boss acts, but what he or she views as valuable and important—and then mirror it. If it's important to your boss to work late, then subtly let him or her know that you are working late. If customers like to be schmoozed or if technology is really important to them, become an expert and let them know it!

When opportunities arise, it's a good idea to give yourself some credit in an indirect, nonposturing way. But it's also a big help to have someone there to push you a little from an objective point of view, since you're probably still not comfortable doing it. You can see the difference between subtly calling attention to your talents and achievements versus bragging.

Many of the senior women I spoke to said that a large number of their conversations and informal meetings took place in hallways and elevators or other informal gathering places.

Diane, a director, agrees that women need to take advantage of opportunities—even in places like hallways and elevators—and talk to senior managers whenever possible. As a manager, she adds that management by walking around is also important to her.

Many participants said that women can easily learn to take advantage of these situations with more senior managers and colleagues, instead of being intimidated by the contact with more senior management. This is something that we can easily practice!

A friend of mine at Merck feels that femininity brings something to the workplace that didn't exist before, such as higher-level teamwork and team units that resemble the family structure. She says that women do it all the time at home. Older women may still "look like masculine leaders" because that's how they succeeded, and they have maintained that image. However, at Merck, there's a group of women who purposely wear red jackets at team meetings, for example, to introduce color into the group and to show an easy leadership style, but one of authority. The color you wear may depend on the type of meeting and the authority you want to show. Subtle details in appearance can mean a lot.

Along with increased visibility comes some degree of risk. We need to stretch ourselves, take a stand, and possibly be challenged on particular stands. Women are frequently uncomfortable with the confrontation that sometimes accompanies increased visibility. Let's face it. The more visible you are, the greater the chance of others not agreeing with what you're saying or doing. But that's OK; you'll get used to it. For example, if you want or need to take a stand on a particular topic, what happens if others challenge you? Are you ready for it?

Women are generally assumed to be the peacekeepers. So it can be particularly uncomfortable for them to be placed into a confrontational environment. When we examine the topic of negotiation in Part Two, for example, we will see that men frequently play with a different set of rules—rules that women often don't know. The same can hold true of other potentially confrontational situations. What happens if you are extremely committed to an idea or position during a meeting and someone else is equally committed to an opposing view? You will often see two men in this situation battle it out, seemingly hostile to each other. Yet later they may have a drink after work or play a game of basketball together. You may think, "How can they be so amicable after such a big fight?" Many women in the same situation would be unable to talk to the other person for quite a while without feeling uncomfortable about the conflict. But again, go back to the playing fields of these "boys" and you will see that it's just part of the "game." That's what is supposed to happen! You fight it out, then it's settled. Women often assume that personal feelings are involved—but usually they're not. We really need to learn that business is business and that we must separate our feelings from the work environment as much as possible.

WHEN YOU HAVE CHANGED, BUT YOUR BOSS DOESN'T SEE IT

A common complaint among women is that they have difficulty with others in their organization seeing the changes they have made an effort to instill. This may be especially true of employees who began at relatively low-level positions in the organization. Or perhaps the employees started in clerical positions and were recently promoted to management. They may be doing what they need to do—going to school at night, learning technical skills, taking lessons on presentation skills—but they're still thought of as the same people in the same position. It may be very helpful for you to look around and assess exactly who is getting noticed and promoted. Is there a certain profile? Then—and again, here is where your mentors or advocates and cheerleaders come in—ask people you value and trust for an honest assessment of how the company sees you. Be prepared for the truth—remember, it's a learning experience. (This is why you want to ask only those people who are looking out for your best interests and development.) Maybe you need to be more involved on a team or on committees. Perhaps you need to interact in various ways with more senior managers. You may want to contribute an article to the organization's newsletter or highlight your non-work volunteer efforts, for example. It's important to let senior management know about you.

Have you made a real effort to improve your technical skills? If your computer or other technical skills need some work, this might be the time to take a night course or other continuing-education opportunity. Most management positions require knowledge of budgets, spreadsheets, or other general financial information. Take the time to learn one of the computer software packages that your manager probably uses—and let her or him know that you're learning it. Ask if you can help with the budget preparation—or at least some aspect of the process. You will gain the basic knowledge that will help you in your next position. Learn everything you can about the Internet or other information resources. Surprisingly, many people still do not know about the wealth of information available on the Internet, information which can give you a lot of background on your business. Become a good researcher. Read business and professional publications to gain additional insight into your field. Be able to discuss the latest developments with your colleagues and bosses. You don't have to know everything, but you should know at least a little about the major themes in your industry. I try to photocopy pertinent articles and send them to various senior people who might find them interesting. Frequently people will thank me for the information. By passing on information, not only are you keeping others updated (helping your network), but you also gain visibility as someone who keeps up with the latest information and takes the initiative.

Perhaps there is just something that is missing. Has your personal style developed with you? Of course, it is important to be compared favorably with those in more senior positions, so pay attention to the way they speak, dress, and carry themselves. These elements may not be apparent to some people, but "little bells" may be going off in others' heads that you're not quite up to par. Therefore, when you are in a situation where you need to command more respect or create a presence, it may be a good idea to wear a suit or other business attire and appropriate accessories. It's surprising, even today, to hear people say that clothes don't make a difference. I definitely still think they do. If you look at two women—one of whom is wearing business attire and the other a miniskirt and a sweater—who will you think is at a higher level? It very well may not be the case, but people will usually make that association. Now, some may take exception to the idea that clothing matters, especially in this age of business casual, but if you don't look the part of the professional, people won't see you as a professional. Once you have gotten to a certain level you can probably be a little more free, but when you're still on your way up, it's better to conform to what other senior managers are doing. (In Europe, when in doubt, overdressing rather than underdressing is still the way to go.)

I want to underscore that dressing well doesn't mean spending a small fortune on clothes, but it is very important to portray a certain image—a polished, professional image. It's important, as well, to mirror the organizational culture. The look is going to be far different in advertising than in banking, for example. When in doubt, look at the very successful women in your organization. There are enough times when a woman can feel insecure in her position, especially in a predominantly male environment, so in my opinion it's better to eliminate at least one source of feeling out of place!

Not surprisingly, all the senior women I interviewed were very appropriately dressed, even though a number of them specifically stated that they made an effort to maintain their femininity as well. However, it is especially important to keep up a professional appearance. Work is no place for sexy, suggestive, or frilly attire. You may laugh and say, "Oh, I would never dress like that!" But look around—plenty of women do! You don't want to invite the possibility of having people think you're a lightweight!

This may be a time, as well, to elicit constructive criticism on your general appearance. Are your hair and makeup dated or too young-looking? Are you wearing too much jewelry or makeup? Do you need to take diction classes to lose a regional accent or grammar classes to improve your speech? You may not even realize that you look or sound different from others, but they will notice right away! (Remember the film *Working Girl?*) Ask people you trust to help you do a makeover if that is needed. Ask them to compare you (constructively) with senior managers in your organization. Make a list of what you may need to do and do it! By the way, don't think that it's any different for men. They are also frequently judged on their appearance and comportment, and they too should mirror other successful men in their organizations!

It may also be helpful to study how successful managers in your organization handle situations. Be sure to emulate the ones you admire. Perhaps it's the way they deal with people. Maybe they really listen to others. They may be very organized. People have frequently commented that I don't ever seem to lose my cool, that I always seem to be pleasant and calm, even in stressful situations. It surprises me sometimes that people remark on that, since I certainly don't generally feel calm on the inside. But looking calm is a very helpful asset. When the research participants were asked what they really liked about themselves, many of them (women and men) said their sense of humor, or their balance, or their fairness with employees. It's really important to know how to do a great job, but still take the time to talk—and listen—to employees and make them feel important. That's a very impressive skill that we all can practice. The important thing is to set a goal at the beginning—a real and attainable goal of what you need to do, to change, to develop, and to grow.

VISIBILITY AND YOUR BOSS

A potential risk associated with increased visibility is alienating your own boss. What happens if he or she begins to feel threatened by your new efforts and likely successes? This can be a tricky situation if it is not handled with care. If possible, ask your mentor or advocate to assess the pluses and minuses of your proposed actions. A mentor may be more politically aware of problems that you are unable to foresee. In an ideal world, you are an integral part of an effective team. Bosses may feel less threatened if they know that, although you are ambitious, you are still part of the team and you want to make the boss look good. Let your boss know what you're doing, if possible. I have always asked my boss what I could do to help him or her. I have frequently complimented bosses publicly and shared information that could benefit them.

Whenever possible, try to look at issues from you boss's perspective, as well as your own. Many of us have been fortunate to have bosses that we liked. A likable boss makes relationship building much easier. However, there are also many people who have bosses whom they don't very much like. What do you do? Well, try to analyze what the difficulty is. Is it a personality conflict? A major difference of perspective? Or is the boss just a creep? That may be possible, too! Try to get an outside, unbiased opinion if you can. Ask others—especially those who can get along with your boss, but not necessarily the boss's "cronies"—what they would suggest to improve the relationship. Frequently, it may be an issue of communication. Maybe you need some one-on-one time out of the office to get to know the boss a little better. It does take time, energy, and effort to get to know someone well, but it frequently does pay off.

You may be surprised at the response when you try to develop a positive interaction with colleagues. You may, for example, suggest that a group of people get together for lunch and get to know one another better, including people who are decision makers or otherwise well connected. These people can be from your organization or outside your organization. Include your boss. This type of outing will allow your boss to network a bit as well. You may also observe where your boss is getting bogged down and offer your help in certain areas. Not only will it aid your boss, but you will be adding to the job description on your résumé. Asking about your boss's interests and hobbies—and learning a bit about them—may be a good way to develop common ground. Provide information on upcoming events or books and articles on a favorite topic if you happen to see them. There is a fine line between developing a professional rapport and "brown-nosing," however. So ask your advocate if you have any doubts about your strategy. Make sure you understand your boss's own goals and expectations as well. You may even want to ask what the boss needs to focus on, as far as his or her boss's expectations are concerned, then see how you can assist. Be proactive. If there's a project that the boss is working on, spend some of your own time doing background research or read an article and photocopy it for your boss. Show that you're interested in developing new skills and gaining new information. Be detail-oriented! You may not have to sweat the details, but your boss probably does. Check over your work carefully—it may be embarrassing for your boss, as well as for you, if work on a project is done incorrectly. Check your figures, your calculations, and so forth. Many of us have learned the hard way—fortunately, not with critical issues—that mistakes happen when we're in a hurry to get things done on schedule. Everyone has had that sinking feeling that a project or document has just gone out of the office with an error—and now it's too late to correct! Always give yourself a little extra time to proofread, check, and verify information.

Understand, as well, that some personality types are never going to mesh well. If you can handle personality differences and work within the framework, great. Try to do whatever you can to develop a positive strategy to work well with your boss. However, if you have tried everything and you and the boss are still at each other's throats, it may be time to seriously change to your networking mode and look elsewhere. This, again, ties into your risk-taking challenge. Your job may be very comfortable and you may enjoy it—except for your boss. If it's becoming intolerable, move on.

Some of the women I interviewed said that they took on jobs that no one else wanted and worked hard to make them successful. It may be very important here to utilize several of the other necessary success skills. For example, you may want to use your networking or mentor connections to get a sense of what the smart political move would be before taking on a more risky project. Does the project have the support of senior managers? Are they willing to provide the necessary resources? Or is the project rumored to be destined for failure? A bad choice of project could backfire on your chances to advance. But success on a good project could really catapult your career. Be sure to check with more experienced colleagues to get as much input as possible before you risk your reputation and your job!

MAKING PRESENTATIONS—AND OTHER TERRORS!

So, what if you feel uncomfortable taking on some of these responsibilities? Can you prepare or practice for visibility? One area that many people feel uneasy about is speaking in front of others. (Don't worry, public speaking is one of the top three fears that most people have! But you can prepare for it!)

A couple of years ago, the European Women's Management Development Network held its annual international conference in the United States, and the U.S. board was responsible for all the details. Dr. Helen Solomons, the U.S. president, encouraged the board members, especially those who were not particularly comfortable speaking in public, to practice their presentation skills with a consultant. They were going to be speaking frequently to hundreds of international delegates, which was not necessarily the forte of several board members.

Helmine, a senior consultant who was the conference coordinator, is an engineer and software expert with terrific technical expertise. She was not especially relaxed at first about having to give the welcome speech to several hundred international attendees. Through advice from the consultant, practice, and encouragement, Helmine overcame her nervousness and delivered a wonderful opening presentation. She admits that she would not have done it if she hadn't had to. Although she acknowledged that she was never going to feel especially calm in front of large groups, it was a wonderful challenge and learning experience, which greatly heightened her visibility and her confidence level.

To prepare yourself with presentation skills, look into taking a public speaking course at your local college or other continuing-education provider. Join Toastmasters or other organizations whose role it is to assist you in public speaking. Practice making presentations at your professional group or association, club, church, or synagogue. Choose a topic you enjoy and it will not seem as daunting. Ask others to help you in the preparation and to offer a positive critique—accept helpful criticism without taking it personally. Remember, this is a learning experience. Interpersonal communication is one of the greatest assets for those looking to move ahead in organizations. How many times do you hear "I could do better than that" or "I know as much or more than they do." But if you don't show your peers and senior managers that you are talented, that you have the capability and background and can do the job, they may never know.

Many of the senior women I interviewed said that women can easily learn to take advantage of informal situations with more senior managers and colleagues, instead of being intimidated by their contact with senior management. This is something that we can easily practice!

INVITING YOURSELF TO BE MORE VISIBLE

One manager became frustrated that more senior managers at her organization weren't asking her for advice in her areas of expertise. She made suggestions that were generally ignored. She made proposals, but she wasn't a senior manager, so they were not embraced and taken seriously. But she was playing the game by her rules, assuming that since she probably knew more about the topic than anyone else in her department, people would listen to her expertise. Wrong!

It can be frustrating to try to make yourself more visible. One manager who succeeded overcame all the odds. First, she didn't have the official credentials at the time (the right degree and title). She didn't have a senior position. She didn't have an advocate pulling for her. She was waiting to be included in strategy meetings which dealt with the issues that she knew a lot about. It didn't happen. So she took a chance and asked her boss if she could be included in the next strategic planning meeting about the issue. (She found out about the upcoming meeting by chance.) He said sure, no problem. So she went prepared with the numbers, information on trends, data on possible strategies, and so forth—all photocopied for the attendees: senior managers. As the meeting began, she didn't really say too much. However, as the discussions continued, she realized that she did know a lot more about the topic and she started to voice her opinion, backed up with the photocopied information. Ironically, almost every time that a question was raised about an issue, she had the information already prepared. When one of the most respected people at the company supported one of her suggestions, it really made the other members take notice. The attendees had to include her as a participant. She was assigned to work with several of the senior people there on various projects and studies. The visibility and preparation were critical to gaining acceptance.

First, try to invite yourself to important meetings. Ask your boss or other senior manager to invite you. Second, come prepared if you can. Third, if you feel somewhat comfortable, push yourself to speak up, especially if it's an area you know about. Fourth, try to arrange for an advocate to underscore the importance of what you're saying to the other team members (you can set this up in advance). Finally, make sure you are given credit—publicly, if possible—for your contributions.

It's relatively easy to speak out when you're in a comfortable environment with friends or colleagues. The risk factor is probably pretty low. However, every time that you are in a relatively new environment, you take a chance when you speak up. If you take the chance and speak out, a couple of things can happen. People may say that it's a great idea or suggestion, and your visibility will be increased. Or people may simply ignore you. Worse yet, they may say that it's a really stupid idea or suggestion! (Some women take criticism very seriously, so you have to be fairly tough-skinned if this happens.)

It's a big help when you're speaking at a meeting to have a

respected person agree that what you have said is absolutely on target, or that you have made an excellent point. Such support ("staged" or otherwise) can give you an enormous amount of credibility among more senior executives. As you gradually gain experience and respect, you'll feel more comfortable speaking up at meetings and other gatherings. You may want to practice speaking up in less stressful, lower-risk environments at first. But keep in mind, even as you gain experience and confidence, that you will continue to find yourself in new and challenging situations as you move up to new positions. So you need to become really comfortable with the risk-taking aspect of speaking up.

Sometimes, however, a new environment turns out to be surprisingly pleasant. I was invited to be a member of the Wharton Expert Network at the University of Pennsylvania Wharton School. The network provided an opportunity for second-year MBA students to interact with "experts" in various fields and gain insights on an international level. Since I was a newcomer among seasoned experts, mostly men, I decided just to learn the ropes the first time I attended. However, it turned out to be a highly interactive, low-stress environment, especially surprising given the caliber of the attendees. I found myself frequently commenting on various international management issues and even giving advice to these top students. It was a very interesting opportunity to gain visibility and also to do some networking!

INFLUENCE AND VISIBILITY IN THE ORGANIZATION

The resource theory of influence states that women generally do not have very much control (i.e., financial access) over the organization's resources, so they don't often have much influence within the organization. As a result, they become somewhat isolated, interacting less with those who can really help them advance. On the other hand, once women begin to move into higher-level positions, they tend to gain more influence, and therefore do not experience these communication barriers as drastically. It's like that Catch-22 early in your career when people tell you, "You can't get a job without experience, but you can't get experience without a job." The idea is to learn the necessary strategies to move ahead and gain influence, so that you will be in greater control of the organization's resources, which will consequently allow you to be taken more seriously and experience fewer barriers. So, have you been reading carefully?

> *Dana, a senior vice president, says that things often do open up and get better. People value the individual, rather than the stereotype. Even men who had difficulty getting used to Dana as the first woman in her position (and many other positions) changed as they developed a one-on-one relationship with her, instead of the group. When you gain greater visibility and respect, barriers do start to break down.*

Some research points to the relatively low participation of women in scheduled meetings, especially at fairly high levels. This is generally true of meetings where major decisions are discussed and strategic policies are set. Women may be at a serious disadvantage by not being invited to these meetings because of their perceived (or real) lack of influence. Despite all the complaints about meetings, they are frequently a control or power thing. The meeting is by nature exclusionary to those not "in the loop." It's almost a closed network by itself, considering that most of the time, lower-level employees can't just invite themselves to high-level strategic meetings. The people who have "made the cut" and gotten invited to these meetings may actually not want other people to be invited. Since most high-level meetings have traditionally included primarily men, it may actually be true that women are not invited as frequently and consequently miss out on a lot of decision making. The power, either by design or by default, often continues to rest with men in the organization.

So in order to make some real changes, and also get ahead in your organization, learn from others—and your own experiences—about how to become more visible. Remember, if they don't know you're there, you'll never get ahead!

SUMMARY

- Take advantage of teams and committees and volunteer for projects to increase your visibility and also develop your network. Doing so gives you a chance to stand out, especially if the team or project is endorsed by senior management.

- A professional portfolio, highlighting your accomplishments and expertise, is an effective way to increase your visibility by letting others know about your complete package.

- Assess which traits and skills are valuable in your organization and reflect or mirror them in your own behavior.

- Take advantage of opportunities to interact with senior managers, even in hallways, elevators, and other informal environments.

- Look around and see who is getting promoted. Learn what their skills and education are and what their general profile is.

ACTION PLAN

How do individuals and groups gain visibility in your organization?

What can you do to become more visible? (You might write for the company newsletter, give presentations, volunteer as a team leader, and so on.)

If you feel uncomfortable about subtly "blowing your own horn," how will you practice?

How will you use your network or mentor to help increase your visibility?

Ask to be included in key meetings, projects, and committees. Ask for more responsibility.

Analyze your organization to see if there is an area in which it can utilize your expertise, especially if you can increase productivity or reduce costs.

Think about how you are going to improve your skills

(through presentations, technical skills, budget preparation, and so on).

How can you make your boss look good or help the boss with her or his job?

SUCCESSFUL PEOPLE KNOW HOW TO DEVELOP AN EFFECTIVE NETWORK

IT'S NOT NECESSARILY WHAT YOU THINK!

Interestingly enough, some of the research participants had strong negative feelings about the term *networking*. It appears that networking has become the cliché of business card exchangers—manipulative, self-serving people who are looking to get ahead. I want to change that attitude and view!

> *In an article in Fortune magazine, TV's Martha Stewart, Charlotte Beers of Ogilvy & Mather, and deal maker Darla Moore discussed their views on networking.[11] Beers eschewed the advice for women to network, while Martha Stewart stated that she never even used the word, let alone belonged to a network group. Moore felt that women's networks have done nothing for women professionally. She favored finding a niche and becoming the best in your field in order to gain recognition. (I personally do not agree with Moore's view that women's networks are not effective. I think that it depends on the goals of the organization and who makes up its members. In addition, your network should definitely not be limited to women.)*

How could networking cause such a reaction? Well, we really need to look at what today's effective networks are all about—

they're not what you think! For a lot of people who do not, in their professions, meet the kinds of people who can assist them in advancing, making contacts is essential to gain recognition and visibility. But the big difference is in how people develop their "network." Networks can include groups of like-minded people in hobbies, leisure pursuits, professional associations, education, and special interests, among many others.

Almost everyone will tell you about "networking events" in which the participants scope out the room or scan the attendee list and name tags to zero in on someone who can specifically help them. While of course the ultimate goal of this type of networking is to make contacts with people who can assist in their professional development, networkers frequently just don't get it, and can miss some real opportunities. They know how to work a room, but that's absolutely contrary to building an effective network.

> *A professional dinner I attended a couple of years ago included a speaker on networking. The speaker, the wife of a politician, clearly had significant experience in "working a room." However, her advice and recommendations were somewhat disturbing. She talked about how to effectively enter a circle of conversation, check out who everyone was, and in a couple of minutes decide whether the people in that particular group were the chosen ones with whom to continue the conversation. She recommended that if these people weren't going to be of help, you should excuse yourself politely and find another group.*

While you have no doubt been in situations in which you were cornered by a boor (or bore), the random discarding of those who seemingly cannot immediately suit your needs seems a bit harsh. In several minutes it is difficult to assess someone's common interests and potential for a professional relationship. This type of person generally stands out as rather self-serving, someone who is probably not going to invite the commitment of help from others.

Helen Solomons, president of Harrison Associates, a human resources consultancy, is the U.S. president and country representative for the European Women's Management Development Network. Dr. Solomons has done significant research on the effectiveness of networks, especially international networks, based on relationships. She has also learned the benefits of effective networking as a result of her significant international work over the years. A native of England, she says that she was a bit shy at first with networking, feeling a certain cultural difference. As she emphasizes, however, effective networking is the result of relationship building, not just the business card exchanges that we so frequently hear about.

I asked Dr. Solomons if there was a turning point in her career when she realized the value of an effective network. She answered right away that there was. She started out as an artist and then took 10 years off to be at home with her two children. When she returned to the job market, she realized that she needed to update her career skills and that earning a degree would help her. She finished her undergraduate degree and continued on to receive her PhD at Bryn Mawr College. She reminded me that this was in the late 1960s and early 1970s, when the environment for women returning to work was very different than it is now. She didn't even know that there were other women who felt as she did. At Bryn Mawr, she worked in the Career Planning and Placement Office. Through her boss's contacts, she got a job after graduation working part time at the University of Pennsylvania. At this time, however, she didn't even know what networking was.

While there, Dr. Solomons found out about a terrific new position at Penn, which was developed by a group of senior university women seeking a way to match highly qualified women looking for university positions with appropriate openings. Dr. Solomons recounts the interesting way in which this group came about. Several senior university women were snowed in at the airport on their way to a meeting. They started brainstorming about ways to facilitate the advancement of women in higher education. They not only came up with this new idea, called HERS, but also found a way to fund the project from the Ford Foundation. They developed a relationship between the women who were looking for the jobs and the people who were hiring. (Remember that at this time most of the people in hiring positions were men, as were most of the visible candidates.) Despite terrific competition from other highly qualified PhDs, Dr. Solomons received support for the new position from her mentor, who was well connected in this founding group. Cynthia Secor, the executive director of the new initiative, introduced her to the term *networking*.

As Helen Solomons discovered, establishing an effective network, like having a mentor, can be critical in the success strategy. We have frequently heard about the "old-boys' network" and there is probably a great deal of validity in its effectiveness. This network has often been viewed as a sort of club, in which only selected members may join, in either a formal or an informal sense. Examples of these "clubs" are alumni groups at prestigious schools, professional organizations, and even family connections. The members of these clubs have an almost unspoken bond. When they get a call from an "inside" networker—someone who is a fellow alum of a particular school, or a member of their organization in another city—they are quite likely to accept the call or suggest lunch or arrange a meeting. It is a network of inclusion.

> *Judith Rodin, the University of Pennsylvania's president, indicates that networks are especially important. They provide access, visibility, and support. She said that she never had difficulty being part of the old-boys' network, since her experience at NYU, Yale, Penn, and Columbia gained her acceptance as an insider. (Keep this in mind if you're planning to go back to school—or planning for your child's education!)*

Access to these circles has been restricted for the most part to insiders. However, what if you are not a Harvard or Wharton MBA or have not been born into a fifth-generation prominent family? Successful career management often necessitates exploring alternative methods of creating or accessing resources.

There are numerous professional organizations which include in their rolls exactly the types of people who may be able to assist you in your career. But how and where do you begin? Here's where your mentor or adviser can play a critical role. People who are in senior positions probably did not get there without an effective network, no matter how it actually developed. You should certainly ask them to recommend organizations that would be helpful in your career development or people whom you can contact. Most people are very pleased to be asked their advice, so they should be happy to provide this information. In effective network management, once you have made contact with several key people, you can ask them to recommend other people who may be willing to help in your development. In this way, you have begun to exponentially expand your resources.

However, remember that effective networking involves building a relationship. It makes sense that if you have developed a relationship with someone, he or she will be far more likely to help you in your professional development.

> *Geraldine Bown, a very successful English consultant, is an extraordinary person who strongly feels that whenever possible you should help someone else before asking for help yourself.*

> *Judy Woodruff, of CNN, has worked very hard to build relationships in her career. She often reaches out to people and takes time to develop one-on-one relationships.*

I have always remembered that advice, which I think is critical in building the kind of network that will help you in the long term. You need to make an effort to really listen to what people are saying when you meet them. Even if they are not in a position to help at that time, there is a possibility that you may provide some advice or valuable information for them. It's especially important to be able to help others. Critics may say that they don't have time to be helping everyone else without concentrating on themselves. However, it is important to remember that networking is, ideally, a relationship of give and take. People may not be able to help you at this point, but who can tell in the future?

> *The former president of Bryn Mawr says that being thrown together with other people on panels, committees, or advisory groups is not a bad thing. It can be very helpful to use e-mail to extend your network and broaden your knowledge base. She got to know people through collaboration.*

Helen Solomons advocates "making serendipity work for you." Specifically, you never know the interesting people you will meet, so enjoy the moment rather than concentrating on what others can do for you. In addition, you never know what people may do in the future. Dr. Solomons has met countless people over the years who have become famous and are now highly sought after. As a result of maintaining her relationships, however, she always feels comfortable calling them freely. She agrees that you should also think about what you can do to help others in your network, without necessarily thinking about what they can do for you. They will be very grateful, and you never know if and when you may need to ask a favor in return. And don't just talk to people in your network when you need them. Make an effort to keep in touch periodically just to say hello. Dr. Solomons also recommends being a good listener. People enjoy talking about themselves. She feels that people can sense that she has a genuine interest in them.

Dana Becker Dunn, a senior vice president at AT&T, typifies the idea of relationship building. She has built a terrific internal network as a result of taking the time to get to know her colleagues and subordinates and really listening to what they need. Frequently she will slip important information that she has to a colleague during meetings to help that person address issues or questions more easily or effectively. She is truly committed to helping her team. Talking to Dana, you can't help but be impressed, not only by her exceptional background and expertise, but also by her extraordinary ease and friendly manner.

Karen House, president of the international division of Dow Jones, Inc., also typifies someone who makes an effort to develop an effective network. She clearly has been extremely generous of her time, and she agreed to an interview for my original research as a doctoral student. We got together about a year later to talk about my research results, among other things. At that time she asked me if during my research I had met any very interesting senior women. (As a former reporter, she was always interested in knowing what was going on.) She said that most of the time she attends press events and does not have the opportunity to meet senior women in other fields—meetings which she enjoys. I was able to provide her with the names of a number of women whom she would have much in common with and enjoy talking to. Although she was far better "connected" than I was, I was still able to provide an extension of her network that she may not have had at that time. Who knows? At a time when she wants to pursue a topic for one of the Dow Jones publications, Karen may be able to look at my list and pick up the phone for information from these women in other large organizations without having to spend time doing her own research or making her own inquiries. It is an ongoing process of give and take.

Can the old-boys' network work for women as well? We will examine that in depth in Part Two. But a number of women have said that they did not feel initial acceptance into the "club." Many older men still want to maintain their seats of real power and may resist the entrance of women.

A former Philadelphia judge feels that women may sometimes lose out in the old-boys' network. She adds that men are often out there doing all kinds of "guy things"—playing golf, making deals, and so forth. She feels that certain zones—the access to real seats of power—are not going to be easily penetrated. She gives an example of a private men's club in the early 1980s, at which she was attending a male colleague's dinner reception. The Union League of Philadelphia, a bastion of "old-boys' networkdom," had a separate entrance and dining room for women which, although pleasant enough, was actually in the basement of the building. She arrived for the event and was subsequently told by the male concierge that she would have to go outside (on a winter night), walk to the other side of the building, and use the ladies' entrance. She said, "Why should I walk outside in the cold and dead of night when I can walk 50 feet straight in front of me to get from point A to point B?" He insisted that she couldn't use the front entrance. Not one to take fools lightly, she said, "Oh, no? Just watch me!"

Annoyed at this kind of unequal and undignified treatment for women, the judge rallied other women leaders in the city. Finally, all the clubs in Philadelphia were forced to admit women. She still doesn't belong to any of the private clubs in the city, but feels comfortable with the fact that she is welcome to join as a member.

DEVELOPING AND KEEPING TRACK OF YOUR NETWORK

Helen Solomons observes that there are a lot of different kinds of people with many different kinds of networking needs. They need an effective system to keep track of a network. It is ideal if you can access your network information via computer database, either through software that is now available or through a small, hand-held "wizard." How many times have you jotted down names and phone numbers on an old business card or the back of an envelope because it was the closest piece of paper at hand? Just try to find a name later, though. It's usually right after you have decided to get organized and cleaned your office or home work area that you discover you need the information. You've known where it was for months, but now you can't find it.

There should also be certain goals associated with your networking. First, Dr. Solomons underscores the importance of relationship building. You can join professional associations, student organizations, work groups, and so forth. You can use whatever vehicle is at hand. As a student, for example, you may volunteer for student organizations and conduct research on interesting topics, or do interviews for newsletters or newspapers, or assist at conferences and have the opportunity to meet influential people and develop professional relationships with important "old boys." In such situations, everyone begins to know your name and you can gain important visibility. This can be especially important when you're doing a job search. Dr. Solomons adds, however, to be thoughtful and careful. When initiating a professional relationship with influential men, keep it strictly professional.

It may be very helpful to stay in touch with your alumni associations. These contacts may be able to help you develop leads for a job search by identifying fellow alums at organizations which you may want to target. This is a wonderful vehicle for meeting people who may be willing to help. Many people don't even realize the benefits. Dr. Solomons also recommends that you start a small group of your own—either in person or especially now on the Internet—if you are interested in a particular topic. For example, women who are interested in maintaining a work-life balance may enjoy sharing their experiences or suggestions. Dr. Solomons is involved with a luncheon group that encompasses no responsibilities, no agenda, no program. It just provides an opportunity for colleagues to get together and share. Attendees are generally asked to bring someone else along who has similar interests or who is doing interesting things.

It takes a lot of time and effort to develop an effective network. Sometimes you just don't feel like going to an event that could enhance your network. You're tired, you're too busy—there are a million excuses. But it's important to try to make a real effort, especially when it's easier just to go home and relax. Very shortly before writing this, my sister Lynn asked me to go with her to a professional association networking event. Both of us were tired and really didn't want to go. I reminded her of what we had just discussed. Resigned to going, we ended up not only meeting some terrific (and helpful) people but having a really good time as well! So, frequently when Lynn and I just don't feel like going to various events, one of us usually will coerce the other into going, and it almost always proves helpful. This is an excellent case of having an advocate or support person assist you with your career management. It frequently helps to have someone kick you in the proverbial pants to make sure that you make an effort to get out and network. I can't tell you how many times I have agreed that whoever said "it's not what you know, it's who you know" is absolutely right! There are many cases in which people I know have gotten a lead, a job, or valuable information only because of the people *they* know.

> *Everyone needs a network for all kinds of things. Mary Ruff, a wonderful editor, has given me information in publishing that I would have never known on my own. She claims that the publishing field is notorious for using networks. Everyone knows someone who knows someone else, who knows everything that's going on in the industry.*

Some people look at their calendars and rolodexes at the beginning of the week or month and schedule times to meet with friends, acquaintances, and others they would like to or should meet. This can take some planning, but it's a good habit to get into. It makes good sense that the more people—especially the more senior people—you know, the greater visibility you will have. (Think about the old-boys' network again. The boys know, socialize with, and help one another. It works!) Don't be uncomfortable asking a more senior person to join in your lunch group, for example. You may first want to develop a certain rapport with that person, then build up to having lunch. It's even better if someone you know is fairly well connected and can include you in the same type of gathering in his or her circle of senior management.

I frequently pass along information or names of interesting contacts to many of the people I meet. I have done this repeatedly with the senior people I have interviewed. Since I have had the benefit of talking to senior people across industries, I often ask them if I can pass along their names to other senior people in the same type of role in a different company or industry. Or if I just think that they would enjoy meeting or talking to other senior people, I will often send their names to some of the people in my network. If I meet a terrific woman in finance at one company, I may pass her name along to a female executive in finance at another company, an executive whom she may never have met but whom she might enjoy meeting. I've gotten a number of responses from the successful women and men I've interviewed, thanking me for passing along the names of other people. Don't forget, everyone enjoys adding to a network.

Visibility can be an integral part of an effective network. If few people are aware of your talents, you will not receive the attention and subsequent recognition essential to moving ahead. Similarly, if you do not have an effective network, you may be limiting yourself to opportunities within your immediate scope.

> Rene Redwood, former executive director of the Glass Ceiling Commission, feels that an effective network is a critical part of visibility and vice versa. She says that her network gave her the visibility she needed for her executive position in the Department of Labor. She admits, as well, that an important aspect of her network is friends and colleagues who support and encourage her. Although Rene says that a certain amount of networking comes as a natural part of her position, she continues to work at expanding her network. Despite a grueling schedule, she makes time to take advantage of speaking invitations and other opportunities of special interest. Additionally, she is extremely committed to helping others with their networks. Rene feels that visibility leads to the expansion of her network.

It's an inextricable combination. What skills do you need to improve your visibility? How will you gain them? Helen Solomons advises initiating action rather than just waiting to be asked to join. It may entail a different way of thinking, specifically "Why don't I just start something?" She adds that networking is not a contest to see how many people you can meet in 5 minutes, although there will always be people who are constantly looking over their shoulder to see who has just entered the room—and who can help them. Instead, give the person you're talking to 100 percent of your attention, at least for the time you're talking! Don't collect people, relate to them. Good networkers give others the impression that they are the most important people in the world when they're talking to them. Dr. Solomons cited Hillary Clinton for that talent, for example, when she had the opportunity to meet the First Lady.

Dr. Solomons recommends that you convey a sense of yourself quickly and think about what image you want to project. You don't necessarily have to bowl someone over with everything that you know. You can always get the person's card and follow up with lunch or a meeting. Find out about other people and make them feel comfortable. Building a network means having people trust you. There is a big difference between a circle of acquaintances and an effective network. Women may need help in understanding the importance of a two-way relationship. Men generally know that it's always a trade, but women don't always know. Although you shouldn't take and take without returning the favor, neither should you always give and never ask for anything in return. You may risk feeling exploited if you think that you aren't gaining anything from your network. Remember, it is a two-way street.

SUMMARY

Helen Solomons recommends these tips for building effective networks through relationships:

- Relationship-based networks are more important now than ever, since in the changing workplace your next job or lead will probably be through your network.

- There are new roles for the new women's network. The old-boys' network is based on "jumping the queue"—getting ahead by knowing people and having connections. Women's networks level the playing field.

- It's your network; you have built it. No one can take it away from you.
- Your network should be natural, not always planned.
- Know and practice networking. You'll develop a strategy that works for you.
- Use your networks creatively to serve your needs.
- Technology can help you build networks, especially internationally (the Internet, e-mail, faxes, and so on).
- Make serendipity work for you. Enjoy meeting people for the pleasure of it.
- Put aside one day a week in which you spend an hour or two maintaining your network through phone calls, correspondence, e-mail, and more. Do it faithfully!
- Be sure to consider alumni associations and professional organizations, among others, to build up your network.
- Women can begin to create their own networks; they need not rely on an old-boys' type of network.

ACTION PLAN

Assess your current network. Do you have a good relationship with a number of people who are well connected or influential? How can you augment it?

Do you frequently offer to assist others in developing their network? Do you really listen to what others are trying to do with their own careers and think of people you know who can help them?

What type of network would you like to develop? Is it personal, professional, or something else? Do you keep meaning to make an effort and then fail to get around to it? Why not?

Do you know about organizations that would be helpful to your career? Do you take an active role in participating in events? Do you plan to attend various functions, and then decide you "don't feel like it" when the time comes around?

Do you think at the beginning of the week of several people to have lunch with or meet after work or on the weekend (people who may be helpful to your career)?

SUCCESSFUL PEOPLE HAVE LEARNED TO COMMUNICATE EFFECTIVELY

Many of the women I interviewed discussed effective communication as a powerful tool as they moved ahead in organizations. However, as you can imagine, there were many different personality and communication styles among the research participants. There is no one way of communicating effectively. It depends on the individual, the organization, the situation, the goal. It is important, however, to realize that effective communication depends on the understanding that what you're saying and how you say it may be quite different from someone else's viewpoint. Communication problems are among the top issues that organizations deal with today. Flexibility and adaptability in this area are critical, especially for women, in order to facilitate success. This is one skill we really need to master!

Judith Rodin, president of the University of Pennsylvania, believes that effective communication is critical in this era— being a thinker and a doer is no longer enough. You need to be able to talk passionately about what you believe in. You need to be able to excite, inspire, believe in others. Communication is the key. She can't emphasize this enough.

ONE-ON-ONE COMMUNICATION

There are still times that, for real or perceived reasons, women are discriminated against in organizations. In my original research, fully 100 percent of the senior women interviewed said that discrimination and bias were still evident as an issue in the workplace, although not all of them had personally experienced it. However, much of their success stemmed from how they dealt with the bias. A number of participants added that this discrimination was often unintentional, the result of lack of knowledge rather than actual bias. A number of women agreed that this one-on-one communication really helped their bosses or other senior managers understand and appreciate their perspective.

Effective communication can frequently facilitate a difficult or uncomfortable situation. Communication leads to better understanding, which in turn leads to improved teamwork and productivity.

> One senior woman at AT&T cites communication as a critical component of success. An incredibly talented and hard-working executive, she has been the first woman in many of her positions, so she has frequently faced stereotypes about women in senior management. She says that it's always a positive step when her male colleagues say, "You know, you're OK!" She knows that she has successfully overcome the stereotype and has been accepted into "the club."

> Jane, a senior executive at another major utilities company, talked about the positive effects of one-on-one communication and how it helped her career. When she told her boss that she was having a baby, he "naturally assumed" that she would not want to return to her current position on a full-time basis. He said, "You'll probably want to cut back your hours and take it a little easier." Fortunately, she had a good relationship with him and she said, "Would you say the same thing to my male colleagues?" He laughed and said, "You know, you're right. I wouldn't have brought it up with a man." Her frank and open communication with her boss helped him overcome the general perception that women would automatically want to significantly reduce the amount of work time and responsibility.

It is generally easier to perpetuate stereotypes when talking about generalities, rather than dealing with specific problems on a one-to-one basis.

A senior vice president of CoreStates Bank International Division feels that women need to be specific about their own goals and expectations. If a woman is interested in an international assignment but would like to wait a couple of years until her children are a little older, for example, they recommend that she be up front with her boss.

Several women added that people can't read your mind. If you want a particular assignment, ask for it. They say that some employees may become annoyed if they're not asked to take on plum assignments, more responsibility, or international travel, for example. Yet these people may have never indicated an interest in those areas to anyone.

If you don't indicate otherwise, your individual situation may lead people to assume that you do not want new responsibilities, because of family demands or other factors that preclude such moves. Don't forget, a lot of senior managers are men, and many men—because of their own upbringing or home situation—may still see a difference in roles between working women and mothers. These men may not consciously be stereotyping you, but they honestly may not know anything different. You may have to give them the benefit of the doubt at first. If your boss doesn't ask you, let her or him know what you want! Be clear.

Several executives also add that if a manager is offered plum assignments overseas, for example, and turns them down without discussing the major reasons with his or her boss, the offers may stop coming. It may be easy for your boss to assume that you will not want to spend time away from your family. If it is just a temporary situation, or if you have made arrangements for your family, let your boss know you are interested. If you don't feel that you want the position at this time, but are definitely interested at a future date, let your boss share in your anticipated career timetable.

It's much easier to develop a rapport with your boss if you take the time to communicate. It's amazing how many barriers and differences can be overcome with communication alone. If you are interested in more responsibility, an international position, a sales opportunity, and so forth, just share that information with your boss. It is critical to communicate your career path or interests with your boss so that he or she can help you with your plans.

IMPROVING ONE-ON-ONE COMMUNICATION

Sometimes, improving communication may be as easy as suggesting that a colleague or boss join you for lunch, for a game of golf or tennis, or a walk after lunch, if you have the time. It can often be effective to leave your work environment temporarily to gain fresh perspective on your professional relationship as individuals, rather than as products of your office environment. It can be extremely productive to discover similarities and shared interests—a bond that may actually facilitate a more effective team as well. It's often amazing to learn how much you have in common—common interests, common friends. Don't forget that this may also lead to networking, a support structure, and possible mentors and advocates.

> Edwina Woodbury, chief financial officer at Avon, always uses the Myers-Briggs testing instrument as a team-building exercise with her employees in order to assess where they're coming from and what they can add to the team. She has found it to be very effective in improving communication as well. She also says that she enjoys an informal communication network at Avon: 80 to 90 percent of the issues she faces are resolved in hallways. Instead of sending memos, she goes right to the source to maximize effectiveness.

> Madelyn Jennings, former vice president of human resources at Gannett, likes diverse teams to add maximum breadth of perspective. She adds that homogeneous work groups get to answers quicker, but heterogeneous groups are more creative.

BEING HEARD IN MEETINGS

How many times have women said, "I was in a meeting and voiced my opinion on a particular matter. No one acknowledged it. Then 10 minutes later a male colleague said the exact same thing and they all thought it was a great original idea!" This happens all the time.

> *Five minutes before I began writing this part of the chapter, a friend called me from her meeting and said, "Two of us started to make a comment at exactly the same time—I deferred, since the other person was a more senior member. Wouldn't you know it? He said exactly what I was going to say and, of course, all the senior managers commented, 'Wow, that's such a great idea!' At that point, what could I say? 'Hey, I was just thinking the same thing!'"*

Have you ever waited for your turn to speak in a meeting, only your turn never came? Let me tell you, if you don't speak up, it's never going to come!

What can you do about it? Well, there are several schools of thought on the matter. Of course you can just use the lost opportunity as a learning experience to practice feeling more comfortable with jumping into conversations. Try watching *Crossfire* on CNN or *Business Insiders* on CNBC, among many other examples. It's not only entertaining, but the positive confrontation is a good thing to practice. You'll probably notice that whoever talks the longest and loudest to make a point generally gets the floor!

In some instances, women who find themselves "all alone" in a boardroom choose to funnel their ideas initially through highly visible male allies. In this way, they pass the information to a colleague whom they know will either verbalize their perspective or give them credit for having come up with the idea. Other women may think that this engenders the age-old problem of women not being recognized for their own opinions and contributions. It probably depends largely on the individual situation and the women and men involved.

Several of the women surveyed felt that channeling their information through a male counterpart, especially a man willing to credit his source, at least got the idea to the table. They even felt quite comfortable with not being given credit for the idea, as long as the position came to the table. In some cases, the respondents had to do this only initially, since after they themselves gained acceptance in the group, they felt more comfortable initiating their own ideas. One of the key factors here, however, may be the preliminary relationship building with other members of the team. Building relationships is part of networking, mentoring, and learning the politics of the organization. If you know that you have a strong ally who also happens to have the ear of the decision makers, it may be beneficial to work with her or him, with the understanding that you will be recognized as the one who initiated the idea.

Some women may feel that this type of behavior—having a man speak for them—has persisted long enough and represents a cop-out on the part of women. You may feel very comfortable speaking up for what you need or want in your organization, or making suggestions to senior management. However, other organizational cultures may not foster the same openness and thereby may inhibit some women—especially those not yet comfortable speaking out—from voicing their ideas. They may prefer to do initial homework on the best way to get an idea to the table and still get recognized for it. Still other women are extremely well respected and feel very comfortable in their frank approach, but are politically astute and realize that someone else may actually be able to bring their idea to the table more quickly. Such women take advantage of that assistance.

This may continue to be a politically charged issue, but it is clear that there are several routes available. Women need to be politically aware of what works and what does not in their specific situation and organization. Remember, utilize your mentor to find out what works for you!

RELUCTANCE TO PROMOTE YOURSELF

A friend tells of a colleague who was one of the most amazing self-promoters she had ever seen. In truth, the man did hardly anything at all, but to everyone else, it looked like he was running the show! He always made sure that everyone knew which conferences he was attending, what he was working on, and so forth. You may know the type! People who didn't know the real situation thought, "Wow, this guy is really on the fast track!" While that is definitely *not* the way to go, it can prove to be a valuable lesson on the importance of self-promotion. It is definitely linked to visibility, which is discussed under Success Secret Two.

Men frequently do not have the same socialization as women regarding humility. Many young girls are taught that it is not polite to brag—people may not like you. Well, take some tips from men on the importance of self-promotion and visibility. It is at times quite difficult to practice promoting yourself without coming off as a "brown-noser." But practice we must!

I'm talking mainly about letting people know what you're doing and how important it is to the organization, your team, your boss, whatever. Don't forget, if you have difficulty in promoting yourself to a large extent, get an "agent"—a friend or colleague who can do your promotion for you. Let your colleague spread the word about you—and you do the same for your supporter! It's often easier to brag about someone else than about yourself!

SORRY!

All right, admit it! Do you frequently find yourself saying "sorry" for things that you didn't even do wrong—or worse yet—for something *someone else* did? Don't worry, many women do the same thing! I can't tell you the number of times that I have said that myself. There's the kind of "sorry" that is OK, as in "I'm sorry, I didn't hear you," which is more of a symbol of politeness. However, do you find yourself saying "I'm sorry, maybe I gave unclear directions" when a subordinate does a project or assignment incorrectly? You know all along that your directions were perfectly clear—the subordinate messed it up! Or your boss is quite late for a meeting and you tell the other attendees as they're cooling their heels, "I'm sorry, I didn't realize that she was going to be so long"—like you have any control over your boss's schedule!

There certainly are times when "I'm sorry" can be used to restore balance to a conversation. However, in many cases, it can be perceived as putting yourself down. In her book *Talking from 9 to 5*, Deborah Tannen cites numerous incidents of women ritualistically using an apology in what can be construed as a self-deprecating way.[12] In her extensive research, Tannen has documented that men frequently do not apologize in social or professional exchanges, which may frequently put women in a "one-down" position—a disadvantage—since women frequently do apologize for a variety of reasons. It may really help if you let a few friends in on your plan to reduce the number of times you say "I'm sorry" so that they can gently remind you each time. You may be surprised at how often you say it in the course of a day. This will probably at least heighten your awareness of the frequency of and specific situations in which you find yourself saying "Sorry!"

BUSINESS IS BUSINESS, NOT PERSONAL

If you're like many women, you have not been socialized in the same way as men have. Participating on sports teams is an example. Boys or men are out for blood when they're on the playing field, then they're best friends off the field or court. This attitude continues in the workplace. It is not uncommon to see two men seemingly at each other's throats over an issue, only to get together for a beer after work. Now this approach is not exclusive to men, but it is certainly a more common male behavior pattern. Women are often amazed at how men can shift gears so easily! How can they do that? They're often just socialized that way!

Similarly, some men (and women) may offer their opinions as fact. Typically, they make an extremely strong, confident statement at a meeting and wait for someone to challenge it. They present their idea in such a way as to suggest it is already written in stone, intimidating others from challenging it. Another strategy is to downplay or belittle the opinions or suggestions of others in the expectation that one's opponents will back down. This is an intimidation strategy. People may try to find fault by constant questioning in order to make their own stance appear stronger. Or it may simply be a means by which they can ascertain the strength of someone else's convictions or preparedness in a project, for example. (How committed or prepared is this person to take on the project?)

I've seen this type of behavior a lot and you probably have seen it too. Many men and women who approach discussions or decisions in this way expect a certain rebuttal or resistance. They may appreciate and respect someone who stands up for his or her opinion, and may even acquiesce in light of the confrontation. This is, as Deborah Tannen calls it, "ritual opposition." She states that fewer women than men are comfortable with this approach. In fact, many women who lack experience with ritual opposition may view these challenges as personal attacks.

Many women are not prepared for, or experienced in, these types of encounters. They feel that everyone has to like them all the time, and that confrontation should be avoided whenever possible. But the opposite reaction may result. The woman who avoids confrontation may frequently be seen as weak, lacking the gumption to stand up for her convictions. Yet gumption may be a critical component for leadership positions.

Few of us really enjoy confrontation, but some women have certainly learned how to effectively stand up for what they think. Women can usually confront someone successfully if it is an issue that they really believe in. It's probably best to plan your "attack," but sometimes it just happens. Many women feel that they may be fired if they confront a more senior person. In some cases this could happen, depending on the existing culture toward women or a history of bad blood between the parties, for example. But in the vast majority of conflicts, it is probably not going to happen if you stay focused on the task and not the person. (This may be a good scenario to develop with your mentor or advocate if you have doubts about your credibility or fear a negative outcome.) Remember, confrontation is not a personal attack, just a business issue.

Many women have found that taking the risk and standing up for something they really believe in is a critical first step. If you are well prepared for your argument, if you don't totally lose control, and if you keep the issue from getting personal, many men will actually respect you more for the confrontation. Remember, men are used to it from their socialization!

I confronted a senior administrator several years ago on a student-related issue about which I was adamant. I went into his office to discuss the matter, but he stood up and walked past me and

*out of his office—as I was in midsentence. I followed him right out
of the office and started very loudly confronting him with the issue,
which was not at all my usual communication style! After this
incident, a group of senior individuals met and agreed with me on
the issue. I felt very uncomfortable for a while every time I saw the
administrator in the hallway, as many women would after a heated
confrontation. But some time later, I had another issue to discuss
with him and he was not only extremely accommodating—as he has
been on every subsequent issue—but very pleasant. When I look at
other men and women who deal with this man effectively, I see that
they stand up to him as well. I have noticed that he usually walks
on the people who don't stand up to him. This is a critical part
of "understanding the opposition" during a confrontation.*

Ironically, this approach can sometimes disarm a success
strategy if women come on too strong or in the wrong style or
situation. Both women and men are accepted in a professional
capacity most often when they conform at least somewhat to
gender norms. Men who are less assertive in the workplace can
sometimes be construed as "wimpy" and risk not being taken
seriously by senior management. Conversely, women who seem
overly assertive or confrontational may be perceived as bitchy
or overly emotional by both men and women at the workplace.
The most effective combination may be an equal distribution
of masculine and feminine characteristics—an androgynous
leader. This is admittedly a difficult balance for most people,
but it may come about as the result of trial and error, of emulating the behavior of a successful leader within the organization, or of soliciting effective advice from your mentor. You
need to develop your own style—whatever works for you.

> *A senior executive at American Airlines says that she would
> rather be respected than liked. "Likable" is a word that Barbara
> doesn't like. She says, "I don't care if people like me. I want them
> to respect me."*

You may want to keep in mind another important fact.
Bosses, especially male bosses, may feel somewhat uncomfortable giving frank feedback on the performance of women. Going
back to the socialization issue, some men may still see women in
a more domestic role and feel that harsh criticism will be diffi-

cult for them to handle. It is, therefore, important to articulate your desire for constructive evaluations and suggestions for your growth and development. Men usually feel comfortable giving this kind of feedback to other men, since they can more easily relate to how men will react. If women are to compete at the same level, they must be prepared for the criticism.

PREPARING YOURSELF IN THE EVENT OF CONFLICT

It is absolutely critical to be extremely well prepared if there is even the slightest possibility of a challenge—in a presentation, a proposal, or a negotiation. Knowing that your opinions or assumptions may very well be scrutinized necessitates that risks be reduced whenever possible. You really need to be prepared and know your stuff! No shortcuts! If you are prepared, you develop a keener sense of your own capabilities and can effectively respond to any challenge. However, if you are unable to adapt to this kind of ritual opposition, and you have not prepared as fully as you could have, you may be undermined by the "pros" who thrive on these exchanges. They may be waiting to eat you alive!

> *Karen, an executive at The Wall Street Journal, agrees that you have to really know your stuff. People can be really tough on you and quiz you.*

A friend who is now the president of a construction business used to work for a company whose corporate culture was underscored by this kind of ritual. The senior managers would routinely belittle and even ridicule team members who were making presentations to the point of forcing many of the participants to completely doubt their worth and even causing some very strong women to break down in tears. Everyone just anticipated being attacked, which certainly did not make for effective teamwork. Instead of working together in an atmosphere of mutual respect and trust, which would invite creative solutions, most of the participants were afraid to go out on a limb and consequently made less definitive points or arguments, which ironically only invited more attacks. After a while, several team members realized that this was part of the strategy—albeit a negative one. They made the commitment to be as prepared as possible, assuming that they would be attacked anyway—and just tried very hard not to take it so seriously. In this way, they found that at least they could effectively articulate their position. Ironically, when several of the team members did take a strong position, they were complimented on their stance.

> *Lynn has seen evidence of this physical posturing in various situations as well. She was present at a high-level meeting in a conference room several years ago. One senior executive (a man) was presenting a point and decided to create a physical presence by standing and then strutting around the conference table. Then, as if not to be outdone, his client counterpart also stood and began posturing, almost as a physical challenge. It's a control thing, I think! Lynn said that it was almost humorous, because the men probably didn't even notice that they were mirroring each other's behavior, that it was most likely a subconscious act. But to Lynn, it was very obviously an attempt not to be outmaneuvered.*

It is extremely important here to acknowledge that some organizations reflect this type of culture and some do not. You can learn to operate more effectively in a somewhat confrontational environment—indeed, these situations may exist in even the most team-oriented workplace! It may also be necessary to reflect upon what your values really are. Do you want to operate in this kind of environment, or is the real risk in seeking out another environment which is better suited to your type of productivity? This is an important question!

NEGOTIATING EFFECTIVELY

A good example of understanding the rules is in the negotiation process. Negotiation is frequently a power and communication issue more than anything. Again, think of men's socialization—you're either one up or one down. Think of the adage "Whoever has less to lose in the situation has more control." Women are often not comfortable with negotiation. It may go back to their discomfort with confrontation. It may stem from their insecurity that women aren't as important and therefore hold less of a bargaining position. Or it may simply be a lack of experience in negotiating.

Negotiation is a crucial part of life—not only in the workplace, but in your personal life as well. You negotiate with your kids, your spouse or significant other, your parents, the people at the store when you take back an item, your child's teacher over a passing grade in algebra—the list goes on and on. If you become more proficient at negotiating, you may become less of a victim in many encounters. Negotiation involves communication skills and assertiveness skills. It helps enormously if you have an idea where the other party is coming from (communication). It also helps if you can articulate and stand up for your personal point of view (assertiveness).

When negotiating for a starting salary in a new job, for example, best-selling author and speaker Tom Jackson recommends that you always ask for the top of the salary range, regardless of your experience. Like most people, you probably think that since you don't have the exact experience in that position, you really don't deserve the highest salary that is offered. But if you did have all the experience, you'd probably be bored and be looking for a new challenge anyway.

> *An executive at AT&T said that in her first major position, she felt comfortable with about 75 percent of her job requirements. After her next promotion, she felt that she really knew 50 percent of what she needed. In her latest promotion, she really felt comfortable with about 25 percent of the job requirements, but knew that she could do a good job from her past experience—her track record.*

That says a lot about comfort level with new positions! If you're good enough to get the offer, you should expect the highest salary. However, sometimes, no matter how much you think you deserve a raise, you won't get it. There was an interesting *LA Law* episode some years back. A young African-American lawyer, a Harvard grad, was hired at a very high salary as an associate in the law firm. Another male hotshot, on the fast track in the firm, found out and demanded the same salary from the senior partner—and got it. Finally, a young female associate, a single mother, complained to one of the female partners that she too was entitled to the same raise. The female partner, her mentor, advised against any request for a raise, saying that the young associate didn't have the same commitment, couldn't work the same long hours because of her child, and didn't take the same risks as her male colleague. She didn't have enough ammunition for the request.

If you are negotiating for a raise or promotion, this may be a very good time to talk to your mentor or advocate. She or he can help you examine what you need to do to strengthen your negotiation case—and can help you practice your negotiation skills. It may also help to assess the other party's negotiation style. Try to become a keen observer of successful negotiators in your organization or environment. It can be especially important for you to highlight the values of your product, project, or service— or personal value. Many women still feel uncomfortable "tooting their own horn." You may need to practice appropriate self-promotion as well. (See the discussion of visibility in Part Two.)

Think about the last time you asked for a raise—if indeed you ever have had the nerve to do so. If your boss was a strong negotiator, would you feel that you had a prayer of getting your raise? One of the points that is especially important for women to realize is that they should not link their own salaries and/or promotions to others in the organization, *but should rely on their own merit and accomplishments*. A colleague of mine, unfortunately, did not know about this years ago when she asked for her first raise. She was young and inexperienced about negotiation. She compared her situation with that of a male colleague who had more seniority, but fewer credentials. She was told that seniority was what determined salaries. Several years later, when a new male colleague was hired, he received the same salary as she did. When she questioned it, she was told that he had great credentials, even though she had more seniority. She wasn't too happy about the situation, but it did teach her a good lesson: Never ask for a raise or promotion by comparing yourself with others; do it only on the basis of your merit. By the way, the negotiators were men.

Research supports the contention that women are at disadvantage in the negotiation arena.[13] In a study, students were asked to role-play negotiating for raises. In the scenarios, women generally did not receive the same raises as their male counterparts. In addition, the lowest raises in the various gender combinations (male boss–male employee; female boss–male employee, and so on) were given by male bosses to female employees. It was determined in this study that not only did men end up with higher raises, but they were actually offered more money even before the negotiation. Interestingly, the highest raises were given when the negotiators were the same sex.

Many women in the workplace will concur that these findings reflect their actual experiences.

> *A talented surgeon said that when she realized she would not move up in her position at a major teaching university, she decided to go into private practice. Her boss tried to entice her to stay by offering her more money. He said that, yes, she had been paid less than her male counterparts during her tenure at the university, but that he would raise her salary. That was all the confirmation she needed to make the decision to leave. She knew that things probably would stay basically the same, regardless of her raise. She now has a flourishing private practice and is glad she made the move.*

I have heard similar stories of significant pay disparity even among high-level professionals. Frequently, it is a function of how well the people negotiated at the beginning of their employment.

Deborah Tannen makes a wonderful point about the physical side of negotiation.[14] She cites a CEO who, probably like most senior decision makers, says that he must frequently make decisions on the basis of very limited information. Consequently, he often has to go by gut feeling—how confident those making the proposal or presentation are about their point of view. If they seem sure of themselves, he may risk it. If not, he may not take a chance, despite the actual preparation and scope of the project. Tannen talks about the importance of body posture, speech, facial expressions, and overall enthusiasm for a proposal. You know the kinds of people—the ones who infectiously get everyone excited about what they're doing. You can't help but join in.

POWER DERAILERS

Are there particular verbal and nonverbal forms of communication that can reduce a manager's (especially a female manager's) effectiveness? There are several that many women may need to address in order to be taken more seriously—and I've been guilty of a few of these pitfalls myself. Even though I give seminars on success strategies for women, I still find myself having to adjust my ingrained behavior! So, believe me, we all need to be aware of our potential power derailers.

For example, do you ever listen to someone and find yourself nodding in agreement—a lot? Not only can it become an annoyance and a distraction; it also assumes that you agree with everything being said. If possible, have someone else observe you (again, someone you trust). You may be doing more than you think you are. Another potential power buster is smiling excessively. We want to be nice—that's how we were raised. A colleague, a psychologist, brought this to my attention several years ago. She said, "Just practice sitting here in front of me and not smiling at all." I did stop smiling—or at least I thought I did—but I still had the tendency to show some emotion. It was really hard to be completely stone-faced, but it is something that we should practice, especially when negotiating. I still like to smile a lot, since I genuinely like people, but I can really understand the importance of being able to switch gears and be a little more serious when appropriate.

Another thing that we have all seen—and experienced—is the tendency for women to give out personal information. Women tend to discuss personal matters far more than men. As an exercise, listen to a group of "average" women at a lunch table or lounge at work. What do they discuss? They talk about their kids, their husbands or significant others, clothes (especially where they got them and what a great price they paid!), where they went over the weekend, and so on. If you listen to a group of men in the same setting, you will rarely find them discussing the same personal issues. They'll probably be talking about sports or cars, something work-related, computers, and so forth. Try it. Be aware of the differences between men's and women's conversations. Then, listen to what *successful* women are talking about, either with other women or with men. It will probably, again, be far less personal than what "average" women discuss. While it is nice to talk about your personal life, it probably is a good idea to keep an eye on discussing it too much or too frequently. It may very well mark you as a lightweight.

As we will see in Part Two, it may be a good political move to open your conversation to a wider variety of issues—including sports, computer technology, and business trends—in order to be well accepted into higher-level circles. However, it is important to try to be flexible and adapt your conversational style and topics to the individual group. But keep in mind that in order to gain that flexibility, you need to have a fairly wide range of topics that you can discuss.

One thing that many students learn in an MBA program is the importance of brevity, both spoken and written. You often have to do 2-page summaries, not 10-page reports. You have to do 10-minute presentations, when you could theoretically speak for 30 minutes. Learning how to be more brief in written and spoken interactions is an art. You can develop a better understanding of it if you receive numerous voice-mail messages, for example. Instead of being clear and to the point, callers sometimes give a complete history of the situation over the phone. Try retrieving your voice mail off site before running for a flight or on a 10-minute meeting break! One senior manager says on her voice-mail message, "You'll lose me after 30 seconds!"

Have you ever had someone explain an issue and take 5 minutes to preface it? You want to say, "Just spit it out!" Several years ago the dean of my division asked me for an explanation of a situation with which I had been dealing. I found myself unexpectedly going into great detail, and he gave me a look that combined confusion and impatience. I quickly stopped, presented a short synopsis of the situation and how I dealt with it, and he was gone. I try to remember that scenario and that look any time someone makes a request for information. Look the other person straight in the eye, be brief and to the point. (By the way, that's another good thing to practice— really looking someone in the eye when you speak. It's a statement of power and confidence.) If you are writing a memo or letter, for example, look to see if there is superfluous information and eliminate it. Remember, people don't have time for excess information. (What's that mnemonic used in management? KISS—Keep It Simple, Stupid.)

A confident voice is a real asset. It can set the stage for others to determine your power (or perceived power) level. You may have heard women who end every sentence by raising their intonation, almost as if asking a question. (Some men do this too, but not as often.) Such a style may be seen as tentative and lacking in power, signifying that people are unsure about what they are saying (besides the fact that it is extremely annoying after a few minutes!) Try to be aware not only of projecting your physical voice at a comfortable tone and level but also of modulating your voice appropriately up or down, or keeping it at a consistent level, at the end of phrases and sentences. If you need help, you can always sign up for a speech class at a community organization or at your local college.

In the next week or so, try listening to the tone and intonation of statements made in meetings or in general conversation of both men and women. Do you hear the differences in the statements? Women's speech patterns can sometimes be interpreted as uncertain or insecure. Listen carefully to the intonation more than the content. (But make sure in this exercise that you're not at an important meeting in which you need to be listening to content!) Who sounds more authoritative, more certain? Who gets heard? If you find yourself guilty of consistently rising intonation, try to adopt the style that sounds more powerful in other speakers. This may take practice.

The former president of Bryn Mawr College encourages her female students to serve on committees and to speak up more forcefully, instead of beginning with disclaimers. She notices at times that students at Bryn Mawr, admittedly some of the most elite young women in the country, occasionally say things at board meetings like "You probably already thought of this, but..." or "This may sound stupid, but...." She advises women just to jump into a conversation without worrying if a point has been brought up yet. Women need to practice speaking louder and at greater length.

Men frequently speak longer and more often than women, and are clearer and more succinct in their presentation. Women are not heard at meetings as frequently as men. Women need to be aware that when they say the same things as men—and are not heard—there could be a cultural or even geographical bias. However, women can train themselves to change. It can be an issue of changing the way you say something. For example, you might try speaking more loudly instead of softly, without any disclaimers (as mentioned above), in a more brief format and in a certain tone.

Try to look at your nonverbal communication as well.

> *Gena, an executive at Merck, feels that it is really important to understand your own attitudes and values. Nonverbal communication is 70 percent of the game. You need to project yourself, both verbally and nonverbally.*

Look at people in your work environment, on the evening news, or in other environments to see who has the appearance of self-confidence. Look at the way they sit, stand, and act. Most likely the confident ones will take up a certain physical space, appear comfortable and relaxed, and hold their heads up, shoulders back—no slouching. Now look at people who may be perceived as less successful, powerful, confident. They may look downtrodden or just hesitant and self-conscious. They may take up less physical space (they don't use the arms of a chair, for example). They may cast their eyes down, be hesitant in their speech, have limp handshakes, and so forth. You might try videotaping yourself with the aid of an advocate to see exactly how you can improve your appearance of confidence and success. Do you project the image you want to project? Don't underestimate the power of nonverbal communication. Like it or not, others make an instant assessment of you—for better or for worse—and that's a hard impression to change. You want to maximize your positive attributes and minimize your less positive ones.

Nonverbal communication is something you can quite effectively change, so it's important to start working on areas in need! Remember, this is a process, not a program, so you're striving for a gradual positive change across a number of areas. The more negatives you eliminate and the more positives you accentuate, the more significant the overall change!

ADAPTING YOUR STYLE TO THE ENVIRONMENT AND SITUATION

A *contingent leadership style* refers to a leader adapting his or her management style to a specific situation or environment.[15] The same can be said of us as we examine our behavior patterns and styles in various situations and environments.

> *Diane, a publishing director at Gannett, Inc., indicated that women frequently need to be able to switch gears—to change behaviors according to the environment.*

This is a valid point. Look at your specific environment. Although it is extremely important to be consistent in your behavior, do you adapt well to particular situations?

Salespeople who have gone through a comprehensive training course will tell you that one of the techniques of effective consultative sales is identifying and adapting to the customer's approach and needs. A skilled sales professional can size up his or her customer's style rather quickly and reflect it. You can do the same thing in your own environment.

For example, if sales professionals walk into a customer's office and notice numerous photographs, personal items, and children's drawings, they may conclude that the customer's personal life is important. So they will spend a few minutes commenting on the items and developing a rapport on a personal level before jumping right into business. You can do the same thing with senior managers at your organization. You can frequently get a sense of personality by how people approach you: Are they open and chatty? Do they seem interested in small talk? Are they "warm and fuzzy"? You should be able to tell pretty quickly and respond accordingly. However, if the person is basically a no-nonsense type who likes to get down to business, you can usually tell that too.

You may be fortunate enough to have information on a person's "type" in advance, if you are planning some sort of interaction. If not, try to make a quick decision on the basis of office surroundings or the person's general demeanor. If someone is open and friendly, you may want to ask questions about family or personal interests to break the ice. Few people will mind the extra few minutes to develop the relationship. But if you start to chat with some of those down-to-business types, you will lose precious time for making your point or asking your necessary questions. Also, people may think that you are wasting their precious time with superfluous small talk and become a bit annoyed or resentful. With these people, come in well prepared with all the facts, and be concise, brief, and businesslike. No chit-chat!

You probably are quite familiar with the general style of many of the movers and shakers in your organization. If you want to increase your visibility and develop a professional relationship with these people, it may be effective to mirror their style when you speak to them. (This is a counseling technique.) If you're speaking to technology or finance types, the chances are pretty good that they will have down-to-business personalities. Mirror that behavior. If you are trying to build a relationship, you may want to drop some facts about the latest technology or financial news or trends. But keep it short and germane to their area of interest and expertise. You can always say that you would like to know more about that area or have the opportunity to ask them questions at a later, specified time if you want to develop more of a professional relationship with them.

If, on the other hand, the people you want to approach are open and friendly, you might schedule a time to take them out for a sandwich, for example, to get to know them better. These "people persons" frequently enjoy getting to know others in the organization (or outside the organization), especially as an effective way of increasing their general knowledge base.

Sue, an executive at Tenneco, thinks that women often don't ask questions for fear of looking stupid. Karen, at The Wall Street Journal, agrees that women shouldn't be afraid to ask a lot of questions. You can learn from everyone you come in contact with. Don't be afraid to suggest ideas—the worst people can say is no.

With both groups, you may also want to mirror their actual conversational style. If people are quite serious and methodical in tone and pace of conversation, try to follow their lead. If your usual style is to be enthusiastic about your subject and to have a high energy level, you may speak somewhat quickly. You can drive people crazy by that pace if they tend to think and speak more slowly and methodically. Learn to adapt your conversational style to the person you're speaking to. If his or her personality and style are like yours, that person will relate well and be caught up in the enthusiasm. If you are dealing with the opposite personality, make an effort to speak very slowly and clearly, allowing people time to process what you're saying. It works very well and is something that many women may not think to do.

When interviewing senior-level individuals for this book, I had to assess the situation every time I spoke to a participant. Sometimes there were previous expectations—for example, a colleague would say, "He or she is terrific"—but frequently I didn't know the participants at all, or anything about them. Clearly these people were at least willing to give of their time to talk, so that helped provide some information. Eventually I got a sense of how to approach them—whether to engage in small talk for a couple of minutes or get right to the point: How much personal information were they willing to divulge, and how much time were they willing to spend on the interview? This assessment helped me hit the mark with regard to individual communication style, rather than risk miscommunication with the participants.

In applying this technique in your environment, you may want to examine your personal approaches to subordinates, peers, and bosses. Certain staff members may like to talk about their kids or grandchildren, their vacations, or what they did over the weekend. You will definitely appeal to their sense of self by briefly asking them about their children or whether they had a nice weekend. You don't have to belabor the discussion, but your interest will go a long way in developing an effective team environment. On the other hand, it's a good idea not to get overly involved with personal issues at work, unless coworkers are also good friends. Doing so could minimize your effectiveness as a leader by seeming to confuse the boundaries between personal affairs and work. This is an area that many women may need to clarify, since their social-ization tends to emphasize the importance of developing rela-tionships, regardless of the environment. It can be very help-ful to examine and identify various types of scenarios and adapt your communication style to the specific situation.

You may also want to observe the physical tone and pace of senior individuals in your organization. You'll probably notice that most of these people speak and carry themselves somewhat slowly and deliberately. While I was waiting for a senior execu-tive (on the executive floor) a while back, I became aware of a group of people gathering for a meeting behind me. On the hardwood floor, I could hear some people clickety-clacking at a very fast pace and chatting with others. Then there were others en route to the meeting who were moving and speaking more deliberately. Out of curiosity, I started to look up when they walked by. Sure enough, all the ones scurrying to the meeting appeared to be frazzled lower-level employees, while the others looked like senior management. Even if it was only the image they portrayed (I didn't actually know who they were), there surely seemed to be a fairly clear-cut difference in rank!

> *The technical division president of a large publishing company maintains that communication competence is at the core of everything. You can be respectful to others, but remain true to your point of view. You can be polite, but strong-willed in a business perspective. In her view, it is critical to enter meetings prepared. Never go into a meeting without knowing why it's being held, and what the major expected outcomes are. There should be preparation, communication, and closure.*

SOCIALIZATION—THE NEXT GENERATION

You might be encouraged to know that the next generation of young women is slowly starting to change. Many female high school and college students are very much aware of the impor-tance of healthy competition (especially through sports), the need to stand up for themselves and be assertive, and the importance of visibility and numerous other more "masculine" traits and skills. We can help them by encouraging them to participate in sports, run for student government offices, or manage a large club, newspaper, or magazine. It's especially important for young women to challenge themselves, gain confidence, and increase their visibility.

Whenever I teach classes or give presentations to college or high school students, I specifically ask the young women what their goals and views on competition are, whether they play sports, why they are motivated to engage in certain activities, and who their role models and advocates are. The major thing that strikes me is the great difference in their views and those of our peers a generation ago. Many of these young women are really together—they play sports and are comfortable in healthy competition with their male counterparts. They are hard-working, goal-oriented, and assertive; they are interested in math, science, and technology. Interestingly enough, they do admit that their advocates and role models are usually their parents. So what is happening? Parents, especially those women of our generation who feel that they did not have opportunities or encouragement themselves, are passing along traits and skills that they know to be necessary for success to their children, both boys and girls. (Many parents also say that they want their sons to be more aware of communication, nurturing, and so forth, as well!)

Some women may have just been more fortunate than others to have parents that were aware of the potential consequences of not preparing their daughters for the future. Just try to constantly remind yourself that you can truly undo past experiences and look ahead instead of back. You can definitely begin to control your own destiny by practicing new behaviors. There's no time like the present to start (or continue) changing your attitudes and behavior!

We have greatly benefited from those who came before us. Although we still face numerous barriers and problems in the workplace, it's a lot better than it was for working women in the 1950s, 1960s, and 1970s. No doubt, women in the previous generations wish that they had the opportunities that we now possess. So let's hope that we can all play a major role in the socialization of our next generation—either as parents or as advocates.

Even these young women, however, will need to have effective role models. It is especially important to have models who emphasize the importance of balance in life. *The Wall Street Journal*, for example, recently published an article on how some daughters of highly successful women are starting to rebel against the values of their hard-working mothers.[16] Many of the earlier successful women had to work so hard and conform to the male leadership model that their children now say that they don't want to follow in their footsteps. Their children feel that they missed out on some things at home growing up. There's definitely a message here! The real goal is to try to balance your life and make appropriate choices. We can't have it all. It's critical to examine the skills and attitudes of women who really seem able to balance their work and home lives, find out what works for them, and make our own choices accordingly.

We all need to be role models for the future generation. These young people need to know that it's all right to work really hard, but you must value a sense of balance. That it's all right to be a team player, but you must be an individual as well. It's great if you can be smart, feminine, and assertive without worrying about what guys will think (which is very important in your teens). You need always to keep this in mind—you never know whom you may influence as you go about your daily routine! Always try to be a role model and think about the next generation.

SUMMARY

- Develop one-on-one communication skills. Be clear and specific with your boss and your organization about your career path and timetable.

- If your boss doesn't ask you about what you want to do, tell him or her. Don't assume others know what you want—they can't read your mind.

- Be aware of how your own socialization causes you to think, act, and react the way you do. Be aware, also, of others' socialization to better understand the hows and whys of what they do. Keep in mind that men and women have frequently had different socialization patterns. Learning about these patterns can lead to greatly improved communication and teamwork.

- Start to learn leadership strategies from those you admire. What do they do that you need to learn?

- Be aware that people do not always play under the same set of rules, either by coincidence or by design. You may need to brush up on how rules are developed (e.g., in sports).

- There are several different ways in which you can be heard in your organization: in meetings, in decisions, on your team. These may depend on the situation and/or the organization.

- Women need to practice self-promotion. Visibility increases as others know what you're doing, your accomplishments, and what your potential is.

- Women tend to be at a disadvantage when they say "I'm sorry." Men do not say it as often as women do, and it may be seen as a weakness.

- Women can learn to become more comfortable in challenging environments of conflict, which can be both a negative and a positive thing. However, it is important to establish a positive balance between assertiveness and "bitchiness."

- It is important to learn how to prepare yourself for inevitable conflicts. It is critical to understand the environment, the players, and your own strengths and weaknesses.

- Negotiation is an important part of professional and personal life. There are different styles and approaches to negotiation. Women can learn to become proficient negotiators and give themselves the advantage by leveling the playing field. Also, don't underestimate your own worth and skills in negotiation.

- Verbal and nonverbal behaviors can be critical in forming both initial and lasting impressions. Things like intonation, content of discussion, body language, and adapting your style to your audience can greatly improve your communication success.

- You can develop your own style of communication through input from mentors, people you admire, and your own experience. You will learn what works for you.
- The next generation of young people is learning from us. We must serve as effective role models for both young men and women.

ACTION PLAN

Ask someone you trust to honestly evaluate your communication skills. Use it as a constructive exercise. A valued friend can help you with evaluating your body language, voice intonation, physical presence, and so forth. It may be difficult, but others are noticing your shortcomings too! You might as well start working on them now.

Do you read books and attend seminars to improve your communication skills? Ask others for recommendations on what has helped them.

Do you find yourself saying "I'm sorry" to everyone? (As in, "I'm sorry, maybe I didn't make my instructions clear enough" or "I'm sorry, perhaps you didn't understand.") Once you're aware of the habit, you will probably reduce the number of times you say it.

Almost everything is a negotiation. How do you plan to improve your negotiation skills? (Think about raises, promotions, gaining influence. We all need help on this one!) Try to sit in on negotiations, if possible. Observe others who are successful negotiators. Be aware that there are different approaches and see which one works for you. You can do this in many situations: buying a car, getting a loan, and so on. Practice, practice, practice!

Do you think that men and women frequently communicate differently? If so, how can you try to understand and appreciate the differences to improve communication and teamwork? Do you think that your socialization has poorly or appropriately prepared you to understand different genders and generations? Part of your development is awareness. If you have difficulty in understanding how genders and generations communicate differently, read about it. Talk about it with members of both genders and other generations. Be open-minded.

How are you going to practice being heard at meetings or in groups? Do you feel uncomfortable just jumping in? Do you prefer to "wait your turn"? Try practicing in lower-stress environments, in which you feel comfortable—perhaps in a discussion with friends. You may also want to watch TV discussion shows to see how the panelists communicate.

Do you hate conflict? It's inevitable! How are you going to develop a tolerance for conflict? Do you just walk away or do you need to learn how to face it? Talk to colleagues and friends whom you admire. Ask for their advice. Do it in noncrucial environments. There are also lots of books and videotapes as well as seminars on the topic. Sometimes, you just have to practice through experience. Not all experiences will be good, but at least you can learn! (Remember, some people see you as weak if you always back down, so you may need to practice standing up for yourself. People will probably respect you more!)

Try to remember that you are helping the next generation develop positive communication skills too. Do you need to listen more to your kids, your students, your younger colleagues? Give them the opportunity to communicate by trying to appreciate their different points of view—no matter how exasperating it may sometimes be!

SUCCESSFUL PEOPLE KNOW HOW TO BALANCE WORK AND HOME

As I perused an edition of *Men's Health* magazine (Yes, you never know where you may find helpful information!), I was immediately drawn to an article which dealt with balance in men's lives.[17] Intrigued, I of course turned right to the page. Interestingly enough, the article opened with a familiar complaint—not enough time to get everything done. However, the balancing act for men, according to this article, was finding the right balance between work and *leisure time*. Leisure time—what leisure time? I commented on this to several women and they just laughed. Leisure time very rarely enters into our balancing act—although in all honesty it should!

A major reason to balance your life is so that you will be able to have a better quality of life. Even many high-level male executives are beginning to question why they are working so hard. For what? They want to enjoy their lives and their families more than in the past. Do you frequently feel that there aren't enough hours in the day to get everything done? Do you feel that you're burning the candle at both ends, but not getting a lot done, no matter how organized you are? Do you ever feel guilty if you have half an hour of free time, with nothing to do? (Don't laugh. This does happen once or twice a year!) Mothers who work outside the home may spend an average of

80 hours a week on the job, doing housework and caring for children.[18] Once in a while, they have to regroup and actually learn to schedule time for fun. I know that fun may at times become a foreign word to you, but if you're like me, sometimes you actually forget what it's like to relax and enjoy yourself. Do you ever feel that it's almost a contest of how much work or how many tasks you can get accomplished and how much you can push yourself? It's almost easier, or so it seems, just to keep pushing yourself on the treadmill rather than find alternatives or a solution to get off occasionally and really enjoy yourself! You may feel like you're in perpetual motion.

But keep remembering that life is too short to lose the pleasure in life—you don't want to be like the successful senior men who said that they regretted not taking a step back and enjoying themselves and their families a little more. We women are having more heart attacks than we used to, smoking more, experiencing more stress—in short, we're becoming like the men of generations past. While success is terrific, it's easy to find ourselves faced with many of the negative aspects of ambition as well.

HAVE WE FORGOTTEN HOW TO HAVE FUN?

Part of a better quality of life includes various aspects of play. In its definition, play is for pleasure, an activity undertaken for enjoyment.[19] Play can include the more conventional activities of playing with the kids, playing sports, or playing golf. It can be reading a good book for pleasure, or cooking, or doing needlework. But it can also include much more. It can be intense, it can be invigorating, it can heighten our sense of well-being and reduce anger, anxiety, and frustration. It can lead to healthier relationships, greater creativity, and confidence. Play should consist of a more comfortable opportunity to try new things, taking on new roles or taking risks or challenges that we would ordinarily not take on. In corporate training, for example, games or other activities are frequently used either as ice breakers or exercises designed to make the learning experience easier or less stressful, as well as to reinforce the concepts included in the training.

However, even play is beginning to take on a competitive aspect. Not only do we have less time for play, but we're now beginning to work harder at playing. Instead of going out for a nice brisk walk and enjoying the view, we're working at maintaining our pulse rate at maximum efficiency level. We're out to "kill the competition" in our tennis or racquetball games. We feel depressed if we don't go for our aerobics workout, even though we had to work until 9 o'clock. Even our kids are learning French and computer skills in preschool. Now don't get me wrong. We all have the same crazy schedules and try to fit in everything, but are we losing sight of some basic pleasures? While it's great to keep an eye on staying fit, challenging ourselves, and raising talented kids, are we risking becoming even more stressed out and obsessed with our so-called leisure activities? Especially in this time of rapidly decreasing leisure, we may have difficulty even thinking about doing something unproductive. We better have some quantifiable result at the end of our activity in order to justify our time!

Some time ago, I was walking along the Connecticut shore at sunset with a friend. We were intently trying to maximize our power-walk workout, when suddenly I suggested that we stop to appreciate the sunset for a couple of minutes. We did stop just to look around and really enjoy that time. It was a beautiful view which we almost didn't experience because of our walking pace. It was just a few minutes, but when you have only a specified amount of time, it becomes harder simply to enjoy the little unexpected things along the way.

Various surveys have indicated that we have far less leisure time than in years past, despite advances in technology that promised to make our lives easier and more productive. The average American has only about 16 hours of leisure per week. Any working parent would be surprised at anyone having that much![20] In 1983, one survey indicated that 25 percent of adults reported always feeling "rushed," while the number in 1994 had climbed to almost 40 percent. Does that sound familiar?

What can we do about it? Well, we probably can't do too much about our lack of free time. But we can change our attitudes and outlooks. Do a self-examination. Do you ever have fun these days? If you're like a lot of people, you may not. Why not? It's probably largely due to guilt! We need to stop feeling guilty about setting aside some time for ourselves to do exactly what we want to do. Take a half-hour walk at lunchtime and just listen to great music or an audiobook on a Walkman, or enjoy a pleasant stroll with a colleague. And don't talk about work! Get up a little earlier when it's quiet and read a few pages of a book—or even a chapter. Do some needlepoint in the evening. Play on your computer or chat on the Internet. One of my delightful colleagues could be seen every once in a while outside the office wandering around in a field, just taking in the sights. I'm sure that she didn't have any particular purpose; she just felt like walking in a field! And, although our initial reaction may be "I don't have the time," we may just need to learn to delegate, prioritize, or reduce the guilt. Remember, this book is about learning from others how to be more successful—in this case, how to balance our lives more successfully. We don't want just to observe how others do it; we need to practice it ourselves! Almost all of us are overworked. I know I'm totally stressed out even as we speak! The trick is to learn how to have some fun in life. Read on for some secrets to finding the time.

WHERE TO START?

Many women feel that it's a potential career derailer to admit that they need help—and ask for it. A number of the women I interviewed felt that women were indeed frequently hesitant to request help for fear of looking incapable, incompetent, or inexperienced. But this attitude of "I can do everything" is one of the first ways in which women get caught up in the rat race. Women have to learn not only to ask for help, but to delegate effectively as well. Ask your advocate or mentor for tips on how. I must admit, I don't delegate nearly as well as I should, and as a consequence I end up doing many things that I in fact should not be doing. However, I am aware that this is a personal area of weakness and I am really trying to improve.

> *An executive at a major British corporation advises that we all eventually have to give up some of the areas of our former jobs as we move up, even if it's a task or function that we really enjoy doing. If we don't, not only will we be taking on too many responsibilities, but our boss may continue to see us in our former role!*

It helps if you can identify what excites people working for you or with you. There may be something that a colleague or employee really would love to do that you hate.

> *My former boss is a real "people person." He loves problem solving on a personal level. But he really hates administrative and technical tasks. He admits that he was always glad to have subordinates who liked to do those kinds of tasks. Or else, he said, he would have had to do them himself!*

He was absolutely right to delegate these kinds of tasks. They most likely would have caused him to procrastinate, since that's what we frequently do when we have a project facing us that we don't want to do. Then the project takes on overwhelming proportions about when we will be able to complete it (we've all experienced that). At least, if you delegate, the tasks get done.

Sometimes it's hard to give up control. And sometimes you get burned when you do delegate. But it usually helps if you walk subordinates through the process and explain the overall importance of the task, rather than just their immediate role. If people can understand the importance of doing their part well as it relates to the overall goal, they'll do a better job. That's human nature.

WORK AND HOME

One of the biggest frustrations among managers—both men and women, but especially women—is the constant struggle in balancing home and work life.

Gail Blanke, a senior vice president at Avon, admits that it is sometimes difficult to balance; you need to prioritize. She routinely has a breakfast meeting at 8 a.m., a parent-teacher conference in the evening, and meetings in between. However, her family is her number-one priority. She says that 20 years ago, there were no role models. She didn't think that she would be able to do it, but she learned to balance work and home with two children. She was a manager when her first daughter was born—there was no set maternity leave then, so she designed it. Gail doesn't make excuses. She always says where she is going for family events.

An executive at American Airlines concurs. Early in her career, she went 2 years without a vacation, working Saturdays and Sundays, on the road. She was obviously incredibly busy, working 12- to 13-hour days. She feels that success often comes from visibility. But she had no balance; it was very difficult. Now she no longer brings work home on weekends and nights. She has changed her perspective somewhat to take up golf, watch football, and spend more quality time with her husband.

A top Washington lawyer wanted to spend time with her family. She wanted to have dinner with her kids and be home on weekends, so she took a lot of work home. Her kids, now grown, say that they can't imagine having a mom who didn't work. Her own mom was a role model. She was active in the community, taught migrant workers, and served on the school board. She was a great balancer!

Judy Woodruff of CNN made time for her family even during her highly visible and demanding role as political commentator during the 1996 elections. Although family birthdays and other special events were occasionally inconvenient for the network during that time, she set her priorities, which her organization respected. This says a lot for both the person and the company. Judy doesn't do this balancing act casually. It's a strong commitment to both work and family.

In our mother's generation, the roles were generally quite clearly marked: Men brought home the paycheck and women stayed at home caring for the family. Well, this scenario accounts for only 7 percent of the population in today's world. It's not going to change, so how do we address it?

This balancing act has been the topic of conversation for a number of years, both among people and among organizations. A number of organizations provide flexible scheduling, job sharing, extended maternity or paternity leave, and telecommuting (working at an alternative worksite such as the home). These organizations are often cited as being female-friendly, and a number of employees, both male and female, have taken advantage of the options. However, even in these corporations many senior-level women say that they are unable to avail themselves of a number of the perks available—such as flex time, extended leave, and job sharing—because of the nature of the job and their own critical importance to the organization. Women at senior levels have more demanding schedules and cannot always take advantage of work-family policies. Still, in some ways it can be easier for them to create flexibility in their schedules for their families. For example, if a senior woman has an important family event or situation that she needs to attend or take care of, she may be able to schedule important meetings around that time. Whatever the arrangement, it is clear that these women place the highest priority on their families.

> *Judith Rodin, at the University of Pennsylvania, says that she makes sure to talk to her son every day when she is away about what happened at school and what he is doing, despite her grueling travel schedule. She says that it makes an enormous difference. She adds that parents may need to look at the trade-offs. There are many benefits for children who have the opportunity to travel, meet extraordinary people, and share widely diverse experiences as a result of their parents' careers.*

> *Janice, an executive at Tenneco, says that her children ask her what other moms do if they don't work. She says that her kids are very well adjusted to her role as a single working mother.*

> *Gail, an executive at Avon, never makes excuses when she has to leave work for an event with her daughter.*

> *Diane, at Gannett, is making it a point to help her daughters be more assertive and her son more nurturing.*

Women in more traditional positions, however, may need to take a personal day each time an important family matter or event comes up. If your boss does not share your views on balance and the importance of family, a difficult situation may arise. It may be very helpful to discuss it with your boss, so that you may be able to make alternative arrangements in advance, such as rearranging your work schedule to come in earlier, work later, or take work home in certain situations. (Remember, you have been developing a one-on-one rapport with your boss. Hopefully, you're making progress!) More and more organizations are starting to make these arrangements with their employees.

Frequently, however, it comes back to the issue of choices. With the ability to choose also comes responsibility. In organizations in the past, there was often no choice in lifestyle—either you had a family and stopped working or you chose your career in lieu of a family. Among the women I interviewed in my original research, over 75 percent had children and also maintained high-level careers. But even these women said that they had to make choices. Some women indicated that they were not always able to attend all their children's events at school, for example, but whenever possible they tried to do as much as they could with and for their children.

> *One executive at AT&T said that she rarely took the time to make cookies for her children's bake sales, but she loved to sew and made them Halloween costumes and other special clothes. Other women said that they tried to make vacations really special times with their kids. A number of the women stated that their children were a priority and that they refused to make excuses to leave the office if they had to attend a special event for their children at school. Many of the women created a culture in which other managers—and their subordinates—realized the importance of being able to balance their two worlds.*

Several participants emphasized that they encouraged both their male and female subordinates to take advantage of flexible scheduling and parental leaves. However, a number of the women said that they really had to learn how to turn off their home problems when they were at work and turn off their work problems while at home.

> *A senior executive at U.S. Healthcare says that she really tries to concentrate on work when she's at work and on home when she's at home. It is hard to switch on and off, but it really gives you greater balance.*

It takes a lot of practice! Some of the participants said that their success was not without some sacrifice and frequently made them feel guilty. About 10 or 15 years ago, women were frequently led to believe that they could be superwomen, that it was unfair that they couldn't "have it all." However, the underlying theme among many of the women I interviewed was that you always have to make choices. Perhaps it does seem unfair that many men have been able to have a family, yet have been freed of the responsibility for the care and upbringing of their children in order to pursue a fast-track career. It is still probably true that women bear the burden of work and home.

First, women have almost always been considered the primary nurturers and caretakers. Although that may not always be the case, it is still the most common scenario, irrespective of the position of the mother in her career. That is a fact of life and if you don't believe it, talk to almost any mother—working or not! However, several of the women I interviewed recounted stories of their very senior male peers. They said that, interestingly enough, some of these men were starting to say that they regretted not having spent as much time with their children, many of whom were now grown. If they had to do it again, they would have done things differently.

This feeling is not going unnoticed by many upcoming managers—female, yes, but also their male counterparts. Today's male managers will very frequently tell you that they are making the same choices as women to spend as much time as possible with their children. Perhaps they remember their own fathers and don't want to ignore their children in the same way that they themselves were ignored. Perhaps their wives or significant others have careers and demand more equal time in the upbringing of their children. Attitudes can take a lot of time to change, but at least men are starting to shift their views and values. Men increasingly are beginning to make the same choices as women: Specifically what is their goal at work and at home?

> Lou Dobbs of CNN agrees that many men he talks to—even very senior executives—are placing a great deal of emphasis on quality time with their families, which probably was not the case in the past. He adds that among top-level business leaders, for example, a lot of the macho attitude has disappeared. This attitude does not reflect the spirit of the 1990s. Many of these men really value their time at home.

Don't forget that these people are in leadership positions and are setting organizational policy. Their family-friendly views were probably not as evident a generation ago. So we can serve only to begin significantly changing the policies and practice of organizations of the future.

MAKING CHOICES

Increasingly, we need to make choices. First, if the nature of a job is to work 80 hours per week, we need to examine our own lives and see just how much we want this demanding job. Do we make the choice that this is what we really want and the necessary sacrifices are worth it? Or do we make the decision that we want a professional career, but are willing to stop short of the executive level, with its demands and stressors, in exchange for more quality time away from work? Many jobs have traditionally required a great deal of time and energy to move ahead. I don't know if that attitude will change in a big hurry. However, generally speaking, with greater responsibility and often a higher salary comes the need to dedicate more time to the job, which may not be an unreasonable expectation. This may certainly be based somewhat on personality, goals, and ambition. Women are gaining increasing acceptance into more senior levels—and a number have indeed achieved very senior positions while raising families. However, if many of them say that managers need to make tough choices, we need to really examine our own goals and expectations. Remember that equal opportunity means equal access. Women are increasingly able to gain access to senior positions. Whether we choose to take them is another story. And don't forget, many men who have traditionally had access in the past have chosen not to move into demanding senior positions.

A potential conflict of ideology may also develop, not necessarily between women and men, but among women. Many of the senior women I interviewed stated that it was extremely difficult to balance their demanding schedules with their family life. Many of the women had nannies, since, in addition to their own long hours, they frequently had to travel as well. The issue may become, not whether women do or do not choose to have children for the sake of their career, but how much time they are willing to spend or sacrifice for their career versus their family time. The differential between two women—one who employs a nanny to care for her children and must work 60 to 70 hours a week and one who prefers to be at home more with her children and work a less demanding schedule (at least while her children are dependent)—may be just as great (perhaps even more so) as that between a man and a woman.

Val Hammond, of the Roffey Management Centre in England, agrees with this observation. She adds another dimension, however—that of the woman who has no children. Such a woman is less likely to be able to empathize with working mothers than are men who are working fathers themselves. So, again, a generalization cannot be made that many of these issues are "women's issues." Rather, they are family and work issues.

My two older brothers, both professionals, have made conscious career choices to spend more time with their children. One of them is also the single parent of three boys, whom he has raised himself since they were very young. Both men have chosen to pursue less time-intensive careers than many of their colleagues—and they have no regrets. One brother even turned down a big promotion because it would result in more travel time, time he did not want to take away from his wife and infant son. Though they are men, they have far more experience with the issues of balancing work and family than some women may have in demanding professional positions. I see this within my own organization. It's just becoming more common for men to take a much more active role with their kids—although for many women, this is still not the case!

WHAT ORGANIZATIONS CAN DO

On the other hand, is there a way that we can look at the job as it has always been done and learn how to do it faster, better, and differently? Following a major earthquake in Los Angeles several years ago, a number of the major access routes from one side of the city to the other were seriously damaged and impassable. The result was that telecommuting became an instantaneous necessity. Companies didn't have time to do feasibility studies and test runs—distance working was just done. Surprisingly, a number of companies realized that their productivity didn't suffer. In fact, many of their employees preferred this style of work, proving that telecommuting was a viable method of employment. Frequently it is crisis that creates change.

> *The chief financial officer of Avon feels that organizations should provide flexibility to meet the needs of women and men on an individual basis. Managing diversity means treating everyone, not equally, but equitably. There may be different ways to accommodate different employees: job sharing, flex time, and so on. However, women and men should realize that flex time may affect career track. The best strategy is to let senior management know in advance, especially earlier in your career. Flexible organizations can accommodate good employees, attracting and retaining the best.*

Short of an obvious crisis, what are some other solutions? You can ask your own organization to examine possible options with regard to flexibility. For example, if your job doesn't entail direct customer contact every day, can you arrange to work at home 1 or 2 days a week?

> *Mary, an editor friend, just moved about an hour and a half away from her employer. She has made arrangements to do much of her editing work from her house, coming into the office less frequently and conducting much of her business during business trips.*
>
> *Mai, an executive recruiter, works from home 2 or 3 days a week to spend more time with her son.*
>
> *One vice president we know commutes between her home in Florida and her job in Philadelphia, with the ability to work a fair amount from her home. Technology has been a major factor in these and many other situations.*

If you have a position that can warrant being physically out of the office at least some of the time, you may be able to approach your boss with this type of proposal. You may want to see if any other employees in your organization have established similar arrangements. If you don't ask, you may never know!

Does your organization offer opportunities for flex time or job sharing? If it does, talk to other employees who may be taking advantage of the arrangement. Ask them specific questions about their impressions of the opportunities available to them as a result of their slightly altered career path. Do they still have access to key information? Are they still on their anticipated career track? Get the answers to these questions before you make any commitments. If these opportunities are not available in your organization and it is becoming increasingly difficult to adapt your lifestyle of home and work, you may want to start networking and perhaps create initiatives to start such programs or find another organization that will be more in keeping with your needs and expectations. Frequently a strong advocate in the human resources department can be of enormous help.

> *Terri Sullivan of USA Today and Madelyn Jennings of Gannett have been instrumental in their organizations, setting up numerous effective programs to encourage balance in the workplace. Both human resources executives, they feel a strong mission to provide opportunities to all employees in order to promote an effective diversity of perspective.*

STRATEGIES FOR BALANCE

Much of what we have talked about thus far concerns working smarter, not harder. Although promotions into very senior levels assumes hard work and long hours, there are ways to reduce some of the wasted effort. The more time that you save at work in efficiency and productivity, the more quality time you may have with your family, or time for yourself. In addition, networking does not only apply to the workplace; it should extend to your home life as well. Many managers complain about feeling pulled constantly in many directions. While this certainly does describe today's lifestyle, adaptations can be made at least to lessen the impact of busy schedules. The following strategies will employ your increasingly sharpened skills of effective communication, risk taking, visibility, political acumen, and networking.

Several of the women I interviewed recommended talking to advocates, managers who are sympathetic to the issues facing women in the workforce. Those who have faced the same challenges as we have may have an especially clear understanding of what may be able to help.

> *In a Wall Street Journal article, author Sue Shellenbarger recounted the change in her own management style after the birth of her first child.[21] Prior to her own parenthood, she felt somewhat impatient and frustrated with her female and male subordinates' needs to take off days for their children. However, she acknowledged that once she became a mother herself, she reflected a different—and more understanding—perspective.*

> *Dana, an executive at AT&T, is a mother of a young boy and an artist, a musician, and a masseuse. She creates stained glass and plays tennis, racquetball, and golf. She is also responsible for a very large division of the company. Dana feels that mobility is an integral part of advancement in some organizations, and has been for her. At different times, however, people are mobile or they're not. She has always been accommodated in her career and recommends that women tell management when they're mobile and when they're not. Let people know in advance, so that they can plan as well.*

Try to identify people at work who have experienced the same challenges in balancing work and family. It may be more effective to approach these types of people rather than men or women who have never experienced such concerns. This is not to say that the latter group would not be equally sympathetic. You just have to ask around and get a sense of who will be approachable. Also, don't automatically assume that the women will be more sympathetic than the men. Many men are extremely aware of these issues and indeed deal with the balancing act themselves.

> *Jane, a director of a utilities company, feels that men are starting to change regarding balancing home and family. She also feels that she tries to create an accommodating atmosphere for her own department. She encourages her staff to take advantage of flexibility.*

My former boss, Dennis, was wonderful when I had to deal with my elderly parents' illnesses and emergencies. He had a very flexible approach, since he shared equally with his wife in the care of his children and his other relatives. We had a very open relationship regarding what needed to get done—everything did get done, just on a slightly more flexible schedule at times. I simply worked on some projects at home or in the evenings or on weekends. (An example of his perspective? When Dennis was coaching his daughter's softball team, he told me that many of his fellow coaches were very senior male executives and professionals who felt that their work schedules sometimes interfered with their ability to coach and be with their daughters, which they preferred.) Times are starting to change!

One senior director, Bob, asked his boss, a woman, if he would be able to rearrange the return from an international business trip so that he could see his daughter perform the lead role in a school play. She said, sure, no problem. I recounted this story to a male colleague and he posed the question, "What would have happened if Bob's boss were a man?" Would his male boss have given him the same accommodation? Would he have even felt comfortable asking for the flexibility? Or would an unwritten code have prevented Bob from asking another man, period? Interesting question!

We're starting to see more men in management, as well as women, reevaluating their expectations and balancing their lives more effectively. Although many male and female managers still conform to the more traditional ways of managing, I think it must be underscored that many people are truly beginning to reevaluate their management styles and subsequently are changing the prevailing organizational culture. Since that culture is largely a reflection of the values and attitudes of the organization's members (primarily directed by senior management), it holds true that as senior management increasingly starts to change its values, so will the organization and its culture.

A major component of the balancing act includes time management and network management. There are many seminars, books, tapes, and articles on the topic of time management. The fact is that some people are just better at organizing their time than others. But that's not to say that we can't learn at least something to simplify our everyday lives.

A strategy at work that you have probably heard a million times—but if you're like me, you haven't "had the time to do"—is to get more organized! Something that I have recently started to do—and it's scary that I'm saying "recently," because I should have started this 15 years ago—is to try to handle each paper that I come into contact with one time only, whenever possible. When you concentrate and practice, it really does work—it's amazing! (I just proved it this morning, after being out of my office for nearly 2 weeks.) If it's something you won't read, toss it now. If there's something that will just take you a few minutes and it's fairly "mindless," do it *right away* and get it off of your desk. Many of the senior women I speak to just write a reply on the fax or memo that they received, then send it right back. It's much easier and faster. It's such a feeling of accomplishment and relief not to have your desk or in-bin cluttered with stuff that you will need to do eventually. If you send faxes and memos, develop a generic form and save it on your computer as a cover sheet or shell. You can often just type a short memo or make a quick phone call and address a problem right away. As several of the women I interviewed said, if you can solve a problem or ask a question of someone directly and quickly, do it. (This is a huge advantage of effective networking which I use all the time. You can just pick up the phone and get your answer.)

If you receive phone calls, set aside a specific time each day to return them. Cross out the time if possible on your daily calendar and really stick to it! You'll get in the routine and it will become second nature. If there is information that you give out frequently, have it printed into information sheets and send it rather than having to talk to people at length on the phone for routine calls. Make labels for addresses that you frequently use and keep them handy. Keep your desk clear—it psychologically forces you to "weed out" the junk right away. Put all the superfluous stuff like tape, staplers, and other junk collectors into a drawer. Some organized people use color-coded folders or colored tabs on folders to immediately identify what's inside instead of constantly looking through them. I know that this is all routine stuff, but I've also heard it for years and it has just started to sink in!

At home, think about having a yard sale to get rid of junk that is cluttering up storage areas. I have found that I make more work for myself trying to put my stuff away (in an effort to keep things neat) if there's no place for me to put it. If you have a family and partner, get them involved in chores! Don't fall into the trap of thinking that they can't do it as well as you can. Maybe they can't, but it will at least get done, and that should free up time for you to do other things. Try to get away from total perfectionism. My sister-in-law, Suzanne, who has always been incredibly neat, said that even her neatness standards had to be lowered with a newborn, since she was working 3 days a week. She is much happier, though, since she can spend that time with her son.

> *One executive humorously admits that her family nutrition is based on weekly consumption. They have a vegetarian dinner one night, pizza the next, maybe a barbecue the next. She says that by the end of the week her family is well supplied with all the major food groups!*

It's really amazing how much time we spend on things that can be streamlined or done less frequently. Remember, the goal is to gain a little more free time for yourself and/or your family—not to find more things to add to your stress level!

Network management includes taking advantage of people in your network so that you are better able to balance your life. Many people feel guilty if they ask family, friends, or neighbors to watch their kids just to do something for themselves. At a recent seminar, I asked the women in the audience, "If you had 1 or 2 free hours a week, with no interruptions, what would you do?" Some of the answers were amazing. One woman said that she would take a long, hot shower without her kids banging on the door. Another women said that she would love to take a walk alone in the woods. A third woman said that she would enjoy reading for pleasure, instead of necessity. These don't seem like particularly unreasonable requests, but the respondents felt that these were pleasures they couldn't expect to enjoy for years to come! We tend to think that we have to do everything for everyone else, at our own expense. We have all felt that we were on a merry-go-round which was picking up momentum and we couldn't get off. I suggested to the women at the seminar that they practice their networking skills and set up a group of people with whom they can exchange child-care duties on a systematic basis—for example, if they just want to do something for themselves—a baby-sitting cooperative. If you schedule time for yourself, you'll be able to take it. But if you don't actually schedule time for yourself without feeling guilty, believe me, you'll never get it! It's the same thing with exercise or spending time with your spouse or significant other. Parents often feel comfortable setting up car pools to make sure that their kids are taken to and picked up from events, so the same thinking can be applied to your free time—and sanity! Women especially feel extremely guilty and think that they don't deserve this time to themselves, but you know how you feel if you are trapped in a rut and can't get out. You are probably very cranky and even resentful toward your family, so what good is that? If you even have just a little more time to yourself, you'll feel better, less cranky, and less resentful, and probably end up a better parent or partner as well. You deserve some time to yourself!

In addition to baby-sitting cooperatives, some families are taking the initiative to balance household chores. For example, at a newspaper in Philadelphia, some of the employees with families have joined together in an informal cooperative to cook dinners. Let's say that there are five families in your group. Each of the families is responsible for cooking larger quantities of a particular dinner, which they then give to the other families to freeze. If your specialty is lasagna, you would prepare enough for the other families at one time, reserve one amount for yourself and an equal amount for each of the other families. In turn, the other families prepare their dishes for themselves and the other members to freeze. It's not much harder to prepare a large amount of a dish than it is a single serving. Budgets and menus can be decided in advance, if you like. With just a little preparation and coordination, each family can spend a little time and energy once a week and receive an entire week's worth of meals. This type of co-op may also reduce the amount of complaining about the age-old problem of always serving the same meals! The same kind of cooperative can be arranged for smaller families or singles.

Most of us do feel overwhelmed with alarming regularity. Although sometimes you just can't identify what the reason is, you probably have a pretty good idea of the major stressors in your life that are stealing your time and energy. Once you have identified the problem, you can brainstorm with your supporters to find a reasonable solution. It again comes down to choices. Are you willing to make the effort to let some things go in the interest of having a little more free time?

GENERATION X AND BABY BOOMERS

Recently, I was teaching an introductory graduate class in management in which I started a discussion on the workplace of the future. Since the students were all in their twenties and early thirties (Generation Xers), it was an interesting time to benchmark a little about what they thought about the world of work. Interestingly enough, the class was about 80 percent male. I asked them to identify characteristics of their "ideal" workplace: location, salary, flexibility, environment, and so forth. Their responses confirmed much of what the research is currently finding.

They pretty much agreed that they would like to work for, or start, a company located in a warm climate: Arizona, Florida, South Carolina. They envisioned a 4-day workweek, although they said they wouldn't mind working very hard on those 4 days in order to have the extra time off. Most wanted to have a combination of some structure with a fair amount of autonomy. They wanted to be in a people-oriented environment, in which people were more valuable than—or at least as valuable as—the bottom line. They didn't necessarily want six-figure salaries; they thought that starting at $35,000 to $40,000 would be fine. Finally, they wanted flexibility and balance. Now, keep in mind, these were primarily male students in their early careers.

I told the class about an article I had read in *Fortune* magazine that compared the work attitudes of baby boomers and Generation Xers.[22] The article discussed how Gen Xers view their predecessors as workaholics; boomers don't know technology and they are too rigid. Baby boomers, on the other hand, think that Gen Xers want it all without earning it; young people are lazy and unmotivated and don't want to pay their dues. As I said to the class, it will be very interesting, as the trends of the future and the influence of technology come to pass, to see older people working for younger employees who are more technology-literate. Just think of the dynamics in the workplace then—it's already starting to happen! For women, however, it is very encouraging to see that these same young people on the brink of setting workplace policies are far more open-minded about balance and equality. This is especially true of younger men as compared with their older predecessors. They don't see the same gap between genders as the generation before saw. Likewise, the younger women do not feel—or at least have often not yet experienced—the same kind of discrimination that their predecessors have seen. It may be refreshing to take the opportunity to talk to Gen Xers about balance.

THE WORKAHOLIC

It can be almost too easy to become a workaholic in today's workplace and at home. Most of us have increased our working hours, while we have decreased our leisure time. Even those who have generally laid-back personalities can get caught up in a frenzy of taking on too much. Do you find yourself taking on too many tasks and projects, both at work and at home?

> *I spoke to a man in his twenties at a party a few months ago. He said that in his industry it seemed to be a contest of how many hours you could work. He laughingly said, "It was like one person says, `Wow, I've been working 70 hours a week lately!' And then somebody else says, `Oh yeah? Well, I've been averaging over 80!'" Should people really be bragging about this? (No, not all Gen Xers are this way. Some are laid-back and balanced!)*

Of course, it's true that those who have the most to do—and do it well—are always the first people that others want on their team! Who wants a lazy loser to head up a project? Now, I'm not saying that you should become a slacker to prove a point and not be asked to do projects, but it is important to learn to say no occasionally. If you don't, the overwhelming stress can truly become paralyzing and lead to fatigue, illness, and reduced productivity in the long run.

Do you ever feel that even the most mundane or routine task becomes overwhelming when you're really stressed out? It may sound easy to "just say no," but it is probably extremely difficult for most of us to do so. While you may not have much input into decisions on what you must do at work, you can certainly have a significant influence on what you are asked to do outside of work. Are you frequently asked to do special volunteer projects, such as organize your children's school fund-raiser, or head your professional organization's annual dinner, or chair a neighborhood block party? The list goes on and on. How many of us have said yes without thinking about it first. Then we're too uncomfortable to get out of it, even if we really can't spare the time. How many of us have been halfway through the planning process for the event and swear we will never do this to ourselves again—until the next someone asks! While it is not necessarily that we always want to say no, it is important to prioritize which events or tasks we want to take on.

How to start? Well, this is where an advocate can help. If you can find someone who truly understands the nature of what you're being asked to do, an advocate can give you a good way to analyze what kinds of benefits the task or project can be to you before you accept.

The first thing you can practice is withholding your commitment. When someone asks you to do something outside your normal work-related tasks, reply that you are flattered, but you would like to think about it before answering. Many of us have a tendency to accept a project immediately because it may be interesting or fun. But then, after we have committed ourselves to it, we start to have second thoughts about how interesting it will be or how much this is really going to help our overall goals. You may want to get additional information about exactly what the project will entail. Sometimes the people who are asking for help will give you initial information along the lines of "Oh, it won't take too much of your time." Then you discover that they don't want to do it anymore because they were swamped when they did it! This is frequently true of annual activities: school events, association or club events, conferences, and so forth.

Take some time to ask other people what the actual commitment will be. Take time, as well, to think about the timing of the project or task. Will you have other, conflicting issues in your life at that time? Perhaps you can ask others to find someone to share the responsibility with, so it's not a total burden on you. Most important, ask yourself how it will benefit you. This may seem cold, especially if you are asked to do something really worthwhile such as a charity task, or if, as frequently happens, someone makes you feel guilty if you don't want to participate. But this is what you really need to practice. Is the event or task really going to give you what you need or want, whether it's doing something worthwhile for your community, gaining visibility, or helping out your kids' school? Only you can answer that. But keep in mind that you have only 24 hours in a day. If you are already feeling stretched too thin as it is, getting involved in a big activity is only going to stretch you further. You may risk becoming resentful of the activity and negating the reason you wanted to do it in the first place.

By giving yourself some time to really think about the pros and cons, you will undoubtedly be able to make a much better assessment of whether you can do it. Remember, the plan is to get more fun, more energy, and more balance back into your life. Life really is too short to spend it miserably!

SUMMARY

- Delegate, even if it means having to give up tasks you like. Remember, what is routine for you is challenging for others. Give details when you delegate. Let others know your time constraints.

- Think about what is involved in accepting a volunteer task or event before you commit to it. Consider how much time it will take and if it will fulfill what your interests and needs are.

- It's important to build fun and leisure time into living. Otherwise you risk being less effective or productive in your career and personal life. Even some senior executives are starting to say that they wish they had spent more time at home with family and friends.

- Play should be a comfortable opportunity to try new things and to relieve stress, not yet another outlet in which to be an overachiever.

- Family-friendly benefits may be available at your organization. Talk to people, especially women, who have been able to take advantage of some of these benefits and still be successful.

- If possible, identify potential bosses who are more in touch with balance issues in their own careers and in those of their employees.

- Develop a network of people with whom you can share meal preparation, child care, and other activities in order to give yourself a break (on a regular basis).

- Technology allows greater freedom in the workplace with faxes, cellular phones, the Internet, videoconferences, and e-mail. But with greater flexibility comes less defined distinctions between work time and leisure time.

ACTION PLAN

What would make your life more balanced? More time, more help, better organization?

Who can help you achieve these goals?

If you had several hours free just for yourself, what would you do?

How do you plan to find this time? (Ask friends or family, develop a "support group," and so on.)

How will you develop an effective network?

How will you help others find this time?

Who and what can help you work smarter, not harder?

Do you feel guilty if you do things for yourself occasionally? Why? How can you begin to enjoy more and feel guilty less?

SUCCESSFUL PEOPLE KNOW WHEN TO TAKE SMART RISKS

Have you ever seen videotapes on television of people who bungee-jump off a bridge or cliff or tower? Or have you ever done it yourself? You see the terrified, but excited faces of the people about to jump. Then the camera pans down into the ravine or river to give a perspective of what the jumpers see. It doesn't look good—several thousand feet of open air beneath them! Their feet are perilously perched on the edge of the precipice. Then the moment of truth—in one instant, they make the decision—this is it. They jump. And what's the first thing you hear as the cord expands to its fullest length? Whoooooooooooo-eeee!! They're all smiles, the adrenaline is pumping, they're psyched, they've done it! They're ready to do it again. Now, although most of us will never go bungee-jumping (I know that I won't!), the same emotions take over every time we are about to do something frightening or challenging. It's all relative. We probably don't really want to "take the plunge." Maybe someone else convinces us to take the challenge. We're ready to jump in—and are terrified of what may happen. At one point we make the decision to jump, or turn back. But if we turn back, not only will we risk missing that thrill of accomplishment at the end; we'll also never know if we could have done it. And that's a shame.

A number of the women I interviewed indicated that they were risk takers. Many of them said that they did not consciously think about it, but upon reflection decided that they probably were. However, most women will probably tell you that they do not feel particularly comfortable with taking risks. This may prove to be one of the behaviors that can derail a career. Yet, surprisingly, risk taking can be learned. It may take a while, but practice can certainly improve your chances of overcoming the adversity to calculated, well-thought-out risks. Keep in mind too that risk taking does not always entail huge gambles. It may be something as simple as starting a new project that you have always wanted to do, or taking a class, or making presentations in front of people. (One of my early practice runs with risk taking was learning how to drive a stick-shift car when I was 30 years old. I had always envied others who looked really cool driving their sports cars, shifting effortlessly, so I just bought a car with a manual transmission and forced myself to learn. And no, I had never driven a stick shift before that day, so I was committed to succeeding—or I couldn't drive to work the following Monday!)

> *A successful Washington lawyer gave up her job to go to Yale Law School at 31 years old, as a single parent. She was willing to take the risk of leaving a comfortable position to try new things in a new area.*

In presentations and seminars, I frequently ask women what it is that may be holding them back from doing something they have always wanted to do. Many of them say it's the feeling that they can't do it, the fear of failure, the feeling that they're too old, or not smart enough, or not talented enough. Usually, it's the feeling that they just can't take the first step. That first step is generally where the most risk is. With many women who are going back to college, for example, it's the realization that their lives will be disrupted, their relationships may change, or their families may resent their decision. For women who really want to be successful, it often takes someone to truly believe in them—and actually be a "cheerleader"—to convince them to take a chance and do what they really want to do.

One of my favorite exercises is to put people into small

groups in which they identify and discuss things that they would really like to do, but have not to this point accomplished. The role of the group is to identify strategies that can overcome any barriers to achieving the desired result. It is an effective combination of support group and brainstorming, but more important it breaks down the reasons for nonaction to their basic components. There usually are pretty good reasons for not taking the first step toward accomplishing your goals.

IF THIS IS SUPPOSED TO HELP . . . THEN WHY DO I FEEL SICK?

For more years than I can count, I've wanted to be a really good skier. I am at an intermediate level and a generally good athlete, but I always envy my friends who, when we go skiing, can't wait to get to the slopes. As we approach the entrance to the ski resort, they are euphoric and the only feeling I have is that I'm so nervous I'm going to be sick! I don't know what it is, but I think that if I were to practice and really work hard, I wouldn't feel that sense of dread instead of fun. But I often have some excuse to not make the time or effort needed to become proficient.

> *I asked my friend Robbie LaRocca for advice. She is a national champion water skier and I said, "Robbie, at what point did you stop getting that sick feeling in the pit of your stomach and really start to enjoy the sport?" She said, "Are you kidding? I still feel the same way every time I'm ready to take off!" Then once I start, I'm OK. But that's the fun of it!"*

So *that's* what I've been feeling for all these years before I go skiing—fun! I just didn't know it. I really thought about what Robbie said. The nauseous feeling only indicates that you're being challenged. It's adrenaline. And that's what takes you to the next level of accomplishment. If we always felt comfortable in everything we did, we would never get beyond that level. What women have to do is to become comfortable with that feeling and realize that they can get beyond the fear and lack of confidence. Once we have accomplished something that we didn't feel we could do, it's incredibly empowering. So that's it—

this is the winter that I'm going to prove myself! I plan to fill my head with thoughts of what the successful women I interviewed would do in a situation like this, go with someone who will be supportive as well as challenging, and get myself psyched!

If you look at the concept behind the Outward Bound programs, it is exactly this principle. It pushes you to a new level. It doesn't mean that you have to enjoy the experience, but it usually proves that you can achieve far more than you ever would have thought possible. The Outward Bound people make you climb mountains, or traverse ravines, or swing from really high trees, but mostly they challenge you to new levels. You never come back the same person you were before! This application holds true for success in the workplace as well.

> *The former head of a presidential commission said that she hasn't really known in advance the specifics of many jobs she has held. A chemistry major with strong math and statistical skills, she became involved in politics and was the chief of staff for a member of Congress (who became her mentor). She said that she trusted her problem-solving, analytical, and communication skills to guide her to success.*

THE IMPOSTOR SYNDROME

Sometimes, unfortunately, we are our own worst enemies. Internal feelings of self-doubt probably are as damaging to us as some of the external barriers we experience. We may be paralyzed into inaction instead of trying to forge ahead and take a chance.

> *Madelyn, a vice president of human resources, says that for women barriers are more frequently internal than external. They may include the occupations that women choose. Also, women frequently take criticism personally. She advises women to speak up. There may be some social discomfort—such as an old-boys' network at outings and meetings—but women can certainly learn to overcome it.*

Women do not always evaluate themselves objectively. Some women may feel a constant fear of failure or, worse yet, the fear that someone will find out that they are actually impostors—they're really not as bright or competent or talented as others may think. They have somehow fooled everyone into thinking that they are talented! This attitude may date back to feelings of insecurity earlier in their lives or careers. Many women experience this feeling when they go back to school, for example. They enter the classroom and immediately think that everyone is smarter, younger, and better prepared than they are. They feel that they really don't belong in that environment—until they experience their first successes—their first A on a paper, the first time they master a new skill, or the first time they offer their view on a topic. The same may be true in the workplace. For so long, women were not expected to aspire to senior positions, at least not "average" women! Even now women question themselves—their decisions and the quality of their work, whether they are pushing themselves hard enough, working long enough hours, and so forth.

It may surprise you that some women in very senior positions still wonder exactly what they're doing and how they got there! This is an important aspect of risk taking. If you are approached to take on a new project or position, you should seriously think about taking it. If other people didn't think you were qualified, they probably wouldn't have offered you the project. It is certainly true that your learning curve may be temporarily at a low end of the spectrum, but you will expand your knowledge base, gain new experience, and challenge yourself more. As a result, you will move to a new plateau, improving your background so that you can take on the next challenge. Many CEOs and human resource directors indicate that broad-based knowledge is one of the most important characteristics of prospective leaders. Without that knowledge, you may not even be considered for your next promotion. So take a chance. If you experience self-doubt—which we all do—trust your mentor or your support people to reinforce your positive self-image!

A colleague of mine at a major pharmaceuticals company was offered a highly visible position in an unfamiliar area for her. We talked on the phone for over an hour as she asked me my opinion on whether she should take the position. There was some risk of failure, but even a greater benefit with increased visibility and exposure to more senior management. She agreed that, despite her fear, she really did want to try the position. She just needed to bounce her ideas and feelings off someone else.

I told her that if she didn't take the position, she would never know how she would have done. Anyway, you always need to ask yourself if you want to be challenged and learn something new. If the answer is yes, and someone is offering you the opportunity, then you're ready for the promotion or new job. At least this way, even if my colleague didn't do as well as she wanted to, she wouldn't wonder "what if." She took the position, did a great job, and as a result of the visibility and success, was offered an even higher position one and a half years later. She admits it really was a great career move.

> *Robyn, a senior vice president at a major insurance company, says that unfortunately women don't always know their capabilities. An executive who is willing to take necessary risks, she says that other women frequently ask her if she isn't nervous about some of the risks she has taken with her career or with high-level decisions she needs to make. She replies that although she doesn't always have all the information that she would like to have to make decisions, she trusts her instincts and past experience and makes the best decisions possible.*

By the way, don't assume that only women feel unsure about taking chances with the career choices and decisions they make. One male colleague, an old friend, admitted that when he took on his new position as president of the company, he was very nervous! Men may just hide their fear better.

BARRIERS FOR WOMEN

Some barriers for women are external (organization, family, outside demands). We have talked about different strategies to overcome external barriers, such as improving our communication or developing effective networks or getting a mentor. But what about internal barriers (fear, insecurity, lack of knowledge)? These barriers too can be overcome with some hard work and practice.

Diane, a director of facilities, says that women aren't always sure what they want. One powerful barrier for some women is relying on the organization rather than doing it on their own. It's not only skills, traits, and abilities that are important, but political acumen as well. Diane feels that there is a universality about successful women—they may identify with other women, but identify as managers first, women second. In addition, she feels that you can't wear your heart on your sleeve. Sometimes you need to live with some underlying attitudes or comments or accept teasing and not take it so seriously. Women either intentionally or unintentionally choose one role—mother, sister, wife, lover—and there may be some flipping back and forth. Diane is deliberately asexual at work; she considers herself a sister—one of the guys. She feels that women must pay attention to sexual conduct.

Sheila Gibbons at USA Today agrees. She feels that women may send mixed messages that are not clear and consistent. Men don't always know how to react at times and there may be some confusion in communication.

Madelyn Jennings at Gannett adds that barriers for women are frequently more internal than external. They may include occupations frequently chosen by women. Also, women tend to take criticism personally. There may be some social discomfort, but it shouldn't really be a barrier if women work at not taking it personally. Madelyn also advises women to speak up more.

Another executive believes that a major barrier for women is waiting to be asked. Many women feel that people will ask them to interview for a position if they are qualified, but often that is not true. You can't be afraid to ask. People don't always know what you want to do if you don't tell them.

Bobbie, a senior director at a major pharmaceutical company feels that some older men—still a majority among senior-level managers—may be paranoid, but more often than not it's just discomfort with change. They're probably just setting up fewer roadblocks. For example, Bobbie's boss is not particularly comfortable around women, nor is he a great advocate of women, but he likes her and has helped Bobbie in her career. Bobbie does not make gender an issue. She talks about joining a women's support group when she first started a number of years ago; however, she was not comfortable there. The group was too angry, too militant. In her opinion, a militant approach caused problems.

ASSERTIVENESS AS AN ASSET

One of the single most difficult areas for many, if not most, women to overcome is becoming more assertive. I have organized numerous conferences and workshop series, and inevitably one of the most popular topics is assertiveness. It can mean the difference between being placed on the fast track or no track at your organization. This is frequently a result of socialization that is amazingly difficult to overcome! How many of us think that we are walked on, manipulated, underutilized, overworked, underpaid, and underrecognized because we are not assertive enough to say no to what we don't want to do, yet we cannot strongly state what we do want to do? I would guess that the majority of readers right now would agree with me. Again, we need to go back to our socialization. It's really hard to undo 10, 20, 30, or 40 years of accepted ways of thinking! We're not supposed to be assertive. People will think we're pushy or, worse yet, bitchy. We want people to like us. I don't want my boss to get mad at me. I don't want to be in a stressful situation. I don't want to make waves—I may get fired!

Look at the people in your organization, both men and women, who are successful. I'll bet that all of them would be considered assertive. Some, of course, more than others! Are there successful women in your organization who are assertive, yet still open and friendly? When I interviewed the women in my original study, I often made arrangements through their assistants, many of whom said that they absolutely loved their bosses. These women were fantastic to work for. However, they were clearly not pushovers and were obviously very successful. Every organization has such women and men. If you can, talk to such people about how they successfully balance their open demeanor and their tough business side. Observe how they act with their bosses, their peers, and their subordinates. Try to take notes on how they behave in certain situations.

Michelle, a corporate lawyer, feels that all women have internal barriers to a certain extent, just some more than others. It helps to identify what you're telling yourself. Are you constantly looking beyond this job to the future? Are you telling yourself you're great (psycho-babble)?

A senior vice president at AT&T suggests stretching out your comfort zone. Every senior-level woman on a recent AT&T panel said the same thing. In her own career, this VP moves about every 18 to 24 months, stretches her capabilities, and stretches herself.

In addition, take assertiveness classes whenever you see them offered. They are frequently given at women's conferences or at open training programs. If your company doesn't offer them, ask your human resources department to sponsor an ongoing series on assertiveness training, especially training for women. (But don't think that a lot of men don't want to learn to be assertive too!) Ask to have these classes based on real-life scenarios so that you can practice assertive behavior. Remember, this type of training is a process, not a stand-alone program, so be sure to have reinforcement for the training and perhaps a support group so that you can share what has worked for you and learn what has been successful for other women. This is part of your support network—your cheerleaders. Don't forget, you really need others to keep you motivated and psyched to be more assertive!

It may be helpful to practice your assertiveness in various situations, in addition to the workplace. In fact, if you practice your assertive (notice, not aggressive) behavior in lower-risk environments, you may be more inclined to push your limits without increasing your sense of fear. For example, you may find that you frequently back down when you have been treated unfairly in a store or some other service environment. Have you ever paid for a service which was not completed? Have you been bumped from your airline seat or been told that your hotel was full, despite a reservation? Have you been in a restaurant and received poor service? Let's not even talk about when you have to take your car in for service! These are all pretty low-risk, yet high-annoyance situations in which you can practice your assertiveness. You don't have to scream and shout (although occasionally it may actually come to that), but you don't have to back down either.

It is surprising how often you can get what you want when you just ask for it. It is usually much easier if you have a coach to help you through such a scenario the first time or two. It may really go against your basic personality, so as with anything, you may have to practice. If you find difficulty, just start small. Expect good service and good use from the products that you paid for. The next time you take your car in for service, ask a lot of questions of the service manager. If you want a better table in a restaurant, or a better hotel room, or better service, just ask for it. Then you can start making progress. If you have already graduated from this level into "Assertiveness, Part 2," practice taking on more responsibility at work, or saying no to a project, or asking for a well-deserved raise. Again, try to discuss your approach with an advocate and, as in all things, be as prepared as possible in order to anticipate any objections to your proposal. An advocate, mentor, or support network is the very best way to accomplish these goals, because we generally hate to take such risks unless we are almost forced to do so for our own good!

Many women may be under the misconception that others will think negatively of them if they are assertive. First, you need to work on the fact that people don't always have to like you. That's an important part of assertiveness and risk taking. More important, most people will probably take you far more seriously if you exhibit consistently assertive behavior rather than always backing down. They may even be pleased that you finally stood up for yourself, instead of backing down. Talk to your advocate or mentor and see if he or she doesn't agree. Not so long ago, whenever I felt that someone was walking on me or taking advantage of my even temper, I would blame the other person. Now if it happens—and believe me, it still does!—I try to be more analytical and think about how I let it happen to me, not blame the other person. I ask myself: "Is it really important enough to make a statement? Or is it something I can use as a learning experience, because I didn't really care about doing it one way or the other?" Remember, we're practicing and learning. It took us a long time to get to this point in our behavior, so you can't expect to change it overnight. There will be some backslides, but the aggregate gain should be considered.

Part of assertive behavior is seen in positive body language. Take time to observe those around you—really look at them. What does their body language say about them? Do they stand

and sit straight or do they slump over? Do they look directly at you or constantly glance away? What about their handshake? Do they smile a lot or not at all? Do people notice them when they enter a room? Why—or why not? As you observe people, especially women, who seem to be confident and well poised, take written notes on what seems to give them that special appearance. Also, make notes of the people who seem to blend into the woodwork, or are mousy and intimidated, to use as a contrast. Try honestly to assess yourself as to where you fit between these two. When you sit, practice leaning back in the chair and taking up some physical space. Lean forward when you make points. Always look people right in the eye. Smile enough to be pleasant, if the situation calls for it, but do not smile a lot (as many women do), since it may be interpreted as an effort to seek acceptance. (Check how often men smile at each other in the same way that women do. They don't! It's amazing the difference, when you take time to notice it.) I still like to be very pleasant to everyone, despite what some of the research says. I just try to smile a little less than I used to (which was most of the time!).

If you're brave and determined, have a trusted friend videotape you in a normal situation—not staged—such as during a typical encounter at work or at a networking session, or during a presentation or workshop. I know you're thinking that others will find it odd that you have someone videotaping your behavior. Just let them think that the videotaper is doing some sort of project—"a day in the life" or research for a sociology class. No one will think twice about it if you come prepared with a story. See how you sit, stand, speak, walk, interact. It's amazing how the camera picks up things that you never see! The first couple of times I was interviewed on local TV I was very glad that it wasn't going to be seen by too many people—the interviews were definitely my learning experiences! But they did give me an honest assessment of how I needed to speak, sit, dress, and act. I sometimes fall into the habit of speaking too quickly, which does not give me as much credibility as I'd like. So I make an effort to speak more slowly. I always enjoy people who speak engagingly, but clearly and slowly. People do take you more seriously when you slow down, so that's one thing I am always aware of.

It may feel very odd at first when you are practicing more assertive behavior. It may seem like you're actually in someone else's body! It may also seem that you're coming on too strong, but keep in mind, that is your opinion. Others will probably not notice it very much at first. A number of women have said that they feel a bit "stand-offish" or cold when they first try to change their behavior. But in reality, if they are even somewhat more reserved, it probably seems just about normal to most people, not as if they're nasty! It's all relative to your past behavior.

OVERCOMING PERSONAL INSECURITIES

We're human. We are sometimes insecure, sometimes jealous, sometimes nervous, sometimes resentful of others' success. All of us! Keeping that in mind, we need to address what causes us to be insecure, jealous, nervous, or resentful—and do something positive to counteract it. It causes a great deal of stress when we see others around us getting what they want, while we are working really hard only to be less successful. Sometimes we're even afraid to admit our insecurities to ourselves, for fear of looking petty or shallow. (But, as I said, we all do it!) How does that happen? What are we doing wrong?

Well, I'm not a therapist, but I honestly believe that, despite some things that can't be changed or overcome, you can do a lot to improve your self-image. It may help to identify exactly what it is that you are insecure about. Be really honest with yourself. If you have a very trusted friend, share that insight with her or him.

What might your insecurity be? Do you feel uncomfortable because you don't have the same credentials or background as your colleagues? Do they have certain degrees and you don't? Do they belong to a certain clique or socioeconomic class and you don't? Do they have international experience but you don't? Are they more professional or better dressed, or do they have better public-speaking skills? Maybe you're uncomfortable about your weight. It could be just about anything! Once you have honestly identified what it is that you're insecure about, start brainstorming (preferably with someone else) about how to overcome this insecurity—for example, acquiring skills that you need to master or by matching the skills of people you are uncomfortable around.

After you figure out what it is that you are insecure about, you need to set up a plan of action. If you're uncomfortable about not having a degree to the point of distraction, bite the bullet, make the commitment, and go back to school! If it's your experience that you're uncomfortable about, and you can't find a job, you can volunteer or work as an intern for the experience you need. If you're uncomfortable about public speaking, you can take a class. It's really a great feeling to challenge yourself. You get energized and you gain a positive outlook. Work with a friend or colleague to push yourself. A young colleague of mine, Steve, is a marathon runner who has talked me into doing a triathlon (swimming, biking, and running). This annual event, sponsored by Danskin, is designed to encourage women of all ages to get into shape and enjoy the benefits of healthy competition. Many of the women, like me, probably never have competed but are looking for a new challenge. This is exactly the kind of activity that women can do to be challenged. It's outstanding that organizations see the need and are willing to support women in their efforts. Training for this kind of event is also a great reason to get into physical shape! I have never competed in an organized event—ever! So, at 40, I am really excited about setting this kind of goal. I can't wait!

The most important thing to realize is that in order to feel more secure, you really need to practice the skills you're lacking until they're top-notch. Remember the four P's—performance, perseverance, practice, and patience. Once you feel that inner security within yourself, you will be amazed at what you can accomplish!

WHEN DO I TAKE A RISK AND LEAVE A BAD SITUATION?

A while back, I spoke to a young woman at a conference who said that she wasn't sure she had made the right decision about quitting a job. The young woman was in a beginning management position and had planned to continue her education in graduate school, which her boss had promised to pay for. However, she said that the department secretary became romantically involved with the boss, and gradually changes began to take place as the secretary took on more power. Eventually, not only did her boss renege on the offer to pay for her graduate school classes, but she lost her position to the secretary. The young manager was clearly frustrated and upset. Her friends and colleagues advised her to tough it out and stay where she was. However, she made the decision to leave and go to another department. She asked my opinion, since we had talked about the topic in the seminar. I told her that I absolutely agreed with her.

Although we may think that it is our duty to tough out a bad environment, there sometimes comes a point where it is a no-win situation. Do you really want to continue to work in this kind of environment? Is the situation likely to change? You may have enough problems dealing with balancing your time, learning the politics of the organization, finding a mentor, developing a network, and increasing your visibility. You don't have time to be fighting a negative environment as well. You want to be in a positive, supportive environment. If you truly can't see an alternative and it's not going to get any better in a big hurry, start to work on your success strategies and get out!

Of course, many people will say, especially in this time of downsizing, that they don't have any opportunities. They can't afford to lose or leave their job. They're right; it is a major consideration, of course! Few people can afford to leave a position capriciously. However, many people still think of career development as something that happens by chance. If you have begun to develop your personal strategies for your career, you should be well on your way to affording yourself options in your job or career path. It is not necessarily an easy process and it may take 6 months or a year—or more. But if you have the luxury of foreseeing the inevitable, don't delay. Start right away with developing your strategy. If you don't have that luxury, it may be even more critical to start as soon as possible. Even if you don't foresee a negative situation down the line, keep in mind that situations can change for the strangest reasons (see the above example). So it really pays to always be prepared. Get that network started—get to know people, especially key people, in other departments, organizations, or associations. Start your visibility campaign. Find several advocates. Start to learn who controls the power and who makes the decisions. Get the education or training you need. Take on new responsibilities to gain experience. It's especially hard to get motivated when things are seemingly all right, but as you can see, the situation may change quickly. You don't want to be left holding the bag!

In my research I have found that CEOs and presidents of organizations generally create organizational culture. If your managers don't believe in and support a positive, flexible organization with open communication which fosters a positive environment for women, forget it—you're probably going nowhere fast! You may think that you can change the organization, but unless you're a senior decision maker, you can't. Maybe you have a boss who's a creep. Maybe it's not an innovative organization. Whatever the situation, start to consider your options.

Start doing research on the Internet, or at your library, or through professional associations and publications. Find out the companies that facilitate the promotion of women. You should be able to find this information in publications such as *Business Week, The Wall Street Journal, Fortune, Working Woman,* and *Working Mother.* At least you will know that the culture in these organizations supports women!

> *Judith Rodin, president of the University of Pennsylvania, notes that you don't always need to follow your long-range career plans. Sometimes taking more educated risks may open up more opportunities.*

Remember, once you start to take more educated risks, you will develop into a new person. You will never again be the person you were before. You'll be stronger, more confident, and more capable, and probably feel a lot better about yourself.

SUMMARY

- Women frequently hesitate to take risks out of fear—fear of failure, or fear of being too old, not smart, or not talented enough. It's difficult to take the first step. We need to get used to the feeling of some discomfort in order to move on to our next level of accomplishment.

- Accomplishment as a result of stretching ourselves and taking some moderate risk is empowering.

- We are our own worst enemies when we allow self-doubt to keep us from challenging ourselves.

- We frequently need to ask ourselves if we want to try to master something new. Although there is always a learning curve and the opportunity to make mistakes, we will eventually be able to master the skill. Remember the four Ps: practice, performance, persistence, patience!

- Being assertive is a critical skill. We have to speak up for what we need or want, but not take it too personally if it leads to conflict.

- We must identify what we are uncomfortable or insecure about, then set up an action plan to address it.

- Sometimes we need to take a risk and leave a bad situation after we have identified the problems and made an honest attempt to rectify the situation. It's important to have an effective network and a supportive environment to move on.

ACTION PLAN

What have you been dying to try but never gotten around to doing? Why not?

Do you have a "support group" of people to encourage you? Do you surround yourself with positive people?

Is there a practical reason that you don't always reach your expectations (insufficient experience or education, for example)? Analyze what is holding you back.

In which situations can you begin to practice assertiveness? Don't let other people be the ones to speak up—because it's easier or because you're too afraid! Identify specific situations in which you should have been more assertive and spoken up or taken action. Write down what you would have done differently, especially if this situation is likely to happen again. If it's an expected situation in the future, try to have someone supportive with you to keep you focused and practice beforehand.

If you're in a bad situation, talk to others about how to get out of it—and start to prepare yourself to do it. Do it right now!

SUCCESSFUL PEOPLE UNDERSTAND THE POLITICS OF THE ORGANIZATION

VISIBILITY + MENTORS + NETWORK = UNDERSTANDING POLITICS

Julia, a senior vice president in a major bank, says that politics is not a dirty word; it's the fabric of the organization. There are always personality quirks. You just have to understand the power base.

Janice, a senior director of corporate communication, agrees that someone has to break into those circles, but once you break in you're very well accepted.

The former president of Bryn Mawr advises that knowing who not to go to for information and guidance in an organization can be as helpful as knowing who to seek out. It's important to see the broader organizational issues and to view your experience within a larger context. Let senior management see your capability and interest. Get to know the people who make the decisions. Accept invitations on teams and committees. Indicate your broader interests. Find out why people do what they do. Be willing to work outside the ordinary hours.

One congresswoman feels that there may be a reluctance on the part of women to press themselves to move ahead. Men may be more inclined to do so through their socialization. But she advises

*women to adopt a different style from men, even as they push
ahead.*

It must be stated that, in order to really understand the
politics of an organization, you need to see visibility, mentors,
and networking as a potent combination. These three areas
are inextricably connected. It is rather difficult to become visible in your organization without at least some help from more
senior levels—which you can gain from having mentors and
an effective network. In turn, the better your network, the
more visible you are likely to be and the more recognition and
help you will receive from important mentors. We will continue to see this theme throughout the chapter and indeed the
entire book.

I asked the women in my original study if they felt that
there were barriers to women moving ahead. If so, what were
they? Some of the participants said that they felt there were
indeed barriers, including discrimination and a lack of awareness of women's potential by certain male managers. In addition to these external barriers, several of the respondents said
that, unfortunately, some women "just don't get it."

Their comment was not meant in a derogatory way, but
simply to suggest that women overlook the importance of visibility. Women think that as long as they do everything well,
they'll get ahead. You get the education, get the experience,
work hard, long hours, and sacrifice—now where's the payoff?
Why aren't you getting ahead? This is an extremely common
misconception about the inner workings of the workplace.
Many women equate promotion and recognition with hard
work, that somehow they'll be rewarded for commitment
alone. Well, certainly you do have to work hard and have the
right background and education, but that's only a step in the
right direction.

> *A senior executive at Merck talks about the "good student
> syndrome"—you work hard, but where's the reward? Political
> influence is critical in your career. There's a track, including
> image and self-projection, that goes beyond just doing a good job.
> It's not enough to be at the "right place at the right time, just
> lucky." You also need to know what it is that successful women are*

doing right that you're not doing. After looking at a lot of books and tapes, this executive got the reinforcement to do what she needed to do. She's still scared sometimes, but tries to deal with it. She has a career plan for the first time. There's a very fine line between pushy and assertive. You have to show assertiveness, but also show who you are as a woman. Nonverbal language is very important.

This isn't only a woman's issue. There are many men who don't succeed for the same reasons. It's essential to understand the critical visibility things going on in your groups. You need to understand and show competence in the required skills for success in your department. Identify what you want to do, then work toward it. Don't wait for others to do it for you; they won't. The executive at Merck depended on her group to develop her and to teach her what she needed to know, but she had to raise her visibility herself. Old paradigms don't work anymore, so organizations are tapping new resources. But they're not doing so out of an altruistic design. If these organizations could have continued successfully in what they were doing, they would have.

Successful women often do what makes perfect sense to many men. They learn the politics of the organization. What exactly is organizational politics? Among other things, it's knowing who makes the decisions, who has the power, who knows what's going on. How do you learn that? Well, if you've been reading carefully, you should already have a pretty good idea. Frequently, political acumen is a combination of gaining visibility, having an effective mentor and advocates, taking risks, and establishing an effective network. These things can work together to help you understand organizational politics.

Diane, a director at Gannett, advises women to change pitch, to adopt more than one operating style. We need to change gears. We don't always "get it." Women need to level the playing field.

Mentors and advocates are often extremely valuable sources of information regarding organizational politics. Since they are frequently more senior, well-connected people, they are likely to have access to the "inside scoop"—what's going on—and can consequently advise you on what to do in order to succeed in your career.

An executive at AT&T says there is a "club"—you have to be invited in. She has been invited in but she won't change to fit the existing mold. She feels that being invited shows that things are actually changing. She advises getting white men committed to and involved in diversity training—in addition to women and minorities. The male "majority" may hold the key to changing the environment.

Visibility also plays a major part in being political. It is generally extremely difficult for women to promote themselves, even subtly. In the film classic *Chariots of Fire,* a talented young runner from Oxford in the 1920s—an Olympic hopeful—wrote highly flattering press releases about his own performances (under a pen name) to promote his visibility and credibility as a successful runner: the one to beat. Perception became reality. All the other runners, Americans and other British athletes, knew that he was their biggest threat to victory. It was an extremely subtle, yet effective sequence in the film. Perception frequently does become reality. If other people think of you as talented, you take on that persona. Think of many great artists. Have you ever seen paintings worth many thousands of dollars and felt that your kids could do a better job? Who determines greatness and worth? Why are certain models who are tall and thin, but could even be called homely, phenomenally successful? Why are some bad films called classics or dissonant musical pieces called masterpieces? Probably because other people—maybe even self-proclaimed experts—call these paintings or models or films or compositions exceptional!

We also need to have our supporters, our "cheerleaders," start to tell other people—influential people—how great we are. Even if we have difficulty in promoting ourselves, we can have friends or colleagues spread the word for us. Sometimes we play down our own accomplishments out of humility. But we can't afford to be humble—there's a lot of competition out there!

A good friend of mine was in charge of press releases where I worked and sent quite a comprehensive story about me to the press about work I was doing for a conference of the European Women's Management Development Network, an international organization. She wrote things about me that I never would have written myself. They were true, but I didn't think that they were a big deal and I certainly wouldn't have wanted to appear to be bragging. (Remember our early socialization!) But she thought that they were important and generously wanted to give me credit for them. Hence, the positive perception became reality.

Understanding that other people—especially decision makers—need to perceive you as talented, ambitious, and smart, you may want to start looking around for a suitable and supportive "agent" to promote you. Of course, you are expected to return the favor whenever possible.

Another strategy is to examine the success of those who are already in senior positions. Are there qualities and skills that they have which you don't? What are they? Are these people more visible? If so, how? Do they spend a good deal of time schmoozing clients? Or making presentations to senior management? What is their management or leadership style? Is it more congruent with the organizational culture than yours? What is their network like? Do they belong to professional organizations? If so, which ones—and can you be invited to join as well?

Another potential problem for women is the fear of making the first move. It's like asking a man on a date—you think that you just shouldn't do it. (Again, women sometimes have a difficult time separating their personal and professional behaviors and feelings.) Socialization may have a lot to do with this. We may feel too aggressive in taking the first step in any relationship—business relationships included. It may be difficult to overcome that feeling, but it is very important to take the initiative in business situations. It can certainly be overwhelming to take the first step in networking, for example. Think of a time when you found yourself at a business or social outing and didn't know anyone there! It can produce an almost paralyzing sense of fear if you don't approach it in the right way.

Lynn is constantly in situations where she must attend professional functions or meet with clients, many of whom are strangers. However, what most people don't realize when they meet Lynn is that in her younger years she was one of the most

*painfully shy people on earth. Gradually, however, she came out of
her shell with a lot of practice and encouragement. She still may
not like going into a room full of strangers, but she hides that
feeling really well! She is also very active in helping others,
especially women, by introducing them around the room and
facilitating their development of taking the first step. She knows
firsthand what it's like. It may be hard, but if Lynn could do it,
believe me, anyone can!*

From another perspective, making the first move is an
aspect of risk taking. It's going out on a limb, doing something
that you wouldn't ordinarily think that you could do. How can
you start? First, it's probably a good idea to enlist the help of
someone who's good at socializing. I had a college friend who
was amazing: If he went to get a drink at a social event, by the
time the bartender handed it to him, he had already started to
work the room. I never forgot his easy manner and the way
that he could just strike up a conversation. Most people feel
self-conscious about making the first move in a conversation,
but if you think about it, probably just about everyone else in
the room feels the same way. Most people will probably be
thrilled to talk to someone else. Once you have a few positive
experiences (and you really need to force yourself to practice
this one), you will realize that most people are very open and
responsive. If you can, go to a professional or work-related
event with someone who knows other people there. Ask your
associate to help you meet the people that you should especially get to know. I try to do this whenever I can. Networking, as I
mentioned before, is absolutely critical in ultimately becoming
more politically aware. Don't forget two of your four P's—I can
speak from experience that persistence and practice do work.

TAKING SOME RISKS—AND MINIMIZING OTHERS—AS YOU MOVE AHEAD

When we talked earlier about certain risks with increased visibility, the positive or negative effect of your boss becomes
apparent. As I mentioned before, sometimes success—even

success with your boss—is a matter of luck. Some people just end up with loser bosses. But as you move up in an organization or from organization to organization, your network and mentors may be able to give you information on which career moves—and indeed, which bosses—will help you succeed and possibly minimize your risk. You may actually begin to make your own luck.

> *When Lynn started a job in a new company, she was lucky enough to have a great boss—who unfortunately left just 4 months later. However, she had consciously begun to build an effective network so that when she was offered various new positions, she could ask people she trusted what they would advise. So it became less a function of luck and more a function of research and networking. The risk was somewhat minimized as she gained more information about the decisions she needed to make regarding her own career development.*

Sometimes women have a difficult time stepping outside of the box when it comes to their job descriptions. They may feel that if someone else is already doing a particular job or task, it becomes outside of their possible domain. However, in this era of increasing need for flexibility and adaptability, combined with the decrease in specific job descriptions, it becomes more essential to be able to cross over into other work functions. Think about the differences, for example, between the basic, entry-level types of functions as opposed to the role of more senior decision makers. The entrepreneurial visionaries are no more essential than the people taking the more mundane, monotonous jobs. They are both necessary, despite all the hype about empowering workers to the lowest level possible. In all honesty, there will always be those workers who are happy knowing their exact boundaries, working 9 to 5 without taking on extra responsibilities—in other words, they don't necessarily want to be empowered. Then there are the more assertive, entrepreneurial types, the people who generally do not fit a particular job description. It is critical, therefore, in this changing work environment for women to become more comfortable with less well-defined rules, fewer boundaries, more adaptability, and greater risk taking if they are to aspire to more senior-level positions in organizations. Unfortunately, many women do not receive formal or informal training in this type of behavior. Our childhood activities prepare us for generally more structured, passive roles.

OVERCOMING BIASES

Quite honestly, most of the women I interviewed agreed that even in the most forward-thinking organization, discrimination may be evident. Even if the organization espouses diversity in its policies, changing the attitudes and practices of others is a totally different matter. So, until we have figured out a means by which we can totally eradicate individual biases, we need to make sure that discrimination does not derail our careers. It is still my belief that the majority of discrimination takes place simply out of ignorance—being unaware of how different personalities, perspectives, and attitudes affect the workplace. I have spoken to many men and women who, presented with a diverse perspective, truly do make an effort to understand other points of view. (Of course, some people may be so deeply entrenched in their perspectives that they will never be able to change. Hopefully, such biased people will be dramatically fewer in number and less influential as the demographics of leaders begins to change!)

Many of the women I spoke to had experienced bias or discrimination at some point in their careers, but it didn't stop them from succeeding. Why not? Well, many of them admitted that they had approached various situations with a proactive stance. How did they achieve success within such a male-dominated environment at the top?

First, let's set the stage for what many of these women were faced with—and indeed are still frequently faced with. Keep in mind that the average senior manager is still the white male in his fifties or sixties. He has spent most of his career surrounded by those who are generally like him—other guys. They talk about sports, they hang out, they have lunch. With a wife who traditionally has worked in the home, our executive has had limited exposure to professional women at his level. It is not surprising, therefore, that this man holds the opinions, attitudes, and values that he does. However, the majority of traditional senior managers will probably be fairly open-minded about accepting women into senior levels, even if it takes some persuasion. But what about the senior manager who is biased against women? How can he be changed?

For this man, everything is fine as long as everyone is pretty much like him. Then think about it: Maybe 5 or 10 years earlier, a woman managed to "sneak" into a senior-level position. (She probably had a "thing" with the boss, our executive thinks. How else could she have gotten here?) He's not happy about the situation. How can he tell his jokes? How can he make his comments about the hot, young secretaries? The new woman has changed everything by being in his meetings. He doesn't like it. But she's smart—really smart! He may not agree with everything she says, but she does bring up good points about several issues, he must confess. She's not like other women. She is really prepared, she knows her stuff, and she stands up for what she thinks. She's almost like one of us! Maybe she's not so bad after all.

I'll bet if you talk candidly with male managers, they will confide that many men do feel this way. But, with the right approaches and strategies, a woman can be extremely well accepted into the "mainstream" of senior management. Many women have been thus admitted into the club.

So how *did* these women get ahead? Well, they often said that they had to work harder than their male counterparts. Many emphasized that their work had to be perfect, no room for mistakes. They learned to move in a man's world—maybe they enjoyed sports, they were able to talk about "guys' topics," they showed their ability to be tough and to make tough decisions, they were competitive. Now, you may think that they had to adapt to a male model of leadership to fit in. Well, some of the women I interviewed possessed quite typical masculine characteristics—they were competitive and athletic, and could make tough decisions. But the vast majority were a terrific combination of masculine and feminine traits. They are assertive, but build teams. They really know their stuff. They are good communicators and strong negotiators. They take risks, but listen to others. They look to the bottom line, but not at the expense of the employees. They work well with both men and women.

Sometimes, when women are faced with discrimination, they try to ignore it, fight it, or work around it. This can be a highly charged issue. There are certainly several approaches to the problem, but I can report on how many of these very successful women have handled it effectively, without either losing their credibility or limiting their path to senior positions. The majority of those who faced the discrimination problem felt that it was simply due to lack of understanding on the part of their male coworkers. They frequently were involved, either directly or indirectly, with changing the attitudes and thereby the culture of the environment toward women.

> One former congresswoman became "accepted" by male representatives of the House. She changed them, they changed her. The dynamics started to change. They couldn't help but find some of her "women's ideas" practical and reasonable. Colleagues with whom she was at opposite ends of ideology would say, "You're so reasonable!" She began to change viewpoints individually in this way. It's joining the club. Congress is very "personality driven." If you get along with people in general, you'll probably get along with people in the House. There are a lot of effective ways of doing things. However, there is a different sense of expectations for women, as well as different approaches. She adds that there is no one right way of doing things. Successful people try more often and learn to accept failures. Now heading the bipartisan Women's Campaign Fund, she is helping women aspiring to politics develop exactly those skills.

In addition to working hard and working smart, which was assumed, these women developed a reputation for being top performers by anyone's standards. They not only did the right things, but also developed the right networks, had high-level advocates, and took appropriate risks. They were genuinely well respected by their peers, male and female alike. Consequently, their perspectives and opinions were well received and accepted.

One of the senior women I interviewed attended a workshop on sexual harassment, which was a part of an organization-wide training program. When a film was shown identifying a situation of sexual harassment, one of the men in the audience stated that "this kind of behavior doesn't occur in our company." She countered that yes, indeed, this type of behavior did exist. Her colleague was amazed, but he took the observation as the truth, because she was so well respected that her opinion carried enormous weight. Other women who had not earned as high a level of respect would undoubtedly have been taken far less seriously with the same opinion.

Therefore, if there are highly respected women—and men—who believe that a certain amount of bias exists against women in the organization, it is critical to be sure to get them involved not only in the organizational change, but in your personal career advancement as well.

A senior executive at Dow Jones says that her organization has definitely become more comfortable with women. Male managers are of an age that they're not uncomfortable with women. Senior management is committed to dismantling the old-boys' network. However, there still may be a tendency to see women as having jobs, while men have careers. It is important to realize that being treated equally does not necessarily equate with equal opportunity.

A senior executive at AT&T says that some men are not used to the idea of women in senior management. Although they are less prevalent, if you find yourself hooked to a boss like that, move on. Five or ten years ago she heard "I've never worked for a female boss, before. I'm nervous about it." This has changed. For about the first half of her career, she didn't have a plan. Although she considers herself "one of the guys," she says it's OK to be feminine. Also, it's better to choose your battles, to pick the target when it matters. She thinks that during job interviews, people look at candidates who are like them. You need to maximize the number of spots on your résumé that will bond with someone else.

So, how can you learn to move in the world of management—especially male management? Some women have suggested that learning about sports does benefit, even if you are only an enthusiastic fan. A number of the women I interviewed played golf, which they considered to be extremely helpful in doing business. (I personally have not yet made the commitment to golf, which I probably should do. I received golf lessons for Christmas a few years ago, but after the first two lessons I decided that I didn't have the patience to learn a new sport at that time. I may take it up later!) Other women note that it is important to keep your emotions in check, to be able to make the tough decisions, and to be able to be "one of the guys." This, again, is not to say that women need to take on a masculine persona at all. However, it may be important to be aware of the differences—some subtle and some not so subtle—between men and women in the workplace.

Women should be able to accept joking criticism, teasing, and other "male" types of interaction without taking it too personally. Don't forget, most men treat one another in this way; they're just not treating you any differently. Women should also keep their sexuality out of the workplace. Without realizing it, some women may unconsciously or consciously flirt or present behavior which may be appropriate for personal relationships, but unacceptable for business or professional relationships. Particular care should be taken to keep these two environments separate. This may seem rather evident. However, since some women have not been in the workplace for a significant amount of time, they may be somewhat unaware of the boundaries between work and social behavior. Several of the participants in the study indicated that they were frequently viewed as a "sister," almost as one of the guys, but obviously not quite. They enjoyed that role, since it indicated that their male colleagues talked to them as equals, realizing and appreciating their unique outlook as women, but not regarding them from the same perspective as that of women with whom they might be involved—a wife, girlfriend, or mother, for example.

But why do women have to be the ones to adapt to the organizational politics instead of men changing them? The answer is simple. More men dictate the culture of organizations at this time. However, as more women move up, the organizations will undoubtedly change. So in the future it looks like it won't necessarily be "politics as usual."

SUMMARY

- A combination of visibility, effective networks, and mentors frequently helps people understand one another, and consequently work more effectively in their organizations.

- A colleague or friend can serve as your "press agent" and contribute to your visibility and credibility via effective promotion. You can do the same thing for a friend.

- Examine the qualities and skills of successful people and emulate them.

- Look beyond traditional jobs and job descriptions. It is also important to know and understand your own abilities, interests, and limitations.

- Women still need to do it better than their male colleagues, with no room for mistakes. There can be no excuses for people making assumptions or doubting their ability to attain success.

- Women need a change of pitch, more than one operating style. We need to change gears. We don't always "get it." Women need to level the playing field.

ACTION PLAN

How are you going to learn about the politics in your own organization? (Ask a mentor or an advocate? Keenly observe which people are getting ahead and what they're doing?)

What steps are you going to take to begin to become more politically astute? Increase your visibility? Establish a working relationship with a senior or highly respected manager? Expand your network?

Who can assist you in increasing your positive press? Can you help others too?

How, and with whom, can you begin to change attitudes? Do you interact with people who may need to change their views? Write down strategies on how you or others may be able to change.

Ask yourself several hard questions: Do you fit a negative female stereotype? Do you overreact or take things too personally? Do you work harder or longer on unnecessary details to make sure that your work is perfect? If you have answered yes, work with advocates or mentors and begin to practice what your organization expects in order to get ahead. Or make the decision that it's not worth it to you, and move on.

PART TWO

PUTTING THE SECRETS TO WORK

MEN AND WOMEN AT WORK

Much has been written about the ways in which men lead as opposed to the ways in which women lead. How they communicate. How they negotiate. How they get ahead. It seems that everyone is fascinated with this topic! If each sex is aware of the differences, it will be much easier to understand the other's behavior. But keep in mind, as you read about men and women at work, that this chapter is *not* about encouraging women to learn to act like men! In the past, male-dominated organizational cultures have created environments of fierce competition, lack of communication, individualistic attitudes, and incredible bureaucracy. Do we really want to perpetuate that kind of environment? I don't think so! What we are talking about is learning how men and women frequently view things and how they interact. Keep in mind that many of the stereotypes of men and women are changing with our changing roles in the workplace. Also keep in mind that gender *roles* are often more important than actual gender—there are a lot of nurturing men who are terrific team players and there are plenty of women who can negotiate and make tough decisions with the best of them! We're out to break the stereotypes, not reinforce them! We're looking to create a terrific balance of masculine and feminine characteristics and traits. That's what makes the best leadership, and those effective leaders create the best organizations.

Are men and women really that different at work? Well, it may depend on who you ask and where you work. You've heard it all before—old-boys' networks, male bonding, sports and military models versus "a women's way of leading." Are these concepts—or should they be—mutually exclusive? Many of the women I talked to said that gender shouldn't be an issue at all. Other women agreed, but added that it's a positive thing to celebrate the differences and varied perspectives that women bring to the workplace. Everyone agreed about the value of flexibility and the need to be able to work well with men and women equally.

So how is it that some women turn out to be so different from men, while others are only minimally different? We need to look at women's socialization. This is an enormously important aspect of our behavior—we really need to understand what we're all about!

GENDER ROLES

Gender encompasses a number of things beyond biological sex. It includes the "appropriate" roles assigned to us by the culture in which we live. Society may often dictate what is appropriate for our gender. However, gender roles are specific to individual people. These roles are often the result of our physical makeup, our life experiences at work or at school, our role models, our sexual and romantic experiences, our peers, and our family. We may need to examine our own values, attitudes, and personal history more closely in order to get a better sense of who we are and why we view the world—especially our work world—the way that we do.

From our early lives, there are certain expectations which frequently reflect our gender. We initially learn to behave in a certain way from our families. Have you ever noticed that people tend to be more careful and tentative with girls than they are with boys? Some people say that boys act in a different way from girls even at a very early age. But sometimes the way in which a child is treated seems to have as much, if not more, to do with how a child behaves. As adults, we may generalize and think that women behave in a certain way and men another. But we may not always take into consideration the incredible number of factors which have influenced our lives along the way. Enormous time and energy have been spent in researching whether the differences are innate or acquired through socialization. Psychologists continue to deliberate over the theories of nature versus nurture. Whatever the answer, it is fairly clear that boys have frequently been socialized in a different way from girls.

It's pretty clear that socialization can play a significant role in the development of skills to be used in the future. If just one or two of life's variables are changed, the resulting changes in behavior and attitudes can be enormous. This is something for parents, especially, to be aware of as they help their children develop.

Part of the socialization process may consist of positive and negative life experiences that affect the way we view things and form our attitudes and points of view. Negative experiences can be seen as baggage from our past, things that we may not even be able to identify. This baggage may not even be something particularly destructive, just something that affects the way in which we view things. Negative life experiences can explain why we overreact to seemingly innocent or inconsequential things, either at home or in the workplace. Perhaps when you were a child, your parents were overly protective and strict. Now that you have matured and gained your independence, you sometimes go overboard in wanting freedom to do whatever you want to do. It may dramatically influence your choice of career, your choice of friends and lifestyle, and even how you raise your own family. Then what happens if you have a boss who reminds you of your particularly strict father or mother? Your personal experiences may cause you to overreact to the boss's control, whereas others may not even be fazed by the same behavior. This is especially true between men and women. Much of the problem may be due to poor communication, lack of self-esteem, lack of experience, or lack of awareness of differences in personality. Think of your own personal experiences. They have undoubtedly shaped your attitudes, your expectations, and the way in which you look at things.

This concept often has an ironic twist. My brother and sister-in-law gave me a gift of dinner at a very nice restaurant when I received my doctorate. When I made the reservation, the very pleasant young woman took down the information. I gave her the particulars and she asked for my name. Very pleased to be using my title for the first time, I said that the reservation was for Dr. Brooks. She very nicely said, "Great, we have a reservation for Dr. Brooks at 8 p.m. We'll see him on Saturday."

EARLY SOCIALIZATION (HOW IT MAY AFFECT YOUR SUCCESS)

There are usually three areas in which women have difficulty. First, studies have shown that there is still discrimination against women in the workplace. My own research has confirmed that, as I mentioned earlier. (But time and effort are ever so gradually beginning to change these attitudes.) Second, many women have just recently started to have the experience, background, and education to know how business works. We're making a lot of progress in this area as well. However, one area which remains difficult to overcome is our own socialization—our upbringing, our values, our culture. Our own "baggage," if you want to call it that, is a hurdle that many of us really need to overcome. I think that girls today will have an advantage over most of us who are older. When I see them playing sports with the boys, learning computers, and playing with more gender-neutral toys, I am extremely optimistic that these activities will be a true equalizer between young men and women. (Still, I cringe at times when I go down the doll aisle in Toys R Us and see the ongoing portrayal of women as dressed-up "bits of fluff"! I know, I shouldn't be so judgmental.) Let us hope the next generation will develop a more positive outlook on life and work. Meanwhile, as discussed earlier, many of us grownups have some serious socialization issues to overcome.

In the past, girls were frequently praised for being honest, obedient, humble, and respectful. We may have thought, as we grew up, that it wasn't ladylike to be competitive. So girls and young women tended to avoid competition and confrontation in order not to lose their femininity. Boys, on the other hand, have generally placed great value on showing independence, assertiveness, self-reliance, and competition.

In her book *In a Different Voice,* Carol Gilligan discusses the sex-role differences between boys and girls.[23] She reports on the results of a study by Janet Lever, conducted in 1976, of 10- and 11-year-old boys and girls at play.[24] Twenty years later, these children are now moving up in the workplace and may be in management positions. (This is an important fact, considering that their socialization will have developed their management and leadership styles.) Lever observed that the boys tended to play in larger and more age-heterogeneous groups, played out-of-doors more frequently than girls, played more competitive games than girls, and played games that lasted longer than girls' games. Boys also tended to play games that required a greater level of skill. When disputes arose, the boys were generally able to resolve them fairly quickly and effectively. The boys were seen to quarrel frequently. They shouted at one another, even pushed and shoved one another, but it did not appear to disrupt the play for an extended period of time. The worst-case scenario usually just resulted in repeating a play. The boys genuinely seemed to enjoy the "legal debates," which usually included all players, regardless of skill or size. They learned problem-solving and conflict resolution skills.

While I was writing this chapter, I went to watch some friends play softball. They were all professional men (no women), and I really laughed as I watched the behavior on and off of the field. I could understand their behavior pattern perfectly without even being a psychologist! They looked for weaknesses to exploit in the other team. They congratulated members for good plays, yelled at members for stupid mistakes (sometimes the very same players they had just congratulated 5 minutes earlier), reassured one another for a good try that didn't work out, cheered one another on, and got into verbal fights. It was a microcosm of their world at work. And they had been practicing this for years! (One thing I couldn't help but notice was the ubiquitous guy comment: "Come on, you're playing like a girl!") These exact rules apply at work and at play. If we played "girls' games" instead of "boys' games" grow-ing up, we didn't learn what we needed to prepare us for work. It's often just a bigger game.

In Lever's research, on the other hand, girls were often observed playing noncompetitive games such as jump rope, or other turn-taking games which did not necessitate one girl's success at the expense of another's failure. Since disputes were less likely to occur, most girls were poorly prepared to participate effectively in any dispute. Girls, unlike boys, tend-ed to end the game in the event of a dispute, rather than pos-sibly risk the relationship. Girls also tended to play in smaller groups, perhaps with just one or two friends, developing a sense of relationship building and sensitivity.

Lever established that boys generally developed and refined the skills of healthy competition, independence, and organization as a result of their play. They gradually prepared themselves for participating in various activities in large and diverse groups, experiencing socially approved competition. (Sound like your workplace?) Girls, as a result of their specific games, did not generally learn the same skills.

Betty Harragan writes that girls' games are outgrown early in childhood and are not resumed in adulthood because they basically have virtually no intrinsic value—they teach noth-ing.[25] (What are the skills learned in playing dolls, house, or hopscotch, for example?) She states that the objectives of girls' games do not include performing under competitive stress or playing to win; they simply aim to improve a skill in a vacuum. As adults, women often still think that if they work hard and practice self-perfection in a limited arena, they'll become suc-cessful.

So, do we really need to examine how men are frequently able to play with their enemies and compete with their friends? Just go back to their games. Traditionally boys have always been allowed to "play with their enemies and compete with their friends," says Gilligan.

I've asked a lot of men, just out of curiosity, if it's true that most men feel perfectly comfortable on a ball field or court with their "enemies"—or at least someone they don't particularly like—

on their team. They say "sure, especially if they're good players!"
Conversely, they usually agree that if their close friend is on the
opposing team, they say "they'll be out for blood. Then, when the
game is over, everything's back to normal. That's part of the
competition—the fun."

Wow, did most of us women miss out on some serious development of competitive skills needed to make it in the workplace! Women who have competed in sports will probably
identify with this to a certain extent as well, although it may
be interesting to do a study to see if women athletes display
the same or different tendencies as their male counterparts
toward teammates and competitors.

In Lever's research, girls' games were generally more social
than boys'—smaller groups or pairs, relationship-oriented.
Young women have traditionally had an uneasiness with competition, as well as a conflict between femininity and success.
Boys learn the organizational skills required to coordinate the
activities of larger and more diverse groups (like running corporations or governments, perhaps?).

LEARNING LEADERSHIP STRATEGIES

Leadership necessitates giving people instructions on what to
do. However, girls have often been taught from an early age,
either directly or indirectly, that if you tell other people what
to do, you're bossy. Fortunately, in the next generation of
young women, we may start to see a gradual shift in this
socialization pattern. Girls are starting to do the same things
that boys do. They are playing competitive sports, are encouraged to excel in math and science, share boys' interests in
computers and technology, and so forth. I think that this may
in large part be due to the reaction that many parents had to
their own socialization—they didn't want to bring their own
children up in the same way they were brought up. So there's
hope for the next generation!

A clear example of the changes in women's socialization
can be seen in the sports arena. When the first women's team

in the America's Cup yacht race was highlighted in a Lifetime Network television special series, the crew members discussed their successes and difficulties. During a particularly close race, in which they lost to another one of the American teams (all male), the women analyzed what they had done differently from the men. The women admitted that, although they were about as competitive and fit as men and women can be, when it came to making a decision about what to do in a critical moment, they used the team approach and discussed it among themselves. But, by the time they reached consensus, the other American team had passed them. They studied what the other (male) team had done differently to win. They noticed that their male counterparts would follow the strongest, most outspoken leader, who just grabbed the command and said, "We're doing this!" The women said that they had to learn sometimes to push others aside when they needed to take charge in a critical moment. It was fascinating to see these tremendous female athletes fine-tuning their competitive edge. Even these women acknowledge that, although the team approach is best, there still may be times when you are ultimately responsible to make a critical decision on the basis of the information given to you. It's what happens every day in organizations. That's leadership.

> *Gail Blanke of Avon, an Olympic-class swimmer, agrees that competition in sports prepares women for leadership and teamwork. A team captain in school, she adds that sports help teach you the value of working together, resolving conflicts, winning and losing graciously, and sticking with it even when times are tough.*

Betty Harragan writes that "losing a game is the signal to practice more, to improvise better techniques, to improve team coordination, to do whatever is necessary to correct the past errors so as to go forward with a determination to win the next one."[26] That's terrific advice! I've really thought about that quote and I think that it's something we can apply to everything in our lives. Women frequently don't understand the physical and emotional "routine" of winning and losing if they have never competed. We may take losses personally or may even be devastated by them. Those who have played competitive sports know, however, that someone *always* has to lose— and it's going to have to be you a fair amount of the time. So we really have to start realizing that, although losing isn't fun, it doesn't have to be devastating either. We have to get used to it! The same dynamics hold true at work. Sometimes you get the job, sometimes you don't. Sometimes you get the raise, sometimes you don't. Today a decision is made in your favor, or you get the promotion, or you make the deal. But tomorrow you don't. It's OK to be disappointed. But maybe it's also a signal to learn what you need to improve.

A young colleague of mine, who frequently asks my advice on various things, recently interviewed for an internal position. I was on the search committee. Although he has a lot going for him, he was not one of the finalists. We discussed some of the major points of the interview. Since I know him so well, I felt comfortable giving him praise on what he did well, but also constructive criticism on what he might want to improve. He really appreciated my candid assessment and we strategized about various ways in which he could achieve these improvements. He took it as a learning experience and continued on. As an athlete, he is used to winning and losing. That's exactly the way to handle it. We all need to approach these inevitable situations as positively as possible.

ESTABLISHING THE RULES

Boys' rules have usually been different from girls' rules. There is generally a distinct hierarchy among boys—at play, in class, in social settings. Boys learn the one-up strategy. For every boy who has higher status, there is someone else who has a lower-status position. Think in nature, for example, of the males of most species. There is a constant battle between the incumbent leader and the challengers. From bears to lions to bucks, the males spend their lives establishing and protecting their status. Among the human species, status is achieved by giving orders, being the center of the action, and possessing the necessary information.

If you compare the differences in socialization in the workplace, it's easy to see the difficulties for many women who have been socialized in a very traditional way—which probably includes most women over the age of 29 or 30. We're playing by a different set of rules! But no one has told us about the differences.

> *At international women's conferences, Helen Solomons and I sometimes make a presentation which involves playing a game on cultural differences. The participants all think that they're receiving the same rules for the game, but each table is given a separate set of rules. People are not allowed to talk during the game, so they can't relate that information even if they do figure it out. Everyone enjoys playing, and during the discussion after the game we focus on the feelings of the participants as they were playing. Responses range from anger to frustration to embarrassment—feeling foolish. People were using different sets of rules, and no one told them!*

Don't we frequently find the same things in our personal and professional environments? Sometimes we are playing by our rules, thinking that other people are doing the same thing—only they're not. And no one has told us! Sometimes others are aware that they are presenting a different set of rules to us, but probably most of the time they just don't realize that we grew up learning a different set of rules. So we need to develop relationships and communicate well with those who are making the rules. (Or develop the expertise to make the rules ourselves!)

GENDER EXPECTATIONS

There are certain expectations with regard to gender. Traditionally, men have assumed certain roles and women have assumed others. Society generally sets these expectations, which are reinforced in a variety of ways. Men and women are seen more favorably when they conform to stereotypical roles than when they deviate from them. In other words, most people prefer men to act "like men" and prefer women to act "like women." There can certainly be an effective combination of male and female traits, but generally people don't like women to be more masculine in their behavior and act consistently tough, for example; and they don't like men to act too nurturing or soft.[27]

Studies suggest that, although male and female leaders may not differ in their actual behavior and effectiveness, how their subordinates view them does vary. Employees are more comfortable with male bosses who are more task-oriented and female bosses who are more social or person-oriented. That may explain why some employees feel somewhat uncomfortable with a woman who is tough and demanding or with a man who is seen as too nice. Even today, some employees expect that the boss is going to be a man and the subordinate is going to be a woman. Interestingly enough, it is often the task-oriented (i.e., bottom-line) individual who is given leadership opportunities more than the person-oriented individual. (Of course, the ideal scenario is a combination of task- and people-oriented leadership.) Unfortunately, women have frequently been stereotyped as lacking task-oriented skills.

In leadership research, it is frequently found that people (both men and women) with a masculine sex-role identity prefer task-oriented leadership, and people (men and women) with a feminine sex-role identity prefer more people-oriented leaders. Therefore, people who are tough, competitive, direct, and more to the point prefer similar types of leaders. Touchy-feely types of leaders would drive them nuts! Conversely, nurturing, compassionate, good communicators would never enjoy working with a boss who didn't take the time to talk to them, encourage them, or nurture them. Leaders who exhibit both task-oriented and people-oriented behaviors (androgynous types) are generally well accepted by the greatest number of employees. This would definitely be considered the ideal combination. In a 1990 study, 500 male and female managers were asked their perceptions of successful managers, male and female. Descriptions of effective managers matched the characteristics of male managers—specifically, self-confidence, leadership ability, competitiveness, forcefulness, objectivity, aggressiveness, and desiring responsibility. Women were frequently characterized by very different attributes: sympathetic, sensitive, understanding, gullible, and loyal. In the research, both men and women were cited as having a strong preference for a "masculine" manager. Ironically, women in leadership roles frequently fit the stereotype of the ideal leader more than their male counterparts.

Karen Korabik, a professor at the University of Guelf, suggests that it is very important to identify what kind of person you are, which leadership or management style you prefer, and consequently what kind of company you want to work for. If you don't feel comfortable with the ideology, the organizational culture, or the kinds of people who work for a company—especially if you're still in the interview stage—don't work there. It won't get better unless there's a major change at the top. Find someplace that's a good fit with your ideals and personality! Don't forget, the organization's culture—its values—is made up of the leadership at the top. So if you consider yourself a very nurturing, open team player who believes that people are the organization's best asset, it's probably a good idea not to work for a stock brokerage firm as an options trader, for example. You'll get eaten alive! On the other hand, if you are competitive, tough, and down to business, don't plan on being a social worker or counselor! You really need to fit well with your profession and organization.[28]

DIFFERENCES BETWEEN MEN AND WOMEN

We've been hearing a lot about "women's way of leading," the "old-boys' club," stereotypes, barriers, biases. Are they real or imagined? Are men and women really that different in the workplace? Well, I did a lot of research on the subject for my doctoral dissertation, and one of the major conclusions I arrived at was that there is more validity to the differences between gender roles than actual gender. What that means is that there are characteristics, traits, and skills that are traditionally associated with men or male behavior, and others that are more closely associated with women or female behavior.

These generally relate to task-oriented items and person-oriented items. However, both men and women possess these traits, just in different amounts. Some people are more task-oriented and some are more person-oriented.

You may have experienced this yourself. Many women possess characteristics that would be considered masculine, but I don't mean it at all in a negative or "unfeminine" way. Women may be outstanding athletes, tough and logical, good in math, science, and technology, analytical and competitive. You probably know many women like that yourself. These women will frequently be in careers that have been seen as more nontraditional for women, such as technology, finance, accounting, and medicine.

On the other hand, you probably also know many men who are extremely nurturing and compassionate. They may be excellent communicators. For example, counselors and teachers may share these traits. These characteristics are frequently based on gender role, rather than actual gender. Gender role can be determined by culture, family upbringing, birth order, exposure to various activities or experiences—a lot of things. Think about the men and women you know. There are probably men who are nurturing, women who are competitive, and men and women who are a wonderful combination of both. Now you know what you're dealing with in organizations. You may have to figure out individual characteristics and personalities of your coworkers and how to interact with them accordingly.

While it is true that *some* women are more nurturing, more team-oriented, and better communicators than *some* men, it is probably not particularly accurate to make a blanket statement that women lead or manage in a certain way and men lead in a different way. There certainly may appear to be traits that are more inherently feminine or masculine, but each person exhibits certain tendencies. Think of a bell curve. Let's say that the left end of the bell curve represents the feminine side of management or leadership style (individual characteristics, skills, traits, and so on) and the right end represents the more masculine aspects. Some women may fall somewhere to the left of center, the feminine end, some may fall somewhere in the middle, which represents a combination of masculine and feminine characteristics or traits, while still others may fall much further right, toward the masculine end—and vice versa for men.

Part of my original research was to assess whether the senior-level women I interviewed possessed male, female, androgynous (a combination of male and female), or undifferentiated (no difference between male and female) characteristics. I used an instrument that identified these gender-role identities. Much of the leadership literature has traditionally indicated that skills and characteristic necessary to succeed are based on male military or sports models.[29] Since there were frequently assumptions, substantiated or otherwise, that women who made it to top positions in corporations simply mirrored their male counterparts in behavior, background, characteristics, and skills, I wanted to find out if the women I spoke to exhibited traditionally male characteristics and skills. The organizations I chose were widely known as female-friendly organizations which had clearly indicated a commitment to the advancement of women. They included industry leaders such as AT&T, Merck, Johnson & Johnson, Dow Jones, American Airlines, Tenneco, U.S. Healthcare, Gannett, and Avon. Only about one-third of the women did possess masculine characteristics as measured by this instrument, which meant that the majority of participants, although all very senior executives in major organizations, exhibited characteristics or skills that were not considered exclusively masculine. Hmm! There was hope for the rest of us!

So I found that you didn't necessarily have to act like a man to succeed in a "man's world," a pattern that has been characteristically true of major corporations. But, as I found in the experiences and advice of the women I interviewed, it certainly does help if you have a better understanding of how men and women differ in that world! As one executive said, it's helpful for women to know how to switch gears and adapt to various situations and environments. Others advised celebrating the differences between men and women, while not necessarily making it a big issue. In other words, realize the differences and use them to your advantage instead of trying to ignore the fact that women actually are different.

BEING HEARD AMONG MEN

In Success Secret Four, we talked about being heard in meetings. Because men and women are socialized differently, a meeting which is exclusively or predominately made up of women will often have quite a different tenor from one in which more men are present. I have found this on professional association boards or committees which are made up predominately of women. Despite the same dynamics of personality and conflict that exist in any meeting, women will often look out for the more reticent ones who may be having difficulty in trying to make a point, so at least they may be heard. Women will elicit others' opinions and allow them the opportunity to speak up. However, men have been socialized with the attitude that someone needs to take control—to demonstrate superiority—even in a team setting. Control is very frequently an issue in meetings with numerous men in attendance.

Women will frequently wait their turn to speak in meetings or other gatherings.

> *The former president of Bryn Mawr College, sees this pattern often with many women, especially her students. She observes that when women are in meetings they need to be vocal, sufficiently loud to be heard, and not wait their turn. This may be a hard thing to learn to do, especially among a lot of men in a gathering, but you can do it!*

The first time I really noticed it was when I was in a group interview for a new dean. Faculty and administrators were invited to ask questions of the candidate. I had what I thought was a really good question, but every time I decided to ask it, someone else (usually a man) asked his question before I could get my opportunity. Then, of course, one of our senior administrators asked my question. Everyone, including the candidate, said, "Oh, that's an excellent question." I learned!

A lot has been written on the differences in management style between men and women. Sally Helgesen wrote a wonderful book called *The Female Advantage* which examines the leadership characteristics and styles of four women who have reached a senior level in their organizations.[30] As I mentioned earlier in the chapter, I believe that the gender-role identity of the person probably more than the actual gender determines leadership style. But what about generalizations about the sexes? Are they based somewhat in fact for many "average" men and women? I think that these generalizations are slowly but surely beginning to change. Women are gradually being accepted as equally influential and effective leaders and men are increasingly recognized as fostering a more balanced environment between men and women. In fact, when I was doing my original research, recommendations on really terrific women to interview came as often from men as from women. Many of the men told me how fantastic these senior women were, so they obviously had no difficulty in the role of women as leaders. Likewise, many insightful male leaders are realizing the importance of a management style which deviates from the traditional sports or military model.

Frank Cuttita, the president of a discount stock brokerage firm, describes his leadership style. He learned a lot about team management when he was in graduate school, but he admits that an MBA teaches you only the theories, not necessarily how things will work in the real world. In a very high-stress environment, he has to deal daily with issues ranging from specific financial questions to regulatory matters to technology problems. This is in addition to the routine tasks of management and dealing with individual personalities and styles, which are especially evident under stress.

Everyone agrees that Frank is a terrific leader. He frequently provides lunch for his employees, which he feels is very much appreciated. He plays on the company's softball team. He really tries to take the time to identify the strengths of those working directly with him and to call on those skills to maximize productivity and team cohesiveness. These traits are frequently seen in effective female leaders, who tend to be people-oriented as well as task-oriented. If you ask Frank's employees what they like about him, they will probably cite his team outlook and his ability to communicate effectively with them—both traditionally considered to be "feminine" traits.

However, when someone walks into his office, Frank is brief, to the point, and decisive. He doesn't waste time on idle chat. He's a tough boss and a good negotiator. He doesn't say "please" when he's asking for something to be done. The environment of a trading floor by nature is tough, aggressive, and competitive—a very "masculine" sports or military model— and he really excels in this type of organizational culture. However, his employees see the effective combination of both styles of leadership, each at the time when it is appropriate. Frank Cuttita has learned to respond in a manner consistent with the situation.

If it is important for managers to be flexible in their leadership styles, it is equally important for employees to be adaptable in working for someone who may have a different style of management from what they would like. If your personal style is more nurturing and you work for someone who is more down to business, you can't take it personally. Otherwise, you may need to either adapt or find another boss. However, it may help a lot to practice effective communication and work at understanding various points of view.

As either boss or employee, you need to understand the importance of remaining consistent in your behavior. As a manager, for example, you may not always be what others would call well liked—but several of the women I interviewed specifically said that they would rather be called "fair" and "consistent" than "popular" or "well liked." In addition, women and men are generally more respected if they act consistently with their gender. Men who are very nurturing may not be considered as aggressive as the accepted norm calls for; they may be considered "wimps." Women who are highly aggressive become "pushy" or "bitchy" or are called "Dragon Lady."

RECEIVING FEEDBACK, TAKING CRITICISM, AND NOT TAKING IT PERSONALLY

One difficulty for some women is taking things too personally at work. Much of it goes back to the need to be well liked. Remember how, as girls, we tried to maintain relationships over disputes; the very nature of our games fostered the need to be nice and spare others' feelings. Boys, on the other hand, have generally been raised to believe that one effective way to get ahead is to tease, criticize, and joke with others to put them down. They frequently don't worry about hurting others' feelings and subsequently learn how not to take things too seriously when they're the target! They learn either to tough it out or to give it right back to the other guy. So right away we're playing a totally different game by a totally different set of rules. Women are trying to spare others' feelings, while men may be trying either consciously or unconsciously to beat out the "other guy" by putting him down. This is something that can be worked on, however. The first, and maybe the most important, thing is to realize that these tremendous differences exist. Once we understand and analyze the dynamics of what's going on, it becomes far easier not only to deal with it, but to learn the strategy.

> *A few years ago, Lynn played tennis with a British friend, a terrific athlete who had not really played much tennis. The product of an all-boys boarding school in England, John had been completely immersed in the old-boys' network and way of doing things. If you didn't learn how to compete and win at school, as well as keeping one up on the other boys, you were in big trouble! Although Lynn plays very well, John beat her. But he kept reminding her of his victory—even several weeks later! Lynn at that time (before she fully understood the rules) simply became annoyed. Then, when my research began on this book, I pointed out the impact of socialization on boys and girls. It was as though a light bulb went off. Aha! Lynn finally understood exactly what John was doing and why he was doing it. He was just gaining his one-up status over someone who was, in theory, better than he*

was. He couldn't let that happen, of course. So, when he beat Lynn (maybe she just had an off day—it happens, even to the pros), he really had to let her know it. Women, on the other hand, would generally never do that to another woman, or to a man. They would probably say, "Great game! You probably just were having a bad day." or "Wow, I guess that was beginner's luck!" See the difference?

When you think about it, it really starts to make sense. Think of occasions when you may have felt that men were giving you a hard time, criticizing you, teasing you. Did you just give it right back to them or did you take it personally? Probably a lot of us have taken it personally, because we just didn't know that it was in fun. Have you ever heard, after possibly taking criticism or teasing from a guy, "Oh, stop making such a big deal about it, I was just kidding"? The woman may dwell on the comment for weeks, but the man has forgotten all about it. If you do eventually bring up how you felt, he probably has no idea of what you're talking about!

A scene from an adventure movie by Alistair McLean called *Death Train* underscores this point. In it Pierce Brosnan plays a tough, seasoned professional adventurer with an international organization, and Alexandra Paul (from *Baywatch*) is the smart, but inexperienced first-time field agent. As a helicopter flies them to their dangerous assignment, Brosnan starts asking about Paul's background. She says that she was an Olympic medal winner (a biathlete), is an expert marksman, speaks four languages, and runs a very fast mile. After confidently talking about her qualifications for the assignment, she tells him that she has always wanted to be a field operative. He coolly adds, "So, what are you doing now?" meaning what does she really do for a living, since she's obviously not good enough to be an agent. The others in the helicopter—two tough guys—just start to laugh, as men would do if a group member was being teased or mocked, but she takes the criticism seriously. What she doesn't realize, however, is that not only is she not yet one of the guys, she still hasn't proved herself enough for Brosnan to respect her as a professional, so this has become her sort of hazing. Does that sound familiar in the workplace?

The problem is not only that many men, because of their individual bias, will not automatically accept women in important positions. It is also the case that some women—and I emphasize some, not all—may still need to fill in one missing part. We may know that we're smart enough, educated enough, and talented enough to do the job, but we still haven't proved ourselves. That may take time. So first it's important to do the best job we can do, which may mean doing it better than everyone else just because we're women. A significant number of the successful women I interviewed underscored this point. They said that you have to work harder, work better, and be perfect, leaving no room for criticism. You can't give an opportunity to anyone to question your abilities. This is absolutely true. As several women added, mediocre men can get by and be successful, but never women!

But almost as important, we also need to know the tricks of the trade, the politics, how things are done. This may mean practicing taking—and giving—mock criticism and teasing, possibly being one of the guys (please note, not acting macho or too masculine—be yourself). We need to understand that this is actually a sort of ritual for men. Some men may see women as weak. Some men may feel that women can't joke around and be one of the guys, that women take things too seriously. Some men may think that they can't "be themselves" when women are around and can't talk about what they normally talk about "with the guys." Fair or not, this may mean that women need to understand and practice being able to effectively "hang out with the guys." But keep in mind that many men are starting to really appreciate and understand how women view things. Open communication can greatly improve this situation.

This, again, is where a mentor or an advocate can help. A woman may have a very well-positioned advocate pulling for her. He or she can make the woman visible, underscore her extensive qualifications to her teammates and bosses, give her confidence, and reassure her about handling the old-boys' club. It will help you enormously if you can have a well-placed, well-respected senior member of your organization giving you advice on how to interact effectively. A man would probably be able to give you the added insight of how men would act and react in given situations, in order to prepare you better for your role. In addition, many, many of the participants in the research said that their advice, or the characteristic about themselves that they most liked, was a sense of humor. It is absolutely invaluable! If you can feel confident enough to be able to laugh at yourself occasionally, you will be gaining an incredibly valuable skill. If people are testing you, this may save your reputation, your acceptance into the "club," and even your career!

MEN AND WOMEN ON INTERVIEWING

It can be very interesting to observe the sometimes dramatic differences between men and women in interviewing situations. I have been involved in numerous search committees and have made a conscious effort to observe the differences in style and approach between male and female candidates. As I have mentioned frequently, gender role is often a better barometer of individual characteristics and traits than gender itself. There are always men and women who are less stereotypical for their gender, but there certainly seem to be consistent trends in behavior.

One of the most obvious differences is assertiveness and confidence, which is often more evident in male candidates than in their female counterparts. For example, men tend to refer to their personal accomplishments and use "I" far more often than women do. When asked what qualifies them for a particular task or position, men will frequently say, "Well, I gained a great deal of experience in that area when I led my team on Project X, which turned out to be a huge success!" Women may be more reluctant to take ownership of the project and will respond, "Well, I have a good deal of experience in that area, since our team was responsible for Project X in my last position." No ownership, no allusion to the direct impact that she may have had on the success of the project.

Not too long ago, I interviewed several young men and women for a fairly entry-level management position. It was very interesting! Most of the young women tended to recite their experience only as one of the members of the group that was responsible for the project. It became so much of a pattern among the women that one of the committee members had to continually ask them to talk about their direct involvement or experience in the job. The male candidates, however, frequently responded with their direct involvement.

> One male candidate's comment on his experience sums it all up: "We had a big, new project that had never been done before, so someone in the office suggested, 'Why don't you have Greg take it on, since he's the expert in that area?' I don't want to pat myself on the back, but it turned out to be a huge, huge success!"

The candidate effectively accomplished two things by answering the question in that way. First, he identified himself indirectly as a leader, someone whom others recommended for big projects, without ever directly bragging about himself. Second, he indirectly indicated that the success of the project was largely due to his efforts as the leader, not necessarily the efforts of the entire team. It was great! Although he lacked certain experience in some areas, the entire committee was extremely impressed with his energy and enthusiasm. Here is something that many men do which women may want to learn—that sense of indirect suggestion or self-promotion.

The former executive director of the Glass Ceiling Commission also notices differences between men and women in interviews. The young men come in and are extremely confident about things that they may or may not have experience in, whereas many of the young women will say that they are very willing to learn. While that may be true, it seems quite apparent that employers respond well to those who are very self-assured and positive about their abilities—whether or not they have actually had the experience—and who can capitalize on their various past experiences to directly address the roles and tasks of the new position.

Successful men and women may take on what would frequently be called more masculine characteristics when they interview. Most are very positive and self-assured. They speak clearly and directly, without using a lot of qualifiers, such as "Well, I'm not sure if this is what you're looking for, but here's what I can do" or "I really don't have too much experience in that area"—period. They have a positive body language, not sitting too rigidly or moving around too much. They look the interviewer right in the eye when responding to questions.

Employers look for people who have a proven track record. Even if your employment history is not tremendously comprehensive, you can still capitalize on what you have accomplished. The key is to present yourself in a very positive way. Describe your work experiences as a combination of skills learned, how you accomplished various projects, what other people thought about them, and success you have enjoyed. Be very positive. This is no time for humility. You are marketing and selling yourself. Many women, unfortunately, exhibit a certain reserve in selling themselves. As women, we have been conditioned to represent ourselves as less capable, and as a result may shortchange ourselves. Not only have we been taught to be more reserved and humble, we also have difficulty letting go of our insecurities and find ourselves limited by our perceived failures and weaknesses. We are often afraid to take risks.

At work, you may want to ask if you could be included on search committees, even if only as an observer, in order to gain insight into effective interviewing styles and strategies. It would be especially helpful to be in on interviews for more senior positions.

DIFFERENCES IN NEGOTIATING

Negotiation is a really important issue if you are to be able to compete on a level playing field. Remember, the accepted rules for men and women are probably different. Not only that, men probably do have a preconceived perception of you as a woman when you enter into a negotiation—the perception that they can steamroll right over you. You may have to be twice as tough at the beginning just to establish yourself as a player.

It must first be assumed that there are various ways of negotiating. In my graduate classes, I sometimes illustrate the differences in negotiating styles between men and women in the following exercise. I ask the students to write down one or several words describing their concept of negotiation. I then ask one man in the class to collect the other men's responses and likewise a woman to collect the women's responses (just for fun). I have these volunteers read their respective group responses. I create two columns on the board or on a flip chart. Not surprisingly, the male responses are frequently comments such as "win at all costs," "crush them," "this is a battleground," and other competitive, military- or sports-related responses. The women, on the other hand, frequently respond with such comments as "win-win," "cooperation," and "hate it." While there are always exceptions to these scenarios, the class generally starts to react with amusement as the responses are read and listed. The exercise clearly identifies the different positions from which the members of the class are coming. (However, I'm starting to notice more similarities between men's and women's responses than before. That's good!)

If we apply these same types of responses and points of reference to the workplace, it is no surprise that negotiators on either side may be experiencing an uneven playing field. As a generalization, many women appear to view negotiation either as a win-win scenario, which frequently may be advantageous, or as a dreaded necessity of life. This is in contrast to many men, who do not necessarily consider negotiation to be their favorite pastime but who certainly view it as an extension of their sports experiences and may actually be quite proficient at the game. Most women, given this scenario, will probably be at a disadvantage in both approach and experience. Confidence in this and many other situations is a huge asset, even if it's only a perception of confidence.

Many years ago, in my first real job out of college, I worked in the sales department of a hotel in Philadelphia. I was very young and inexperienced about many things, as most people are out of college. Probably the single most important piece of information that I gained from that job was advice from a 32-year-old sales manager. He said that when you're talking to a customer and are reasonably sure about the answer to a question, but have a little doubt, don't hesitate. Don't second-guess yourself or use qualifying statements like "Well, I could be wrong, but . . . ." Just jump right in with your response with absolute certainty and a sure, solid voice. You will instill confidence in the customer and make him or her feel more comfortable about dealing with you and the company. That was about 15 years ago and I still remember the manager's advice. Many men react with confidence automatically, whereas some women feel that they must have every fact right or they can't give a confident answer. We may need to practice this type of communication.

DIFFERENT STYLES

It is very helpful to get used to dealing with different leadership and communication styles. As mentioned in previous chapters, it can be especially effective to mirror different styles of communication. Men often just communicate differently from women. Again, it is especially important to learn how not to take things personally.

Some of the men I spoke to—and these are extremely open-minded, well-educated professionals—had the perception that most women were too emotional. Some of them said that they didn't think they would want a female boss. Others said that they wouldn't mind having a female boss as long as she was consistent, not too moody, and fair. I think that a lot of men, even the youngest or most forward-thinking men, still have some biases to overcome, despite their positive association with a number of female colleagues. Perhaps, even unconsciously, they still continue to think of women in the traditional role of mother, sister, lover, or wife, rather than colleague. Many men have not had female bosses and may harbor some doubts about how they would react to such a situation. I think that they may feel comfortable enough at this point with women as equals, but are still reserving judgment on women as bosses.

On the other hand, some women feel that they get along better with men than with women. A colleague of mine, Winifred Williams, who supervises primarily women but raised three sons, agrees that her approach is more direct than that of many women she supervises. Consequently, her male colleagues and employees tend to feel very comfortable with her more direct management style, while some of the women she manages feel that at times she is not sympathetic enough. Remember, it has a lot to do with your socialization.

DIFFERENCES IN CONVERSATIONS

Both men and women certainly discuss a wide variety of work and nonwork topics during their workday. However, there seems to be a general trend as to what these topics include, topics that are often specific to men or women. A number of years ago, I was teaching high school French in a suburban school district. Generally, the ratio of male to female teachers in high school education is roughly 50-50, so I frequently would "hang out" with my male colleagues as much as my female colleagues—with one exception, at lunch. One year in particular was especially notable, perhaps because of the dynamics and personalities of my colleagues who had lunch at the same time as I did. In a modest-size faculty dining room— for literally the entire year—all the men sat at one table and the women sat at another table. It bordered on bizarre behavior for adult colleagues.

Almost all the women (and the men) were married. Basically the women talked every day for a year about their children—which diapers they used, when their kids began to talk, walk, and receive potty training. Every day's conversation just picked up where the previous day's had ended. I'm sure it was very nice for these women to be able to commiserate about the joys and trials of motherhood, but since I was about 25 and single, it wasn't of particular interest to me day in and day out. You may ask, then, why I sat there. Well, imagine the stigma of being the only woman—and a young, single woman—sitting with all married men at lunch. I would have most certainly been labeled—something. I finally gave up and just had lunch in my classroom. (At this point in my life, however, I wouldn't worry about what people thought and would simply sit with my male colleagues anyway. Live and learn!)

The bottom line of this situation was that I could overhear what the male teachers were talking about—sports, politics, work, current events, and humorous stories, but generally not their personal lives. This seems to represent an extreme example of a major difference between what men discuss and what women discuss. Men usually don't discuss their personal lives too much with acquaintances and colleagues, unless they are close personal friends as well. So, if you work with male colleagues, it is generally a good idea to diversify your realm of topics for discussion to include outside areas of interest.

GIVING FEEDBACK

A significant difficulty for men is giving feedback to women—especially, in a work environment, their subordinates or peers. It can be an exceedingly uncomfortable situation for both parties, but particularly for men. Feedback and critiques can be especially important for women as they advance in their careers in order to identify areas where they excel and, perhaps more important, where they need improvement. But women frequently don't have the opportunity to discuss specific areas in which they may receive effective feedback.

Usually when a man wants to give feedback to another man, he just lays it out without ceremony. Remember, most men are used to this type of scenario from their competitive youth. They don't have to worry about how the other guy is going to take it, since he has probably had a similar socialization. A male boss or colleague will just say something like "Look, you're not pulling your weight on this project. You need to get your act together and start contributing." One boss, a man who is fairly generous with his positive feedback, says that he usually doesn't even have to give negative feedback or constructive criticism to his employees (mostly male). The team "polices" itself and requires the team member who's not contributing to pull his weight.

But a man may have a great deal of difficulty in giving feedback to a woman, especially if it involves a certain amount of constructive criticism. His perception may be somewhat limited to a woman's role in the home—such as mother or other caretaker—which may lead him to interpret the woman as being more emotional, less tough, less "like a guy." Therefore, he may have difficulty defining his role in providing effective feedback—for fear of being faced with an "emotional female" who will get upset with his observations. Unfortunately, the woman may lose the opportunity to gain valuable insight and advice as a result.

This situation may be related to another communication issue. Many men feel that women are too indirect and many women think that men are too direct. When feedback is required, a male employee may have difficulty figuring out what some female bosses or colleagues are saying, since many women may wish to soften the blow of constructive criticism by cloaking it among positive comments. A man may become confused as to what the issue actually is and become frustrated. He may just want to know exactly what the problem is and what he needs to do to remedy it.

On the other hand, women may feel that men are unduly cold and callous when doling out criticism. Many women are used to having their feelings spared somewhat by female playmates, as they faced potential criticism while they were growing up. They may be taken aback or put off by what they consider to be overly blunt critiques of their performance or talent. It may be an effective technique to try to be flexible and mirror the behavior of the people you are dealing with. If they are direct, be direct. If they choose to be more aware of others' feelings by being less direct, you may want to follow their lead. You may need to change your approach depending upon the situation.

Individual personality may have a lot to do with how people give feedback, both positive and negative. Some women, especially, may also be waiting for the pat on the back in return for outstanding performance, something that may never come from certain bosses or teammates—both male and female. Other people are more nurturing and often will give generous praise and less severe criticism. It is critical to be aware of and flexible with individual management styles. In addition to this flexibility, it is very important not to take things too personally. The question to ask may be "Do they treat me any differently from anyone else?"

As women, we need to be aware that men may truly be uncomfortable giving us feedback. Justified or not, many men really do feel this way, even the most enlightened men. Consequently, it can be very helpful to establish effective communication along the way to develop a positive environment in which both parties feel comfortable giving and receiving feedback.

Women may need to become more decisive. Men probably know a little more about this area, especially because of their socialization and sports or military background. As I mentioned earlier, the members of the America's Cup women's crew were tremendous athletes and very competitive, but when faced with certain critical paths, they chose to make a team decision. However, they admitted that what they really needed was to have one person just take control and make the decision. Some women may need to develop a better sense of timing about when exactly to stop building consensus and gathering information and simply make a decision with the information available. CEOs and other very senior managers frequently need to display exactly this type of decisive behavior every day when making decisions on things about which they have only limited information. Some women tend to put off making a decision, especially a tough decision, until they have enough information—a scenario that may never occur. Sometimes you just need to jump in and take the risk.

Women tend to be better listeners than men. They are especially good at information gathering and developing relationships and networks which can facilitate effective communication, and thereby lead to good decisions. You may need to "learn to be yourself" as you develop success or leadership skills. Remember, women who do not conform at least somewhat to expected gender norms may not be well accepted. In other words, women who are too tough, too cold, too controlling, or too masculine tend to be ostracized by both men and women. It's better to strive to be an effective combination of masculine and feminine attributes and skills.

BASIC DIFFERENCES IN COMMUNICATION

One major difference between men and women highlighted by the research is that men appear to communicate more frequently than women.[31] Interestingly enough, research shows that men frequently interact more with people above them in authority than women do. We may not know who has initiated the contact with these men, but we do know that women tend to receive more information *from* their superiors. In addition, women seem to consider peer interaction more important than men do. Research has also found that men tend to communicate with people in other functional groups (different departments or divisions) more often than women do. Women seem to prefer face-to-face interaction, whereas men tend to pick up the telephone.

Other research has shown that women may stay in their immediate area to communicate, whereas men seem to prefer to be away from their work location, outside their office setting. Interestingly, in a higher-education setting, female students tend to interact with their advisers or professors in an office, whereas male students frequently talk with their professors in a lounge or other setting. It is very easy to see a correlation between this behavior and the proliferation of the old-boys' network, informal mentoring, and the like. (Remember that many of the successful women I interviewed held a lot of their major discussions in hallways, elevators, and other public places.)

Similarly, men tend to talk in scheduled meetings more frequently than women. They stick more to communicating about the task, whereas women tend to speak more frequently about other topics as well. The research also identifies several major areas about women's communication patterns as they move ahead in organizations. First, as a woman gains additional responsibility, she tends to communicate with people in other departments more frequently. In addition, more senior women tend to have fewer unscheduled meetings, while scheduled meetings increase. It also appears, however, that numerous employees interacting with a relatively small number of more senior managers may cause information overload on the part of the senior managers.[32] A recommendation for women as they advance may be found again in the idea of flexibility. That is, it may be helpful for women to assess the communication style or immediacy or urgency and respond accordingly.

For example, face-to-face communication may go a long way to ensure clear understanding of information which may otherwise be misinterpreted. On the other hand, the telephone, especially armed with voice mail, may be the ideal solution for routine task information. My colleagues all agree that as annoying as it may be at times, voice mail is a great invention for leaving basic messages, relaying general information, confirming dates and times, and so forth. You frequently can avoid things like phone tag and unduly lengthy conversations in this way. It can be a great time-management device!

Some female managers may make themselves more accessible to their subordinates at the time when problems or questions arise. However, this type of open-door policy can also cause significant interruptions in their work. How many times do you find your colleagues, subordinates, and bosses just stopping in whenever they have a question or problem? While it's great in theory to have an open-door policy, it can create havoc in your schedule. Some research indicates that high performers have significantly fewer interruptions than moderate performers. Now that's a surprise! They have more time to get more things done. It might be advisable to try to set up specific times to arrange meetings and have the attendees gather all necessary questions or information. You can then handle everything at one time, rather than during periodic interruptions. Or you may want to leave your door (if you have a door) half open, rather than open all the way. You may also get in the habit of using humorous signs on your office entrance to indicate whether it's a good or bad time to come in. Even a humorous "do not disturb" or "do not enter—I'm thinking" sign will give the right message, but in a relaxed, informal way. Develop a pattern or routine and let people know your system and respect it.

In one of my classes, I asked the students—predominately women in their twenties, thirties, and forties—what differences they felt existed between men and women in their workplace. Interestingly enough, a number of the women in their thirties and forties jumped right up and started to cite various situations they had experienced. One woman said that while she was working her tail off to complete deadlines, her male counterparts were talking on the phone, going to lunch, playing golf, and having fun! And they were the ones getting the recognition, the promotions, the raises. She said that it really irks her. A few of the other women agreed. However, when we analyzed what was happening, a realization took place. We framed the scenario in terms of exactly what the men were doing. Yes, to the women involved it seemed as though the men were just hanging out, having fun, and not doing any work. But to the men—and especially to the company—it was obvious that they were developing important relationships, gaining visibility for themselves and for the company, forming networks, communicating. While the woman was in her office or cubicle slaving to get the work done, they were working smart.

Women and men agree that they take a lot of work home with them or spend long hours during the evening or weekends entertaining customers or clients that other employees never see. Since so many organizations and consequently their employees still frame work in what is accomplished from 9 a.m. to 5 p.m., we may not be aware of what hard-working employees are doing before or after hours. Although I still sometimes feel a bit uncomfortable espousing self-promotion (the socialization thing!), it is very important to let your bosses know—subtly—that you are spending the extra time and effort outside the office. Otherwise, they really may not know.

Are you frequently the first one in your office or the last one to leave? Does anyone see you or know that? Unless you let other people casually know that you're working above and beyond the call of duty, they may just assume you're working as hard as the next person—which may not be very hard! You may want to casually mention, "You know, it's so nice to be able to get so much accomplished between 7:30 and 9:00 a.m., before the phones start ringing" or "Wow, you know how working on the computer is—you think that you're going to finish a project in a couple of hours and the next thing you know, you've gotten into it so much that you look at the clock and it's 11 at night!" or "It's amazing. Just looking at this marketing piece, you would think it could have been done in an hour, not the 8 hours I spent on it!" You're not complaining or brown-nosing, just indicating that you spent a lot more time on your project or at work than it may appear to others. People who appear not to be working that hard as they talk on the phone or play golf may in fact be spending a good deal of their own time on their work.

So, in essence, these men (and women) who appear to be having fun may actually be working smart. (Of course, there is always the possibility that they are just having a good time, but eventually their bosses will catch on. Hopefully it won't be too long before the truth catches up with them!) Try to identify those who are getting ahead and what they are doing. Also try to notice if many of the women in your organization are the ones who are working hard, but not smart. Are they working on highly visible projects? Who are their contacts within the organization? Who knows about their projects, their hard work, their commitment, their creativity? Does anyone know? If your bosses don't know, it's up to you to let them know! (For more information on gaining visibility, see Success Secret Two.)

By the way, in this same class, the women in their twenties added that they really do not see the same disparity between men and women. To them, it's more of a difference between older employees and younger ones. Younger women frequently do not see, or perhaps have not yet experienced, the same differences that slightly older or more experienced women have had.

Try to pay attention in the next couple of weeks to the dynamics in your organization, or in your division, or on your team. You will probably notice that if there's a situation in which men feel that they can improve their work environment, network, meet senior managers, gain visibility, and move ahead, most men will go for it. If they are inundated with work and a senior manager wants to have lunch, for example, they'll go to the lunch meeting and just figure out a way to get the work done later in the day. Women, on the other hand, will say that they have too much work to do and may not take advantage of a networking opportunity. But that goes back to the old thought that if you work hard enough and get the right education and experience, you will move ahead. It's amazing how many women still do make this choice, thinking that if they don't look like they're constantly working at their desks, they will not get recognition from their boss. However, just the opposite is often true. Networking with well-placed people may be just the added boost your career needs. So examine any choices between working hard and working smart!

We can't stereotype men and women. Just because an employee is a woman, we can't assume that she's nurturing. Likewise, we can't assume a man to be tough and decisive just because he's a man. We can't go by preconceived ideas. There needs to be, as well, an effective balance of masculine and feminine traits in any organization. However, frequently men are categorized as being more task-oriented, while women often are seen to be more person-oriented. The organization may pick up on this and even become categorized as a male-centered organization or a female-friendly organization.

A while back, a friend of mine who works at a large financial institution said that the company was in the middle of a consultant's visit to examine its organizational practices and to make recommendations. I was only in graduate school at the time, but I made the same observations as the seasoned consultant from a large firm. It was obvious! The company had developed an organizational culture on such a strong male, military model that the teamwork and effective communication got lost. People did not usually work together as a team, but as adversaries. They were

in it for the short-term bonus, not for the long-term good of the
organization. By the way, it's no surprise that women do not
generally do particularly well in this type of organization unless
they become female counterparts of their male colleagues.

Mary, a medical editor, talks about her previous publishing
position in which there was an ongoing discussion among the
editors about the need for a women's health book. The men
couldn't figure out why such a specific book would be necessary—
or if it would sell.

Even school environments can be dictated by the "male-
ness" or "femaleness" of the course or classroom culture. On a
television special about how girls are sometimes shortchanged
in school through course selection and attention by teachers,
an interesting comparison was made. Thanks to a grant to
study possible imbalances, two calculus-based physics classes,
taught by the same (male) teacher, were compared. Obviously
there were no underachievers in this student group! One class
was conducted in the "traditional" male-oriented format. Only
a few female students were enrolled in the class, which was set
up with desks in traditional rows, with traditional class interaction of lecture, then application. The students were given the
problem to solve individually, then told to raise their hands
when done. The teacher then was to go to each student and
assess the solution. Here is the pattern: The class becomes
very quiet. Then a young man raises his hand. The teacher
goes over. He says, good job, that's the answer. Next student
(male), same thing, correct answer. Next student (male), same
thing. Finally, the fifth or sixth student is a young woman, who
tentatively raises her hand to show that she has solved the
problem. The teacher quietly (but loudly enough for the young
men to hear) tells the woman that her answer is incorrect and
that she needs to go back and recalculate it. You can see the
mortification in her face! It took a lot of courage for her even
to raise her hand in this kind of environment—no less be publicly seen as a failure in front of the other students!

Then, we go to the other class. Same teacher, totally different setup. The class is all female. Instead of desks and rows,
the class is seated around tables with four students each. The

same problem is assigned, only this time there is a lot of conversation and interaction going on. Students are comfortably asking questions of the teacher. Students are helping other students. You can see young women's faces light up as they understand a problem that has been vexing them—now they see it! Later, several young women are interviewed. One student says that at first she wasn't happy about being in a single-sex class for fear that she wouldn't be as challenged or learn as much. But now, several weeks into the class, she admits that she is learning much more effectively. (At about this point in the show, I begin thinking to myself, "It makes much better pedagogical sense to teach all the classes like this, not just the ones for young women. Why don't they just change the teaching style in these and other classes?" Two minutes later, the teacher says, "This format was so successful, we have decided to teach all similar classes like this next year!") Of course, it's using the "female" characteristics of communication, team building, sharing, and helping to meet the frequently challenging demands of learning. It was clear even in this situation that the "masculine"-oriented class was not nearly as effective as a combination of masculine and feminine characteristics!

> *Gay Haskins, a management expert at the London School of Business, cites several differences between men and women. Men, she says, are more activity-oriented, taking initiatives, whereas women are more concerned about what is happening in the group. They want to facilitate a positive atmosphere in which everyone can grow. She adds that the female culture is more collectivist than the male culture. Women don't think as much about position; it's more important to influence. They also frequently need to like the people they work with, whereas men consider this far less important. For women, working together, participation, and cooperation are often crucial.*

PERCEPTIONS OF MEN AND WOMEN

Many women have heard the comparisons of behavior between men and women. Given the same behavior, men are go-getters, women are pushy. He is tough, she is bitchy. He's leaving because he sees opportunities, she's leaving because she's undependable. He's having lunches with his boss because they're solving problems, she's having an affair. He's flexible, she's indecisive. Are these perceptions true? Well, although these are stereotypes, there are still organizations that foster this kind of thinking. Luckily these organizations are gradually being held accountable for change.

On a lighter note, in her book *How Men Think*, Adrienne Mendell sums up a lot about male-female behavior. She shares a great analogy: A man she interviewed summed up a lot of male-female behavior by saying that when he sees a button he just has to push it to see what it does.[33] When I asked a number of my male friends about it, they all said, "Oh yeah, me too!" Think about computers, for example. If you watch a lot of men who aren't too computer-literate, they just jump in and start pointing and clicking, whereas many women who are computer neophytes will often wait to be given instructions before they touch anything. (The men's behavior may be a sign of positive risk taking. Women may want to start emulating this ability to jump into technology.)

On the other hand, it comes as no surprise, for example, that men don't like to ask for help, especially at work, for the same reasons that they don't like to ask directions. It's the challenge. It's not just in front of women that men don't ask directions, but in general. They like to conquer the situation by themselves, not ask someone for help. Men often won't come right out and say, "Could you help me with this?" They'll do it in another, more indirect way. They don't want to look stupid, so they may talk about a related topic, then go to the area in which they had a question. They may try to present the question in a different form, often couched as an observation. For example, they may start a conversation about a related topic, then casually say, "Wow, do you believe that memo? What was that all about, anyway?"

Many, probably most, of the women we spoke to had generally positive things to say about working with men. However, it probably comes as a result of getting to know them on an individual basis over a period of time. Also, women have frequently needed to conform to male environments to get ahead, rather than vice versa. Their leadership styles may often be more congruent with men's in order to make it in these environments.

> One director states, for example, that most men are probably not malicious in their stereotypes. At first they may bluster about having women in meetings, about not being able to tell their jokes, but then they get over it.

> Another executive said that even though her boss doesn't particularly like women in his field, he's always helped her to be more successful.

> A number of women have cited men as their mentors. One woman admires her CEO. When making her own decisions, she frequently asks herself what he would do in this situation.

When I asked some of my male friends and colleagues about their views on men and women, there were some things they told me that really surprised me, or that I hadn't really thought about. For example, several guys in a row observed that women seem to hold grudges longer than men. I had thought about it before, but it was interesting that men had chosen to mention it—sometimes without my bringing it up. Some of them think that some women don't know how to just "get over it" or "let it go." (I started to think that I may have been guilty of holding grudges, as well, without even thinking about it!) But most of the men I talked to had very positive things to say about working with both men and women. It's very interesting, especially when you know people very well, to hear their real thoughts on various things.

How do men see male coworkers? They view working together as a team situation, not as a contest.

> One company president says, "If one of the team members doesn't pull his weight, the other team members let him know about it. The team is forced to solve the problem."

> "As long as they're cool, I like the camaraderie."

> "There's no bulls—t. Like when I was in grad school—everyone was trying to help each other get through the exams."

One man said that he didn't choose to be in an all-male group; it just formed that way. They just gravitated toward others like themselves—they were men.

How did some of the men feel about working with women?

> "We're all equal. We were all selected on the basis of our skills and qualifications to do the job. Accounting is not that gender-sensitive, at least at the beginning."

> "We've all been working together for 10 years as a team. We're all just interested in doing the best job we can."

> "Women are better at working on teams. They're more caring of detail and better organized."

> "When I occasionally hear a sexist statement about women, I just say, 'Look, this is the nineties. They're just as capable as we are.'"

I wouldn't have asked this question of the men I interviewed; it wouldn't have been appropriate without building mutual trust. So I asked a lot of my professional male friends and colleagues, who know me well enough to tell me their honest opinions about what men didn't like about working with women? Some said:

> "I don't like having to deal with those women things. They tend to be less stable in their personality and their treatment of you."

> "They're more moody. Guys are more consistent in their behavior; women are less predictable. A guy can ask a woman a question one day and be fine, then ask the same question and get chewed out in a totally different way the next day."

> "I wouldn't mind having a female boss as long as she acted consistently."

> "Women are always competing with each other. They seem to waste a lot of time worrying about everyone else and not spending enough time doing what they need to get ahead."

> "Do women all hold grudges? It seems that they take a long time just to 'get over it.'"

It's interesting to see some of the reactions of men working with women. Who says that there aren't still stereotypes? But all the men I spoke to really were very open-minded and had no problem working with women who were "cool." This is a very good case for the legitimacy of gender roles, rather than actual gender. Some women really are like one of the guys— they have absolutely no difficulty in being accepted in groups of men and men acknowledge this. Other women are more typically "feminine" in their characteristics, and some men may not fully understand their behavior. Some of the men I spoke to probably were still seeing two sides of women: one through their preconceived stereotypes (men's socialization and early experiences) and another through their firsthand knowledge of working and attending classes with their female peers. Others had no difficulty whatsoever in accepting women as peers and bosses. They may have had very positive experiences with women, both at an early stage and later at school and work. I think that many men have not yet had a female boss and therefore may have difficulty in assessing how a woman would lead. It's probably natural for men to have a certain discomfort at first, based on stereotypes and preconceptions, until they come into contact with effective female bosses and have effective one-on-one professional relationships.

DIFFERENCES IN MENTORING BETWEEN MEN AND WOMEN

There may be some evidence that female managers need a different type of mentoring than their male counterparts. In a study of male and female executives, it was found that women, more than men, tended to gain self-confidence, useful career advice, counseling on organizational politics, and feedback about their weaknesses when in a mentoring situation.[34] As with anything else, if we feel comfortable in a one-on-one situation, we can learn much more about ourselves and our environment than we may have the opportunity to do in a group setting. We may feel uncomfortable or even stupid asking questions or discussing issues in a group. We may feel intimidated and vulnerable. Mentors can help us develop our skills and confidence. Our position in the organization may also have some impact. Women in lower-level positions may need more emphasis on role modeling and assistance with learning their roles, while women at more senior levels may look for career development and gaining credibility and legitimacy in the organization.

Men often seek out mentors, use them as effectively as they can, then move on to the next mentoring situation which will benefit their new status or position. Women, on the other hand, may maintain the relationship, perhaps even past the time in which it is helpful. What this may mean is that women are far less proactive in seeking out mentors, depend on them more, and are less willing to move on even after they cannot learn anything more from the mentor. This, in my opinion, may be due to the very nature of gender roles. Women tend to be relationship-oriented rather than goal-oriented. They see a mentoring situation as developing an ongoing relationship, whereas men may see mentors as more of a path to a goal— their goal—a means to an end. This appears to be a fundamental difference between men and women and their perceptions and goals with regard to mentors.

DO OLD-BOYS' NETWORKS WORK FOR WOMEN?

The old-boys' network has proved to be extremely successful— for men, but not for women. Why is this true? First, men often just feel much more comfortable around other men than around women. They're used to hanging out with men in sports, in fraternities, on golf courses, and in the locker room. Men are predictable in their behavior, no surprises. They can relate to one another. These experiences generally develop into more well-defined experiences in the workplace, as an extension of men's earlier socialization.

Second, men usually use networks that are more task-oriented, those that center on getting a job done. Women, on the other hand, generally prefer networks built on trust and reciprocity, often found in close, personal relationships. From the beginning there is a good chance that men and women will have totally different agendas from a networking perspective. They're often looking for different things from a network.

Third, men and women generally relate more favorably to specific gender roles. Therefore, men may feel some discomfort with women who exhibit more masculine characteristics, such as being tough and aggressive, or with men who are less masculine in their behavior. (However, men generally relate well to women who exhibit a positive combination of masculine and feminine traits, described as being a "sister"—one of the guys, but not too masculine.) A number of women I interviewed said that they specifically chose a "sister" type of relationship. A similar pattern holds for women. They generally relate better to more masculine men and to women who fit a more feminine, nurturing gender role.

What this may mean, then, is that women feel much more comfortable developing networking relationships with others who have had similar experiences—other women, for the most part. Some men admittedly would have some difficulty in sharing their experiences with women, since they have usually not faced the same barriers and biases that women have. In addition, from a networking perspective, many men would not feel particularly uncomfortable contacting an old college friend for a favor, even though they haven't seen him for years. Women would probably not feel as comfortable doing the same thing. They may feel more guilty about not having maintained the relationship and may not want to take advantage of someone.

Many of the successful women I interviewed indicated that, even at their level, they felt some awareness of an old-boys' network. They thought that there was some gender stereotyping of women as less tough, less able to get the job done or make the difficult decisions. However, they generally felt that this stereotyping had not kept them from advancing, since they had learned how to counteract the stereotypes effectively. They added that in a one-on-one professional situation, the man usually started to relate to them (indicating that they were "OK after all"), which helped them gain acceptance and visibility. Therefore, in addition to personal and professional friendships with other women, it may be advantageous for women to increase their networking circle to include senior-level men in a professional relationship. Not only can this serve to effectively expand their circle of influence, it may also begin to dispel the stereotypes that many men hold about women. Senior-level men may even begin to overcome their preconceived stereotypes about women as a result.

These stereotypes may be the result of men's own experiences with the roles of women. They may see women as a reflection of various roles, such as mother, wife, daughter, girlfriend, sister. Several of the women I interviewed agreed that women may fall into these stereotypes. The "mother" role may instill feelings of domineering control or supernurturing, which is inappropriate in the workplace. The "wife" image, on the other hand, may sometimes be perceived as overly dependent upon the male manager. An image of "girlfriend or lover" may be apparent if there is a perception of physical attraction regarding female colleagues or employees. A "sister" role conveys a sense of camaraderie, mutual respect, and equality. Not surprisingly, a number of participants cited this image as their perceived role among male counterparts. It's one that is comfortable and effective. Women's colleagues and bosses feel comfortable with the sister role. They know what to expect.

It is also interesting that, although some women feel that they need to be "one of the guys" in their personality and comportment, taking this behavior to an extreme as a male clone can actually be counterproductive. As I mentioned, many men and women consider extreme masculine behavior to be beyond the norm and inappropriate for women. They feel a greater sense of comfort with more "accepted" female roles. Many colleagues, both male and female, are uncomfortable with women telling off-color jokes, acting too much like men, trying too hard to be tough, and so forth. There should ideally be an appropriate compromise between masculine and feminine behavior.

As noted earlier, men's biases about women are often the result, not of malicious intentions, but simply lack of knowledge. Many male managers, especially those in their fifties and sixties, still do not readily accept women as peers in the workplace. For much of their careers, these senior managers may have experienced more traditional role models for women at home, while they generally saw working women relegated to the ranks of support staff positions. So it makes sense that, after years of this assumption, many older men find it difficult to readjust their perceptions. It may help an aspiring woman advancing within the organization to be aware of their point of reference and assumptions and try to understand where these men are coming from. Communication greatly helps, as does having a sense of humor when appropriate. A number of the study respondents said that they had in fact experienced bias themselves, but did not wear their hearts on their sleeve—they learned how to deal with it effectively. Not necessarily limited to gaining their own personal awareness, they frequently were able to change the attitudes of their more biased colleagues as well. Connie Glaser, in her book *Swim with the Dolphins*, notes that effective communication is especially appropriate in this situation, since stereotypes are based on anonymity.[35] Once a senior-level man gets to know you as a competent, effective, hard-working manager, instead of his previous perception of women in support roles only, the stereotype may begin to dissipate as you gain respect and recognition.

Yes, it is a fact that men in the workplace frequently discuss sports. Many of the women I interviewed said that they were sports fans too, either as participants or as spectators, although several of the women said that they hated sports. But even if these women were not huge sports fans, they often made a point to at least be familiar with what was going on in the sports world. They were current on who was playing which games, who made the great plays, and who won. By the way, participation in sports is also frequently cited as important in leadership development, so if you can get involved, you may not only develop your skills but have a lot of fun as well!

Women should also be aware of what's hot in their professional, business, and technology fields, especially new trends that affect their departments. Professional journals, business publications such as *Newsweek, Business Week* and *The Wall Street Journal,* and technology periodicals like *PC Magazine* can go a long way to inform and update women who need to know what's going on.

It's amazing how much pertinent information you can bring up in conversations just by reading publications in your field. If you know and use the buzzwords attached to business and technology in your area, many male managers will most likely start to see you as "one of the guys" and begin talking to you about the "stuff" they enjoy. Gender will probably become secondary to the topics of conversation and you will be well on your way to gaining entrance into the "club." You may very well say that you shouldn't have to talk about what men talk about. Well, depending upon the environment, this may be true. Unfortunately, until women are extremely well ensconced in senior levels of organizations, schmoozing helps. It can be a very systematic way to be political and gain visibility among the key decision makers. Besides, why not challenge yourself to learn about areas that you may never have explored? It may be fun!

SENSE OF HUMOR

When I asked the respondents which characteristic they particularly liked about themselves, a fair number of them said their sense of humor. Especially in areas that have traditionally been male domains, a sense of humor can make the difference between a difficult, uncomfortable situation and one that can be worked out. Many women should be careful, however, not to turn their colleagues off by trying to conform too much to a masculine type of humor, especially off-color humor. Depending upon the situation, some men (and women) feel uncomfortable with women who try to behave too much like men. Research has shown that men and women frequently dislike those who are not consistent with their gender.[36] However, the ability to joke and tease in a comfortable fashion certainly can make many an uncomfortable situation tolerable.

Men may try to test a woman to see if she can handle teasing. They want to see if they can treat the woman like one of the guys or if she will react negatively. It's far better if you can join in the humor, providing it's appropriate, and be able to laugh at yourself and just give back the same teasing or sarcasm you receive. It levels the playing field—men will accept you on the team more easily. Being accepted by the men in your organization is not your ultimate goal to be sure, but it may prove very useful in creating an overall plan of gaining access to information that you may need, gaining influence in decision making, developing team unity, opening communication channels, and so forth.

> *Diana Brooks, who runs Sotheby's, recounted in an article in Fortune magazine a story about when she first attended a meeting of senior executives as the only woman.*[37] *The president suggested that she make some coffee. She humorously said, "I'll get the coffee if you photocopy these pages for me." He laughed.*

How you respond to such comments may be tied to your perceived role and what that role connotes. It may also have to do with your sense of self—your security, your accomplishments, and your socialization. If you feel good about yourself, you can take yourself less seriously, because you have less to prove. Keep in mind, as well, that adding humor to the workplace can be a distinct advantage. It helps morale and can really build a good team attitude.

SUMMARY

- Gender roles may be more indicative of behavior than actual gender. Men and women may exhibit masculine or feminine traits, or more likely a combination of the two.
- Socialization (life experiences, family, physical makeup, role models, and peers) is specific to each person within the framework of society's expectations of how men and women should behave. Certain societal expectations may reflect our gender, but individual experiences may cause us not to conform to those expectations.
- From an early age, girls have traditionally been socialized to be respectful, polite, friendly, and humble, while boys are generally socialized to be competitive, challenging, and

independent. These traits have been reflected in our games and have often continued into our adult lives. Fortunately, this pattern of socialization is starting to change.

- Understanding "the rules" is important, since men and women have frequently been raised with quite different rule definitions. Women are often at a disadvantage, for example, thinking that if you work hard you'll get ahead. Men generally know that you need to work hard as well as take risks, network, gain visibility, and have effective mentors to get ahead—they know the rules of the game.

- Men and women are generally viewed more favorably (by both men and women) when they conform to stereotypical roles.

- If you are just starting out or looking for a job change, it may be helpful to seek out an organization that matches your personal style. It may be quite difficult to make it in an organization in which your work style is not congruent with the organizational culture.

- It is important to receive feedback or criticism without taking it personally.

- Women have often been socialized to spare others' feelings, while men have learned to put others down in order to get ahead. The rules of the game are frequently very different between genders.

- Women frequently cite their successes as a member of a team, whereas men often give themselves the credit for a success, perhaps as the leader of the team.

- Frequently, while women slave away at their desks to get work done, men appear to be goofing off, having fun. But on closer examination, these men are frequently developing networks, building relationships, gaining visibility, and influencing decision makers.

- Women frequently see a mentoring situation as developing an ongoing relationship, while men may see mentors as more of a path to a goal—their goal—a means to an end. This appears to be a fundamental difference between men and women and their perceptions and goals with regard to mentors.

- In addition to their personal and professional friendships with other women, it may be advantageous for women to increase their networking circle to include senior-level men in a professional relationship. Not only can this serve to effectively expand their circle of influence; it may also begin to dispel the existing stereotypes of women held by male colleagues. Senior-level men may very well begin to overcome some of their preconceived stereotypes of women as a result.

- If you think you're being singled out and treated badly because you're a woman, first see if the boss treats men any differently. Be objective. It could be true or it could just be the boss's personality or leadership style.

- Men frequently identify someone who can help them, then develop a relationship with that person. Women often leave advancement to chance.

SUCCESS STRATEGIES WHEN YOU'RE DOWNSIZED

One of the most difficult things about looking for a job when you don't have a job is the stigma that being out of work is somehow your fault. You may even view yourself as a "loser"—no matter what your skills or your former position! You may think, "Well, if I'm so great, why doesn't anyone want to hire me?" This is an absolutely natural reaction and feeling. People just handle it in different ways. For example, some people withdraw from their friends and family. Although a certain period of "mourning" is natural, it can be extremely counterproductive if it goes on too long. Other people just grit their teeth, get dressed, and hit the streets with their résumé in hand. I would guess that most people fall somewhere in between. They're motivated for a variety of reasons to find a new position, but they may have their down days.

This is when it is especially critical to increase your visibility through an effective network, especially through people who are your advocates. These three areas—visibility, networking, and a support group—are often inextricably intertwined. Although it can be excruciatingly difficult to motivate yourself and get out there to do a job search, the alternative of not working is far less appealing! Most jobs aren't going to find you. How can employers know that you are available for a position? Part of it will be luck, but more of it is letting enough people know that you're looking so that they automatically think of you.

You may want to join a professional temporary organization, which provides short-term positions to professionals. Temping promises to become a booming area as the contingent, project-based environment evolves. Many organizations will need highly skilled people for a specified period of time, contrary to their former practice of employing a long-term workforce. Here is an excellent means of developing new skills and increasing your visibility and subsequently your network of possible employers—not to mention keeping a paycheck coming in! Although a temporary position may be somewhat unsettling as a choice of work environment, it may increasingly become the norm, so it could be advantageous to develop this kind of flexibility.

Another effective way of maintaining or developing contacts is to join or participate in professional associations. These can be fun as well as advantageous to your job search. Not only will you be able to meet and network with others in the areas you would like to be employed, but you may develop a cadre of people who can promote your visibility to others, as well as give you leads on possible positions. In addition, at this time of stress, it can be a good idea to forget about some of your problems for a while and just have a little fun. Here's where your support network can be of enormous help. When you're having one of your bad days and don't want to go out and network, your supporters can usually pump you up enough to get moving.

In Philadelphia, as in many other cities, professional organizations, international chambers of commerce, and various other groups frequently hold purely social activities—pub nights, barbecues, and other informal gatherings—in addition to professional speaking engagements and formal programs. It may lower your stress level to be at a less formal gathering.

A lot of people who are between jobs feel enormously self-conscious about not being in a professional environment at that moment, which is natural. In various networking situations, you may want to develop a "script" about your current status when asked the inevitable question about what you do, which may be perceived as a reflection of your entire identity. Some people I know feel incredibly uncomfortable in these situations. I tell them, "Just extrapolate what you're doing. No one really cares." But they reply, "Well, I know and I care!" A lot of your success will be in how you present yourself. Obviously it is a painful experience. But you will get another job! In the meantime, you may have to temporarily "create" a new identity for yourself. If you do not have a job, you may want to take classes to retool. Now, you can say that you have "taken this opportunity to go back to school," which you've been wanting to do for years, instead of being "just unemployed." The chances are good that people will be far more interested in what you're studying and the discussion will take off from there. If you take a temporary assignment, your position is that you have decided to stretch yourself in a new area, or function, or industry to develop your marketable skills. If you are at home with your children, then this becomes the first opportunity you have had to spend quality time with your kids. You have now created a well-thought-out identity in response to the unfortunate situation of losing your job. People—especially those who may lead you to a job—are far more impressed with a confident (even if only on the outside), well-directed person than with someone who is just drifting, waiting for the next job to drop out of the sky.

Although it is very unsettling not to be working—and many of us have been there—it doesn't mean that you can't be spending that time effectively. The worst thing, although sometimes the easiest, is to withdraw from the situation. But it is critical to call on your existing or new network to get you out doing what you need to do! Increase your visibility by attending professional seminars. Go to your local college and take a class on something you really need or really want to do. Join some new organizations. It's the law of averages: The more people you know—and who know that you're looking for a position—the better your chances will be of finding that new position! Don't forget, increasing numbers of people have lost their jobs at one point in their careers. These people are undoubtedly going to be far more understanding of your situation, and their support should significantly reduce your feelings of discomfort. Anyone who has gone through a downsizing may be far more apt to help you out as well. I think that this can really make an uncomfortable situation far more productive.

UPDATING YOUR SKILLS

Being between jobs is an excellent opportunity to upgrade and fine-tune some of your skills, skills that may be necessary in your next position. As I said, you may want to take classes in computer technology, business writing, or technical writing. You may want to develop your presentation skills or learn desktop publishing or a spreadsheet program. You may really need this time to increase your marketability and improve your résumé.

If you can afford it financially, you may want to volunteer or serve as an intern in the type of industry or specific organization in which you would like to work. This may be an excellent way to network and increase your visibility in the field. It will be a good way to update your résumé as well. Many organizations would be all too happy to have workers with your experience and skills. Keep in mind that this is part of your route to a full-time, permanent position. Professional and charity organizations and associations are always in need of extra public relations professionals, people to help organize functions or run events and do fund-raising.

I know, you may think that it will never happen to you. "I have tenure. I have seniority. I am at the top. I'm well liked and respected." Well, CEOs are fired. Tenured college professors at a small private school who thought that their futures were secure find themselves out looking for jobs when their school closes its doors. The rising star who is so well connected loses favor when a new senior management team comes in. It *can* happen, no matter who you are or who you know!

I have spoken to hundreds of people who either are in danger of losing their jobs or have already lost their jobs. Many of them were completely blindsided by the announcement, and many are managers who didn't see the writing on the wall. Sometimes you can see the signals and sometimes you can't— or maybe you don't want to. In any case, the devastating reality is the same: loss of identity and self-esteem, the sense of drifting without a rudder. I've been there, as has just about everyone I know. Usually, once it's happened to you, you swear that you will never again be taken by surprise in that way. I think that some lessons are learned best when they're the hardest to learn.

In my last college position, one of my duties was to serve as academic liaison to the Pennsylvania Department of Labor for students who had lost their jobs. These people were given the opportunity to be retrained for up to 2 years and often needed help in deciding on a direction to take. I gained a lot of insight into the process, both organizationally and individually, of job loss. Part of my role, when meeting the educational needs of displaced workers, evolved into brainstorming ways in which these students could retrain and effectively get back into the workforce. Now I don't claim to be a career specialist, but after you talk to as many people as I have, you start to realize a few things. It becomes especially apparent to me, with my knowledge of the workplace of the future, that this trend was not going away. So I wanted to see how my strategies for success could translate into career planning and management. They do!

It was not surprising that most of these people did not have particularly effective networks, for example. Many needed serious work on skills development. Most shared a great sense of loss and had difficulty in motivating themselves, but they were seeking training, so that was the first major step. This can be a very big risk, especially for those who have never been to college. Another key strategy, developing a support group, can be foreign to some people. Men, especially, tend to withdraw from the very people who can make up an effective support network. Women are usually better at sharing their personal side, their emotions and feelings, than are men. Sharing can be especially critical at this time.

When you lose your job, and frequently with it your sense of identity, it can be extraordinarily difficult to pick yourself up and start changing your job search strategies. The best time to start, of course, is at the first hint of a layoff. I read somewhere that if you have a sense that layoffs are coming in your company—if things aren't going well financially or if there are takeover plans—follow your intuition. It's probably going to happen! Prepare as soon as humanly possible for your new position. It will probably take a lot longer than you imagine to find a new position, especially if you earn a high salary. Keep in mind, also, that the new world of work is characterized by less job security and the need for flexibility. This may just be your first trial run, so it will pay off to become proficient at always having an effective strategy.

Some outplacement firms or recruitment experts may tell you to give your résumé to everyone you come in contact with—all your acquaintances, the bread man, the plumber, and so on. While in theory this concept may have validity, it doesn't seem to work very well. I believe that those who really care about you one way or another are the ones who will keep their ears open for a position for you—not just anyone. People have their own lives and their own problems. You have probably found that if you sent a résumé blindly to a company, 200 or 300 other people, all with basically the same background, were doing the same thing. So getting your foot in the door is the hardest part. That's when your contacts come into play—your network.

If you are faced with imminent job loss, start analyzing your situation right away! Don't lull yourself into a false sense of security and think that a layoff won't happen or that you can put it off. Most business and management experts agree that, even though some companies are truly committed to their employees, for the most part there is not a lot of benevolence in organizations today. The bottom line is the most important factor, even if it means significant layoffs. An employee must increasingly be in charge of his or her own path. Start honestly evaluating your own skills. If you don't have a degree, are you or will you be prevented from getting the job you really want? To get a similar job in another company, will you need further education or training? Do you have a degree that won't get you a job in today's employment environment? (Or do you have a nearly worthless degree, like mine in French?) A history or psychology degree may make you a very well-rounded person, but I can almost guarantee that it won't get you a job unless you augment your skill base. Do you possess good computer and other technology skills? Do you need to practice interviewing skills? Do you need help with your résumé? Do you have an effective network? It need not be as overwhelming as you may think to really get going on developing these skills. Besides, what's the alternative? Isn't it worth working hard on developing solid career management skills?

NETWORKING IF YOU'RE DOWNSIZED

Probably one of the most critical skills that job seekers need is to develop an effective network. It's really easy when you're in a comfortable position just to let your relationship building go the way of the wind. You keep meaning to stay in touch with your professional contacts. You know that you should check your rolodex each week to make your lunch appointments with colleagues and acquaintances, but you're just too busy! And now, when you have plenty of time on your hands, it's too late—you've lost touch with them. Well, no, it's never too late to resume contacts with colleagues (unless you have burned your bridges). It may just take a little longer or a little more effort to reestablish your network.

A number of students that I worked with as a college liaison lamented that they had let their network diminish. I told them that there was no time like the present to start building it again. Keep in mind, most other people are just as busy as you and they don't really notice how much time has passed. You may feel a bit guilty that you didn't keep up the contact, but neither did they! Just because you need help now doesn't mean that down the road they may not need something from you. (That should ease your guilt somewhat, at least.) Their reception to your suggestion that you reestablish contact may have a lot to do with your original relationship. If you had been quite friendly and built a rapport, they should be very pleased to help you out no matter how much time has transpired. Even those with whom you did not have a strong rapport will frequently be open at least to having lunch or playing a game of tennis. The big thing is that you need to take the first step. It may be hard at first, but that's part of challenging yourself. And keep in mind that you're developing a relationship, not only asking for a job lead. That's a very big difference to get straight in your own mind before you even begin!

Believe it or not, most people have a much more effective network than they think. When you are looking to develop a new network, especially for a job search, begin by examining a few key areas. First, you may want to make a list of the type of industry or the actual companies that you would like to work for. Start thinking about people you know who may work in those industries or for those companies. And remember, someone always knows someone, who knows someone else. Ask your friends, family, and acquaintances—your existing network—if they know anyone in those industries or companies. It's the law of averages. If you ask enough people, someone is bound to know someone else whom you want to know!

Once you have the names of people in various organizations, set up a plan of action. It's critical to remember that these people are busy too, and unless they're good friends of yours, they probably have other things on their mind than your job search. Try to see their perspective. If it's a mutual friend, it may be preferable to send or fax a short note a couple of days before you intend to call, so that the person will have an idea of who you are, who has recommended you, and what it is that you're looking for. Include your phone number in your note, but indicate that you will call the person's office to follow up. This alleviates the discomfort and anxiety of trying to explain who you are and what you want in 30 seconds on the phone. It also gives the recipient an opportunity to reflect at his or her leisure on how to help, as well as to think about other resources that he or she may be able to offer you.

(This method of sending information first, then following up, is a frequent approach in sales. I used it successfully when I started my research project.)

You may wish to meet the person, have a brief lunch, or just speak to your contact on the phone. Consider your strong points. If you feel that your asset is your physical presence and that you prefer in-person contact, try to meet in person. Again, assume that the person is very busy, and try to read his or her personality and agenda. If your contact is open and friendly, you may be able to follow that lead and talk about interests and so forth. If, however, the person is more business-oriented, try to be as concise as possible. (Remember, people gravitate toward others like themselves.) Always follow up with a thank-you note, handwritten if possible. (People like to receive handwritten notes to contrast with all the usual mail they get. Think about it. Which pieces of mail do you open first?)

Another very important, but underutilized, resource is your alma mater. Many people may think that if they have long since graduated, their alumni resource will be outdated. Contact your school for a list of graduates at various companies. The alumni office may offer various services, perhaps free or for a fee. Keep an eye on your alumni magazine or newspapers. Ask fellow alumni whom you may have kept in touch with.

I've done this myself. I kept hearing positive things about the senior management at USA Today/Gannett when I interviewed a number of terrific senior women there for my research. I remembered reading in my alumni magazine that the president and publisher of USA Today was a fellow alum. I wrote him a note indicating how impressive his executives were and what a good job the company was doing for women. He wrote me a nice note in return. I followed up several times with an offer to have lunch when I returned to Washington. We were unable to schedule a lunch date until about the third or fourth time I contacted him. He was delightful and took the time to talk with me about my research as well as his family and other matters. I certainly didn't ever think that I would be chatting pleasantly with the president of USA Today, but I was able to do so because of our shared alma mater.

One of the big pluses of going to an Ivy League or similar school is that you usually have contacts for life. But that doesn't mean other schools don't have a lot to offer as well. You can contact the alumni committee in your area. If you don't know, call the alumni office at the school and ask where your local committee is. The alumni group will probably know a lot of people in your area, so it's a good place to start networking.

If you find that you have to contact someone in an organization without a mutual acquaintance, you can still be successful. Get the name of the person responsible for a particular department or division and send out your introductory note or fax. Although you are actually looking for a job contact, don't necessarily approach it that way. Instead, seek out advice on updating your skills. People often like to be seen as experts. Ask them what they would look for in particular positions in their industry so that you can fill in any gaps in your background. Suggest that you are considering updating your skills by going back to school or taking classes or seminars. Which program do they feel would be most advantageous? Ask if you could take them to lunch, for example, to discuss what you may need to do in the future to become a good candidate either in their company or in the industry as a whole.

Remember, again, this is a process, not a one-shot deal. Some people will be happy to meet with you; others won't. Some people will not be able to give you any information; others will. Ask them to recommend other people in the company or industry who could answer questions or help you. (Now you're tapping into their internal network.) Find out if there is a professional organization that they would recommend joining. Ask for their frank advice on what's lacking in your background that gives other people an advantage in hiring. Keep in mind that you may just meet people with whom you "click," and they may become internal allies who will now be looking out for you. Again, always send a thank-you note for their time and interest. As with any networking activity, it takes a lot of time and effort—but it may be well worth the rewards!

SUMMARY

- You may want to join a professional temp organization, which provides short-term positions to professionals. Temping promises to become a booming area as the contingent, project-based environment evolves. Many organizations will need highly skilled people for a specified period of time, contrary to their former practice of employing a long-term workforce. This may be an excellent means of developing new skills, increasing your visibility, and subsequently building your network of possible employers.

- Maintain or develop contacts by joining or participating in professional organizations. These can be fun as well as advantageous to your job search. Not only will you meet and network with others in the areas you would like to be employed; you may also develop a cadre of people who can promote your visibility to others, as well as give you leads on possible positions.

- Increase your visibility by attending professional seminars. Go to your local college and take a class on something you really need or really want to do. Join some new organizations. It's the law of averages. The more people you know—and who know that you're looking for a position—the better your chances of finding that new position!

- Being between jobs is an excellent opportunity to upgrade and fine-tune some of your skills—skills that may be necessary in your next position.

- If you can afford it financially, you may want to volunteer or serve as an intern in the type of industry or specific organization in which you would like to work. This may be an excellent way to network and increase your visibility in the field.

- Most people have a much more effective network than they think. Start by making a list of the type of industry or the actual companies that you would like to work for. Think about people you know who may work for those companies or in those industries.

- An important, but underutilized resource is your alma mater. Many people think that if they have long since graduated, their alumni resource will be outdated. Contact your alumni office for a list of graduates at various companies.

INTERNATIONAL INFLUENCES

Since a fair number of the women I spoke to were from different countries and cultural backgrounds, I became curious about the possible differences in their attitudes toward success. Despite some differences in perspective, there seemed to be more similarities than differences among the international group.

Everyone keeps saying that the world is getting smaller. It's absolutely true, thanks in large part to technology. I pick up the phone and call my friends and colleagues overseas all the time. Today, a friend called from Hong Kong—you just have to keep a chart handy with the time zone differences! We e-mail and fax overseas all the time. (Europeans especially love faxes!) We can hop on a jet in New York and be in London or Paris in less than 4 hours. We watch the news from Paris, Tokyo, or Bonn every night on television. So, with all the opportunities available internationally, it's no surprise that people are gradually becoming more alike than different. With frequent exposure internationally, it has become far easier to learn, understand, and adapt to other cultures.

Many of the same issues facing working women in the United States face women all over the world. They increasingly want to have satisfying, rewarding jobs, and be able to effectively combine work and home. Certain countries or regions are just at different stages of their development.

Women in the United States seem to be further ahead in terms of equal opportunity, pay equity, and positive attitudes toward women in the workplace, yet European women are far ahead of their U.S. counterparts in terms of parental leave and life balance. Asian women, who have traditionally been relegated to lower-level positions, are starting new businesses in record numbers. In Japan, women are creating five out of six new firms, now numbering approximately 2.5 million businesses. In Singapore, 38 percent of women managers own their own firms and about 20 percent of business owners are women. In China, 34 percent of those who are self-employed are women, and they account for about 25 percent of all new businesses.

> *Pam Chen, a colleague who spent most of her early life and education in Japan, has kept me updated on trends in Asia. She regularly translates Japanese articles on women for me, points out the latest trends for business and professional women, and relates the experiences of her friends who have stayed in Asia or who have chosen to relocate elsewhere. She says that women are gradually beginning to emerge in a new professional role.*

> *Masako, an executive in Tokyo, is a good example of the modern Asian professional woman. She has worked for international companies for 30 years and has developed a wonderful career and reputation. She optimistically adds that there are better opportunities for women—especially younger, well-educated, bilingual women—than in the past.*

> *Taiwanese author Liou Fey Ying adds: "There are now role models for the women of the future. There is a wide spectrum of possibilities: becoming an entrepreneur, a professional manager, a wife, a social activist. The time has come for a thousand flowers to bloom."*

Most women will admit that the United States has been at the forefront of changes in the workplace, followed by Europe and the Pacific Rim. Issues about work and family and a quality work environment seem to be the major focus of women everywhere. A study of more than 7000 European women and men from five European countries was recently conducted by the Whirlpool Foundation in Michigan. A similar study was conducted in the United States and a project is planned for Asia next year. This study, which included participants from France, Spain, the United Kingdom, Italy, and Germany, cited several common areas of interest. Findings stated that 59 percent of working women in Europe provide half or more of their family's income. However, whereas 50 percent of the U.S. workforce is female, in Europe the figure is only 36 percent. And these women work for the same reasons as men do—they need the money. The study indicated that, if money were not an issue, most European women would prefer part-time work. Ninety-four percent agreed that their family was the most important part of their lives.

The study identified several very interesting points. First, in the United States, the greatest workplace concern is that employers may provide fewer benefits, whereas in Europe employees fear that new technology may result in job loss. Another viewpoint: In Italy, 32 percent viewed sexual harassment as a workplace concern, compared with 17 percent in the United States and 4 percent in Germany. Regarding family values, in Italy, Spain, and the United Kingdom, 10 to 11 percent of the participants associated family values with having children, while 30 percent of the French and 48 percent of the Germans made that association. When comparing the important values that parents wanted their children to be taught, 75 percent of the Europeans considered learning respect for others as being important, while computer literacy (at 2 percent) was the least important value for their kids to be taught at home. Most women agreed that they had jobs, not careers. In Spain, if a woman describes her work as a career, it is considered very prestigious, a positive thing, whereas in Italy, describing one's work as a career has a negative connotation for women. According to the study, Europeans realize that the conflict for women is not simply balancing work and home, but wanting more choices and flexibility in their decisions. This is a fairly new message for Europe.

INTERNATIONAL NETWORKING

Helen Solomons has conducted extensive research on networking. She observes that networking actually began in North America. A proponent of networking, she cites an example of international networking while attending a meeting in Brussels.

*She met an influential person who was looking for highly
qualified people to work in Brussels. Just the day before, she
coincidentally had spoken to a woman who was looking for a job
in Brussels, since her husband had just been transferred there. Dr.
Solomons had no idea that she would be able to facilitate a job
match within 2 days! You never know whom you will be speaking
to. This is an important part of natural versus planned
networking.*

Of course, in many parts of the world networking, or actually relationship building, is a way of life. In Asia and South
America especially, relationships form the basis of all business. Business is not done as quickly as it is in the United
States, but can take quite a long period of time to develop. It
often depends on how you perceive time!

*Gay Haskins, at the London School of Business, compares
U.S. and European networks. She finds that Americans are open
and friendly. In the United States, friendships are immediate and
you are almost expected to participate right away, even if you
really don't want to. In Europe, there is a lot of intranationality
networking. At conferences, for example, the British sit with the
British, the Spanish sit with the Spanish, and so forth.*

In 1995, the European Women's Management Development
Network conducted a survey of international women in management to examine their network and what it means for them. The
purpose of the study was to see the role that cultural differences
plays among women in management. Three countries were highlighted—the United Kingdom, Spain, and the United States.

The study found an overall profile of women's attitudes
toward networking, but there were also several striking differences. In general, the women belonged to mixed-gender networks, followed by women's professional networks and company networks. One of the most important ways in which women
access networks is through the recommendation of a colleague, friend, or business contact. Women in management
frequently join networks to learn about relevant issues at work,
to develop themselves, to make business or career contacts, or
to meet others with shared interests. Despite the apparent
importance of women joining networks, there are often barriers

to joining them, as you may imagine. Most frequently women lack the time to participate, or they experience conflicts with family demands (sound familiar?).

While there is much that the participants had in common, there were a number of interesting differences as well. It is increasingly important to be aware of these differences as more and more women find themselves in international environments.

The study identified American women as the "instrumentalists." Americans, considered skilled at networking, place greater emphasis on using a network for self-projection to increase visibility. Americans also frequently use networks for learning new skills or information, rather than for their social benefit. Some other cultures find it surprising that we place significantly less value on the social side of networking!

Women in the United Kingdom were described as the "developers." They often see networks as a vehicle for developing self-confidence rather than as a means to increase visibility. They are also more concerned that a network be outside their organization. (This was cited as a powerful persuader to join a network.)

Val Hammond, of Roffey Park Management Institute in England, agrees with this view. In our conversation, she indicated that it is very important to gain visibility and credibility outside your organization, which a network can effectively help you do.

Women in the United Kingdom also view networks as a place to learn, rather than to do business.

Viki Holton, of the Ashridge Management College, agrees with the study. Americans, in her opinion, frequently make new business contacts, while Europeans frequently want to learn skills. Being English, she agrees that Americans can sometimes come off as very assertive, but it's a cultural thing.

Participants in Spain were identified as the "socialites." They generally place a significantly higher level of importance on the social aspects of networking. Business and learning aspects were far less sought in a network. Rather, the "socialites" preferred to spend enjoyable time with other women. However, interestingly enough, the respondents said that in doing so they were likely to find suppliers for their business—unlike women in the United Kingdom, for example. Remember what we discussed earlier—networks should be relationship-based!

> *Flavia, a director in a publishing firm, feels that networks are especially important in Latin America. A native of Argentina, she literally knows people from all walks of life, all over South America. Not only a strong social relationship but strong business relationships are required to do business in South America. The same is true in Asia. Pam Chen agrees that Asians wouldn't respond well to business ventures without the right kind of introduction and relationship.*

These differences are especially interesting to those conducting business overseas or to those who work in an international environment. We may simply assume that when people are "networking," they have the same expectations, frame of reference, or perspective as we do, while in fact people may have very different agendas. One person might be looking for a very pleasant social relationship, while the other is seeking short-term business contacts. Both participants are bound to be put off and disappointed. It is critical, therefore, to be aware of cultural differences and expectations and to adjust our perspectives accordingly.

MENTORS

There seems to be a great deal of agreement that mentors or advocates play a critical role in women's success. Several participants said that rather than relying on a single mentor, they took particular qualities or aspects that they admired from different people.

> *One woman noted that her sources included both men and women, people she liked and even some she didn't particularly like. She cited one man who, after she hadn't seen him for a while, would always pose as his first question: "So, what are you going to do next?" She says that her image of him is so strong and reinforced that she doesn't even need to see the man—she can hear him from memory! She adds that she has picked up on a number of significant points that were made to her along the way.*

Masako, an executive at a Japanese corporation, said that she really benefited from a mentor who happened to be her boss when she was posted in Rome. She says that her boss frequently let her know that "she could do it." She adds that at that time—in the sixties and seventies—it never would have happened in Japan.

You never know who is going to have an impact on your life. When Gay Haskins arrived in Canada as a young English expatriate working at the World's Fair, she was trained as a teacher, but did not have a university degree. At the British Pavilion, an American from Berkeley stopped by. He was planning to go to Oxford in the fall, so he suggested that they get together when she went back home. He became her first mentor and he said, "Why haven't you been to a university?" So she went.

Several of the women agreed that mentors also improve your visibility. They feel that as organizations change, mentors will become increasingly important as vehicles for understanding those changes. There are pilot mentoring programs in a number of organizations—for example, BP Oil in Germany. Every mentor has four women whom he or she can help in solving problems and answering questions, among other things. The German women have been invited to the next German management conference at BP and also have been invited to participate in a job-shadowing program. These can be relatively easy ways for organizations to provide support and guidance to women looking to advance.

Val Hammond said that one of her advocates kept advising her to think about what only she could bring to a position, not who has necessarily been there before. Even when she questioned whether she could do a particular job in the past, one that she didn't have formal qualifications for, others saw her potential and encouraged her.

One respondent didn't even particularly like one of her mentors, but said that he was enormously helpful and taught her the value of learning to take risks in life.

A few of the respondents added that they didn't really have a formal mentor, but benefited from the insight of various influential people whom they observed and copied. They learned sometimes by osmosis!

GOVERNMENT SUPPORT FOR THE ADVANCEMENT OF WOMEN

Similar initiatives are taking place throughout the world. For example, in 1991, U.S. Secretary of Labor Lynn Martin spearheaded the Glass Ceiling Initiative, a pilot study of the corporate workforce, which examined how middle and upper management positions are filled in corporate America. Specifically, the initiative examined developmental programs, training, assignments, and reward structures—all indicators of upward mobility. The goal was to couple access and equal opportunity with an individual's abilities, hard work, and desire. Across the board there are men and women who will take advantage of these opportunities and others who may not be willing to make the sacrifices and trade-offs required to reach upper levels of management. It's a question of choices.

At the same time the United States was launching the Glass Ceiling Initiative, the United Kingdom was presenting a government-supported initiative called Opportunity 2000. At the initiation, in his keynote speech, Prime Minister John Major talked of a social revolution. He underscored that women must have the same opportunities as men and the same scope for development and fulfillment.

Back home, Lynn and I were struck by the timing of this initiative. Since Lynn had worked for many years at an Anglo-Dutch conglomerate based in England, she still received the annual report. In it, the company proudly showed several group photos of the senior management and board of directors. It was so striking that we just had to ask some of our friends, "What's wrong with this picture?" Of the 20 senior managers, every single one was a white male in his forties, fifties, or sixties. Zero diversity! We all agreed that an American company would probably be too embarrassed to highlight that photograph—it would be harassed! (By the way, the company has since become a member of Opportunity 2000.)

Over 200 companies and organizations have participated in this initiative, which set individual goals for increasing women's participation in management by the year 2000. Some organizations are implementing specific, measurable goals. (London Weekend Television has set as a goal an increase in women employees from 35 percent in 1992 to 43 percent by 2000. NatWest plans to increase women in management from 16.3 percent to 33.3 percent by 2000.) Ashridge Management College, a prestigious management research organization, undertook the initiative.

> *Val Hammond, one of the people involved with the launch of Opportunity 2000, talked to me about the progress of the initiative 5 years later. She said that changes are gradually taking place—some of them subtle, some less subtle. Family-friendly issues are much more visible in organizations now, and they are more frequently seen as not necessarily women's issues. (For example, when Val started working for a bank in 1961, women in banking left work upon marriage.) Interestingly enough, she sometimes sees more support from fathers on the issues than from women who don't have children themselves.*

> *One British executive thinks that it's actually easier for women at more senior levels. There's more civility, less bantering about sports, less bad language. It's sometimes more comfortable.*

In the beginning of the Opportunity 2000 initiative, the organizers would ask, for example, if a company made flexible practices available. If so, to whom—certain women, all women, all employees? The project leaders started asking questions about how many people were actually taking advantage of things like extended maternity leave and the ability to work from home. They found that asking questions was a good way of changing behavior. Organizations really started to think about the issues. Pressure subsequently came down from senior management to actively make huge changes. But the questions constantly have to be asked, or things can go backward very quickly. Middle managers are usually the ones facing the tension between offering flexibility to their employees and attaining effectiveness. Despite the support of senior management, that of middle managers is crucial, because a policy can be skirted in subtle ways if managers see that it makes their job and maintaining the bottom line more difficult.

Similarly, in 1986, Japan passed its Equal Employment

Opportunity Law (EEOL), which prohibits employers from discriminating against women. The law encourages but does not compel employers to give equal opportunity to men and women in recruiting and hiring workers. In 1979, prior to the EEOL, a study was conducted of 1497 Japanese companies employing almost 5 million employees. Only 996 women held managerial positions. Why so few? Traditional attitudes of Japanese society placed pressure on women to leave their jobs upon marriage. In addition, employers feared that female university graduates might be disruptive if they had unrealistically high expectations for women in terms of work assignments and pay.

With the passage of the EEOL, changes slowly began to take place. In 1989, two major surveys were conducted asking employers what they had done over the last 3 years and what they expected to do in the next 3 years to improve the career prospects of female managers. More than half the companies said that they expected to significantly increase the number of female managers.

One major impact that will be sure to create change is the increasing need for new technology-oriented university graduates. In this area, the male-female starting salaries are equalizing, and the shortage of male technological graduates has motivated an increasing number of corporations to look for "substitute labor" among female technology students. Likewise, in science and engineering, some businesses are deciding to recruit women graduates whom they would not have hired previously. The intense recruitment competition in these areas is helping more women find suitable jobs.

It appears that the EEOL may have started to speed up the change in gender-based attitudes that, up to now, have prevented educated Japanese women from finding permanent employment.

Canadian women are also making great strides in nontraditional fields like technology and industry. Patti, a general manager for a corporation in Toronto, believes that a woman's success in Canada is based more on her ability and less on politics than in the United States. Several Canadian women feel that businesswomen in Canada are more direct in their business dealings, a trait that can be unsettling to their American counterparts.

BALANCE

In Europe and increasingly in Asia, many people are having difficulty balancing their lives. However, several of my research participants agreed that Europeans typically give more time to quality of life. There are more holidays and vacations, usually about 25 a year, plus public holidays. In Britain, for example, even senior managers may take 2-week vacations several times a year, which is generally not done in the United States. They also work fewer hours and, in many companies, stop at 4 o'clock for tea. Many people feel that Americans like to work hard and play hard. An Australian friend says that most Australians like to work hard enough to get the time and money to go on vacation and enjoy themselves.

Yet many large aggressive companies are the same worldwide. For example, at a consulting company like McKenzie or Andersen—even in Europe—it's probably easier for Americans, who are used to the fast pace, to adapt. Stockbrokers in London work just as hard as their American counterparts.

Nabuko, a Japanese television producer, feels that she has learned to take things as they come, rather than constantly trying to second-guess decisions and challenge fate. She feels that this somewhat more spiritual perception makes her a more balanced person.

Viki Holton, at Ashridge Management College, says that the British organization has looked into flexible work as a way of increasing balance. Although telecommuting hasn't really taken off too much to date, it may prove to be very beneficial for certain types of jobs in certain companies. Day-care options are not as widespread in the United Kingdom, but part-time work or a slightly shorter workday is beginning to become more commonplace.

One senior director at a major English company feels that women often have to learn to cope in order to succeed. It is especially critical to do two things: focus and delegate. Try not to do things if you don't really have to, and get your family to help. Try to get over the guilt. It is also important to focus on your work when you're at work and on home when you're at home. If you focus on more than one area at a time, it can be distracting to both. You need to separate your energies and do each job wholeheartedly.

Another senior executive agrees. She also underscores the need to delegate. It's important to let things go as you get promoted. Even if you're really good at something and you enjoy it, it still may have to go. Not only will you be taking up too much of your time; your boss may still see you in the lower-level role if you continue to do those tasks after your promotion.

BRINGING DIFFERENCES TO THE WORKPLACE

Many of the participants agreed that everyone has certain internal barriers, but added that people constantly have to reflect on what is unique to them. What can you alone bring to your job or a new position? Developing partnerships with others who have certain skills which you want to learn can be helpful. Try to determine what piece is missing in a particular position and see if you can fill that gap. You may consciously want to look for opportunities, rather than leaving them to chance. An outside network of people may also really help you see a different set of perspectives.

Anita Roddick, founder of the Body Shop, thinks that male entrepreneurs frequently want a smaller version of a large company. Women want to create an honorable livelihood where you can bring your heart and your children to work. However, she sees a hurdle for women in accepting power. She feels that women give up power too easily to men. Women need to increase their self-confidence to embrace power. [38]

Val Hammond recommends that first you have to be extremely competent—you're only as valuable to your organization as you are perceived outside the organization. When you receive recognition from the outside, you gain credibility for both your organization and yourself. Val recommends that you include your colleagues as well. Women need to be in the mainstream of the organization, not on the edge. With her visibility, she has frequently brought up issues of ethics, values, and beliefs. She had to ask male allies to stand up for her ideas some of the time.

Career strategies may need to include certain goals or expectations as well. In a study of women directors in Europe, Ashridge Management College found that women frequently plan only the next step in their career, rather than developing a career plan. In addition, women seem to concentrate on wanting to do as well as possible, whereas men concentrate more on planning ahead and gaining visibility.

> *One British senior executive agrees with the need to maximize visibility. In her view, women need to learn not to be passive. They need to go to meetings to make an explicit point. Many women are not seen as making a contribution. Women aren't often expected to make major presentations. Getting advice and guidance from mentors may afford women the opportunity to develop a professional presentation.*

SUMMARY

- Issues about work and family and a quality work environment seem to be the major focus of women everywhere.

- Despite the apparent importance of women joining networks, there are often barriers to joining them. Most frequently women lack the time to participate, or they experience conflicts with family demands.

- Cultural differences in networking are especially interesting to those conducting business overseas or to those who work in an international environment. We may simply assume that when people are "networking," they have the same expectations, frame of reference, or perspective as we do, while in fact people may have very different agendas.

- The organizers of Opportunity 2000 found that asking questions was a good way of changing behavior. Organizations really started to think about the issues. Pressure subsequently came down from senior management to actively make huge changes. But the questions constantly have to be asked, or things can go backward very quickly.

- Developing partnerships with others who have certain skills which you want to learn can be helpful. Try to determine what piece is missing in a particular position and see if you can fill that gap. You may consciously want to look for opportunities, rather than leaving them to chance.

WOMEN AND TECHNOLOGY

One very exciting aspect of work in the future is the emergence of huge technological advancements. The "technolution" has already begun to dramatically change possibilities of the work environment for men and women. Computers, modems, faxes, e-mail, cellular phones, and access to the Internet have allowed work to be done in more convenient—or even in remote—locations. We have talked, for example, about the incredible impact on lifestyle balance that the possibilities of telecommuting can provide. It also opens up tremendous opportunities for global business. There's just one small problem—a lot of women still know practically nothing about technology.

In a survey by the Georgia Institute of Technology, 17 percent of the American female respondents used the Internet, compared with 7 percent of European women. Commercenet and A. C. Nielsen data show that while men make up 67 percent of Internet users, they account for 77 percent of actual use of the Net—they just use it more frequently than women.

Recently I coordinated a program for 30 to 40 women who were interested in updating their skills and education. As a fun component of the program, we did a hands-on overview of the Internet. Only one woman in the group considered herself computer-literate. About 95 percent had never really used a computer before and felt extremely intimidated by technology. Most of them said that their kids had computers, but they didn't even know where to start.

Well, the good news is that if you're not as computer-literate as you would like to be, you're not alone. You may at times feel stranded in your confusion and discomfort regarding technology. You're not. But you have got to start becoming technology-oriented *right now!*

Technology is now—and increasingly will be—a huge benefit for workers, allowing them to spend more time at home if they wish, spend more time with their kids, or divide their time among various locations. Especially important for entrepreneurs (and two-thirds of those starting new businesses are women), technology allows a new freedom. However, either women will be fully integrated into technology or they will be left behind, relegated into a new generation of "feminizing" jobs.

Though this scenario may be somewhat frightening to some, it will become a reality. But remember, we're all learning to be risk takers. We're getting people to support and guide us to become more successful, so we're on our way to learning the skills and getting the tools we need to become more technology-oriented. I asked Diane Lovelace, a terrific woman who is an expert on the Internet, to lead one of my workshops. The attendees, who started out with terrified looks on their faces that we were going to learn about computers, ended up having such a great time that they didn't want to go to the next session! And that was after only an hour-long introduction to the Internet. They had just taken the risk to come to the program (step 1) and had someone show them what it was like to use technology (step 2). Once they were able to overcome their fears, they couldn't wait for more. I think what really helped in this case was that the program was just for women.

Until women are able to build up their confidence, many new technology users will prefer not to have men around. Some women feel overwhelmed or threatened in a mixed environment. I know it sounds sexist, but at the beginning I think that this is how many women feel. As Adrienne Mendell says in her book *How Men Think,* if a man sees a button, he just has to push it to see what it does.[39] Many women, on the other hand, worry about breaking a computer if they push the wrong button. Men just jump in and play—women want a guide. There is lots of technology information out there for women. If you can't find what you need, ask your local organizations, colleges, or your own company to sponsor programs.

In the information technology world, organizations are horizontal rather than hierarchical. This means that skills that women have frequently excelled in—such as communicating, solving problems, and maintaining effective relationships—are highly valued. Women can reach out to people and work together effectively in a team environment.

There are differences between men and women in how they use technology (although, as always, this is a generalization). Technology is often associated with a masculine perception. The early personal computer (even 10 years ago) used complex mathematically based programs. However, with the increasing ease of using PCs, the graphic appeal, and the point-and-click approach, far more women are using computers. The same is true of the Internet.

When a woman is on-line (in a chat room, for example) and identifies herself as a woman, if she speaks 20 percent of the time, male users think that she's dominating the conversation. If she switches to a "man's identity" on-line, she is able to talk more freely. Since it's anonymous on-line, some women take on a male identity in order to "speak up." It may be a great way to practice assertiveness without any risk, as well. Women who do go on-line frequently are likely to ask questions more often; they feel more confident and comfortable doing so.[40]

It's really quite amusing to see the sometimes huge difference between men and women regarding technology. Again, much of this difference can be more closely associated with gender roles than with actual gender. Men or women with more masculine characteristics are frequently enthralled with technology. They read PC and Internet periodicals—and they are the ones in the computer stores, especially the ones looking at the games. I noticed this when I went to buy computer games for my nephews. I was the only woman in that aisle. During a plane trip, a friend of mine spotted the newly installed computer games in the seat backs, accessible by swiping your credit card through right at your seat! He just had to try them out. Men frequently use PCs as tools or games, whereas women prefer them for communication and information, via e-mail or the Internet.

Perhaps the typical woman computer user starts with an on-line service, such as America Online or Prodigy, to access e-mail to communicate with friends, parents, sons, and daughters. Then the woman realizes that there are special-interest groups to explore, such as health issues, menopause, and parenting. (One colleague used the Internet to find out—successfully—the latest treatments for her breast cancer.) There's a huge network of information out there, often accessible through computers at your local library or college.

High-tech firms themselves are often good places for women to work. With less hierarchy and less of an old-boys' network, they offer many opportunities to write, design, or market software and develop interactive television. And it's never too late to get involved with technology. (There are even increasing numbers of computer groups and chat rooms for senior citizens!) Go find yourself someone supportive to point you in the right direction.

One downside to technology, which will increasingly be a factor as we try to balance our lives, comes from the very issue that is designed to make our work lives more flexible. In my graduate classes, I often ask students about the workplace of the future. We talk about flexibility, but then I ask, "When does your workday end when you can work whenever you want to?" They all agree—never! The traditional workday has been 9 to 5. Now you get to work at 11 p.m. if that's a good time for you. You can receive voice mail day and night, send international faxes after midnight, and hold international conference calls at 4 a.m. You are always accessible, so it can be harder to draw the line between work and home time.

A study conducted by the British Computing Society found that the key attraction for women in information technology was the opportunity for flexible working arrangements and career breaks, along with the opportunity for training and career development management courses.[41] However, Alan Roussell, president of the society, adds that women make up only 11 percent of entrants into computer science programs in the United Kingdom, compared with 45 percent in the United States and 56 percent in Singapore. Interestingly enough, the 11 percent U.K. figure is nearly half of what it was in the mid-1980s. What this shows is that young women really need to be encouraged to gain qualifications in technology fields. And as women move further along in their careers, they need to constantly update their experience.

So what can you do? You can attend seminars or classes on computers and other technology. Have a colleague or a friend show you how to use the programs. I can't tell you the number of people, frequently women, I have helped introduce to various technology. I think that it's often easier to have someone show you, rather than read the manuals. (I can never understand them that easily either!) Get an on-line service, such as America Online or Prodigy, to gain exposure to the vast amount of information out there. Read *PC Magazine* or *Wired.* Use the Internet and CD-ROMs for research and general information. It has to be ongoing—plus it really can be fun. Then, just take some risks and start pushing some buttons—it really does take a lot to "break" a computer!

SUMMARY

- Technology is now—and increasingly will be—a huge benefit for workers, allowing them to spend more time at home if they wish, spend more time with their kids, or divide their time among various locations. Especially important for entrepreneurs (and two-thirds of those starting new businesses are women), technology allows a new freedom.

- Men frequently use PCs as tools or games, whereas women prefer them for communication and information, via e-mail or the Internet.

- One downside to technology, which will increasingly be a factor as we try to balance our lives, comes from the very issue that is designed to make our work lives more flexible. You are always accessible, so it can be harder to draw the line between work and home time.

LOOKING TO THE FUTURE

The organizational landscape is changing dramatically. If you look at changes in the workplace over the past 20 years, you can't help but be struck by the dramatic increases of women in management positions, changing attitudes (by women and men) toward balancing work and home, and the positive rapport among diverse team members. Although many women still see only the negative aspects of women in the workplace—many instances of which are definitely still true—the more optimistic among them see significant improvements in the world of work for women. Although admittedly only a few women are moving into senior levels and boardrooms of major organizations, they are making significant impacts through their decision-making influence and ability to change the organizational culture and attitudes of their male coworkers. It's definitely a lot better than it was a generation ago!

That's the good news. That's what you see when you look at the big picture. The bad news is that some of you may be saying, "Whose organization are you talking about? It sure isn't mine!" Are things still really that different between men and women in organizations? Do men have more opportunities? More clout? More money?

It is true that many organizations still reflect the white, male, old-boys' club at the top. If you watch interviews on CNN or CNBC with CEOs, presidents, and other very senior leaders of American corporations, it's likely that they'll be pretty homogeneous. If you read business and professional publications as well, you'll find that the majority of the stories reflect their readership—white men (which, of course, from a practical standpoint the publications want to do to make money).

Many of the senior women I interviewed are aware of an old-boys' club. However, most of them feel that it is not impossible for nontraditional managers to gain entrance. It may just take a little longer, or they may go about it a little differently. And keep in mind that many senior men may not even be aware that these groups are as homogeneous as they really are. Why? Because it's human nature to surround yourself with people like you. As mentioned earlier (see Success Secret One), senior white men usually feel most comfortable mentoring younger white men, simply because they can identify most easily with them. They see themselves in these younger men—or they see their sons.

A fairly large number of the women I interviewed point to an interesting factor in the changing organizational landscape. They indicate that many senior male managers who have traditionally been fairly narrow-focused in their scope are starting to change their perspectives. Why? Well, their personal environment (i.e., at home) is starting to change. Their wives or significant others may be professionals or executives, for example. Even more interesting is the fact that many of these male executives have daughters who are now entering the workforce (see Success Secret Four). These young women may encounter barriers and biases and relate their stories to their fathers, who in turn may start to reflect upon their own organizational environment and initiatives. Male managers are starting to say, "Hey, are my female employees experiencing those barriers?"

Many younger male managers are starting to change their perspectives as well, for different reasons. First, these men may have gone to college or graduate school with very talented, ambitious, focused women. They're used to healthy competition on an equal plane with women in school. These same attitudes often continue in the workplace. Second, once these younger men enter the workplace, they are usually working in a team environment with diverse groups. They're used to working cooperatively with their female counterparts. As they move up in the organization, these younger men, unlike many of their older male predecessors, are more comfortable with women in leadership roles.

In closing, we can all reflect upon our own personal histories to see which choices led us to where we are today. And more important, what are the choices that we will make today for the future? We may not have an opportunity to change how we were raised, the events that took place as we grew and matured, or the choices we have made. But, look at the wonderful opportunities ahead of us—opportunities that you can make happen! Set goals, make choices, challenge yourself, help others, and help yourself. Take charge of your own development. It will be beautifully unique for each individual.

We hope that while reading this book you have taken the time to reflect—really reflect on who you are, where you are going, what is important to you, what success really is to you. Hopefully, you're just a little different person than who you were before. Maybe you have realigned your expectations or have gained a better sense of self. Maybe you've learned to have just a little more fun in your life. Maybe you will have more support in your life for the tough roads and more friends to share the successes. But most of all, we hope that this has given you the inspiration to start out on your own voyage of discovery. And don't forget to share what you have learned with others, because that's how we're going to make the changes necessary for the future. Very best of luck to you!

ENDNOTES

INTRODUCTION

1. B. L. Harragan, *Games Mother Never Taught You*, Warner, New York, 1977.

SUCCESS SECRET ONE

2. "Up the Corporate Ladder: A Progress Report," *Working Woman*, May 1996, p. 22.
3. C. A. McKeen and C. J. Burke, "Mentor relationships in organizations: Issues, strategies and prospects for women," *Journal of Management*, 16(3), 609–618 (1990).
4. "Up the Corporate Ladder," p. 22.
5. L. W. Fitt and D. A. Newton, "When the mentor is a man and the protégé is a woman," *Harvard Business Review*, 59, 55–60 (1981).
6. R. M. Kanter, *Men and Women in the Corporation*, Basic, New York, 1977.
7. McKeen and Burke, "Mentor relationships," pp. 609–618.
8. P. Sellers, "Women, sex, and power" (profiles of seven women executives), *Fortune*, 134, 42–46 (1996).
9. D. Tannen, *Talking from 9 to 5*, Morrow, New York, 1994.
10. C. Gilligan, *In a Different Voice*, Harvard University Press, Cambridge, MA, 1982.

SUCCESS SECRET TWO

11. "Generational tension in the office: Why busters hate boomers," *Fortune*, 128, 56-58 (1994).

SUCCESS SECRET FOUR

12. Sellers, "Women, sex, and power," pp. 42–46.
13. Tannen, *Talking from 9 to 5*.
14. Gilligan, *In a Different Voice*.
15. D. K. Banner and J. W. Blasingame, "Towards a developmental paradigm of leadership," *Leadership and Organization Development Journal*, 9(4), 7–16 (1988).
16. J. Lublin, "Some adult daughters of 'supermom' plan to take another path," *The Wall Street Journal*, December 28, 1995.

SUCCESS SECRET FIVE

17. *Men's Health*, 8(3), 8(1995).
18. A. McGee-Cooper, *You Don't Have to Go Home from Work Exhausted*, Bantam, New York, 1990.
19. P. Roberts, "The art of goofing off," *Psychology Today*, 28(4), 34–42 (1996).
20. *Ibid.*
21. S. Shellenbarger, "All work and no play can make Jack a dull manager," *The Wall Street Journal*, January 24, 1996.
22. "Generational tension in the office," p. 57.

MEN AND WOMEN AT WORK

23. Gilligan, *In a Different Voice*.
24. J. Lever, "Sex differences in the games children play," *Social Problems*, 23, 478–487 (1976).
25. Harragan, *Games Mother Never Taught You*.
26. *Gilligan*, In a Different Voice, p. 29.
27. Harragan, *Games Mother Never Taught You*, p. 76.
28. J. Rowney and A. Cahoon, "Individual and organizational characteristics of women in managerial leadership," *Journal of Business Ethics*, 9, 293–316 (1990).
29. K. Korabik, "Androgyny and leadership style," *Journal of Business Ethics*, 283–292 (1990).
30. G. Yukl, "Managerial leadership: A review of theory and research," *Journal of Management*, 15 (2), 251–289 (1989).

INDEX